W9-AEJ-722

I FIRED God

I FIRED God

My Life Inside—and Escape from—the Secret World
of the Independent Fundamentalist Baptist Cult

Jocelyn R. Zichterman

with Kathy Passero

St. Martin's Press ❧ New York

www.stmartins.com

Design by Omar Chapa

Library of Congress Cataloging-in-Publication Data

Zichterman, Jocelyn.
    I fired God : my life inside—and escape from—the secret world of the independent fundamental Baptist cult / Jocelyn Zichterman.—First edition.
        pages   cm
    ISBN 978-1-250-02626-2 (hardcover)
    ISBN 978-1-250-02633-0 (e-book)
    1. Baptists—Controversial literature.   2. Zichterman, Jocelyn.   3. Baptists—United States—Biography.   4. Psychological abuse victims—Religious life.
5. Psychological abuse—Religious aspects—Christianity.   6. Abused children—Religious life.   I. Title.
    BX6334.Z53 2013
    286'.5—dc23
    [B]

                                                              2012042119

St. Martin's Press books may be purchased for educational, business, or promotional use. For information on bulk purchases, please contact Macmillan Corporate and Premium Sales Department at 1-800-221-7945 extension 5442 or write specialmarkets@macmillan.com.

First Edition: May 2013

10   9   8   7   6   5   4   3   2   1

Contents

Foreword

Saying we grew up in obscurity seems underwhelming. It suggests minimalism. But the Independent Fundamental Baptist (IFB) movement is far from a small organization. Its churches pervade small-town America, and its members number in the hundreds of thousands. They are your next-door neighbor, that nice family you met at your child's soccer game, and the well-dressed men and women knocking on your door inviting you to church. Many people reading this book will, with or without knowing it, have come into contact with members of the IFB Church. They might even know them well—or think they do. This book may force them to reconsider.

Jocelyn Zichterman's exposé will inevitably draw intense criticism for a number of reasons. Most IFB members hold rigorously to the idea that their churches are *independent* from their fellow "independent" Baptist churches and organizations, particularly when those other IFB groups become entangled in scandals. However, *I Fired God* refutes the notion of individuality they so vehemently claim, meticulously plotting the IFB's widespread network and connecting the dots between its many churches, schools, colleges, camps, and institutes.

Reading through my sister's manuscript was very disturbing for me because I was there. I walked through Jocelyn's childhood with her. Revisiting the horrors of our childhood and early adult years brought back a lot of pain and tears. While the details in this book are vivid, it is impossible to convey the full extent of the nightmare we lived through. *I Fired God* highlights *moments* of terror we experienced in a family under the repressive influence of the IFB. But the reality is, they are just moments. For every dramatic event described in these pages, there were three months of daily horror that go unmentioned. There is no way to compress the years of unending fear, depression, guilt, and pain we suffered into one volume. The stories you are about to read are selected highlights. I can recall thousands more just like them—all disturbing, some humiliating, and many terrifying. As I can attest, Jocelyn's account of our lives in the cult are not exaggerated or sensationalized. If anything, she has downplayed the whole truth, for there are experiences too personal and painful to share with the public.

There are many ways of dealing with abuse. Ultimately, Jocelyn and I both decided that it wasn't healthy to deny what happened to us. What we have been through is a part of who we have become. I've been asked many times how I survived. My method has been to accept the past as part of my development into the person I am today. I refuse to sugarcoat the memories that still cause my heart to race when I hear a garage door open after all these years. I will not minimize the effect the sound a belt buckle has on me when it hits a hard surface even now. I no longer attempt to block out the memories of crying and screaming as the wooden dowel whistled through the air and the rage-filled eyes of my father glared down at me as a child.

Courage cannot be manufactured. It is cultivated. The desire for social justice comes from an inward motivation to see right prevail. This is the spirit of the words you will read in the following pages. No child should endure the brutality we did, especially not under the pretense of religion. No child should suffer at the hands of his or her guardian. Jocelyn's story is written so that others will gain strength to take up the cause of fighting for the innocent—so other children will be protected from harm.

—MELISSA JANZ FLETCHER (Jocelyn's sister), September 2012

I FIRED God

1

IS THE DEVIL BEHIND US OR UP AHEAD?

> My job [as pastor] is to execute wrath upon those
> who disobey. . . . Those of you who want to do right, we
> get along just fine. Those of you who don't want to do
> right usually have a run-in with me. You know why?
> Because I'm ordained by God to stand in this position.
>
> —*Bart Janz, sermon,*
> *"God and Government II,"*
> *Holly Ridge Baptist Church, 2006*

Escaping the Cult: August 1, 2006

I looked down at my hand and realized I was trembling. Terror. That's the only word to describe what I felt. I forced myself to add another item to my long "to do" list, but the pen shook so much that my writing was nearly illegible. Taking several deep breaths and struggling to calm myself, I glanced out the window into a black, moonless night.

It was two in the morning and the house was silent. My husband, Joseph, and all eight of my children had gone to bed hours ago, but I couldn't sleep. I hadn't been able to for more than a week now, knowing that hour by hour the moment was drawing closer when we would leave everything we knew behind and head into a future as inscrutable as the blackness outside the window.

From my seat at the mahogany table in our dining room, I took in my surroundings. There was the china cabinet that held our most cherished wedding gifts. And the grandfather clock we had inherited from my husband, Joseph's, late mother. This had always been my favorite room, and I was sitting in it for the last time. It was where I had read my Bible and prayed every morning over my breakfast tea for the past six years. Now, I realized, I was no longer sure I believed any of the words in the Holy Bible. I wondered if there was a God at all. But I forced those thoughts to the back of my mind. The only thing that mattered was whether we would all survive the journey ahead.

We had been planning it for months—carefully and quietly organizing our departure from the Independent Fundamental Baptist (IFB) church, like captives secretly plotting an escape from their guards—ever since I had spoken up about the brutal abuse I had endured as a child at the hands of my father, Bart Janz, an influential IFB pastor in Brighton, Colorado. Sadistic mind games and vicious beatings were a part of everyday life for my four siblings and me from toddlerhood throughout our teen years—beatings during which I was sometimes forced to lie naked facedown on my bed for hours while my father flogged me until I was bloody and could barely walk, sermonizing between each blow. Determined to keep his "house in order," he wielded power with a Bible in one hand and a thick wooden dowel in the other. A chilling image of him rose up in my mind, eyes black and purple veins pulsating in his neck as they always did when he was in a rage.

I could almost feel raw, angry welts rising afresh on the backs of my legs. Fear surged through me, but I shook it off. There was no time to panic, no time to curl up in the corner and weep. I was determined to save my own children from my fate—from growing up in a community and a faith that not only tolerated but advocated torturing children to crush their will. I had to get them as far away as possible. And I had only a few hours to do it.

Breaking My Silence: January 2005

An overwhelming fear for my children had convinced me to end my long silence about my own past a year earlier. When I finally confided in Joseph, in early 2005, the stories tumbling out in an anguished torrent, he was horrified. He had joined the church at the age of thirteen without his parents' involvement, and, not having grown up in an IFB family, he had no firsthand knowledge of the shattering physical and psychological damage fathers like mine did to their children under the guise of godly discipline.

Learning about my childhood sent Joseph into an intense moral struggle. He loved me and he knew I was telling the truth. But standing by me now would require abandoning his entire way of life. As a man in a fiercely male-dominated subculture, he had always been treated well. He was respected, even revered in the IFB. He had been a frequent IFB conference speaker as well as a professor at one of the most prominent IFB colleges for over a decade. At the age of only thirty-three, he had even received an honorary doctorate from Bob Jones University, the IFB's worldwide headquarters, located in Greenville, South Carolina. So up to this point, the strongest reprimands he had ever gotten from the church leaders had come for failing to keep me sufficiently meek and submissive. He had spent years listening to IFB preachers warn that women were deceivers, Jezebels, put on earth to lead men astray ever since that fateful day when Eve handed Adam the forbidden fruit. He had also been indoctrinated in the IFB paranoia that the world beyond our insular community was wicked and that venturing into it was a one-way ticket to damnation. When Joseph ultimately chose to support my decision to leave the IFB, it was a turning point in our marriage as well as our lives. He knew he was in for the fight of his life.

My husband called my father at his home in Colorado and told him what he had done to me was wrong. But if he was hoping for a mea culpa he didn't know Bart Janz. The man who had made my childhood a living hell now turned his full fury on Joseph and vowed to make our adult lives equally hellish.

He swore he would destroy Joseph's career, ruin us financially, and make sure we never left the IFB. He called the IFB leaders at Northland Baptist Bible College, where Joseph was a professor, to tell them I was making wild allegations and trying to lure my husband away from "the only true church." He painted us in the blackest light possible. The IFB leaders were powerful men and close friends of my father's, and, as far as I can tell, they backed every move he made against us, informing Joseph a short time later that they were terminating his teaching position at the end of that semester. This only enflamed my father's rage toward us and reinforced his sense of righteous indignation. We lived in a small, isolated town in the middle of the Wisconsin woods, five miles from the nearest two-lane highway, where nearly everyone belonged to the IFB. We had nowhere we could turn in our own community for help.

"I'm coming to deal with you publicly in front of the entire community whether you like it or not!" my father screamed over the phone. Joseph tried repeatedly to reason with him. When that failed, he threatened him with a restraining order, but it only threw fuel on the fire.

"This is going to trail you, buddy, for the rest of your life!" my father bellowed. "This is war!"

My Paralyzing Fear

All my life my father had warned me that he would kill me if I ever talked about the abuse I had suffered at his hands. My formative years were full of death threats from him, and somewhere in the back of my mind I had always expected him to carry through. It was just a question of when. I knew the man was capable of bloodshed. I had seen him torture animals to death, even beloved family pets, many times.

Now a new terror seized me: Would he try to do the same to my children? The thought was unbearable. One night a few months earlier I had been gripped with such a paralyzing fear that I had called 911.

"He's coming! I don't know what he'll do!" I screamed into the phone.

The 911 operator tried to make sense of my hysteria. "Who's coming, ma'am? Where is he coming to?"

"My father! I confronted him about abusing me and now he says he's coming to my home! And I have eight children!" Months of stress had taken a heavy toll on my body and my mind, and confessing my fears to a stranger pushed me over the edge. I collapsed into uncontrollable, shuddering sobs while the operator attempted to calm me down.

My life had become like a scene from a horror movie, where you're holding your breath and tensing every muscle, waiting for the monster to spring out. But for me the scene never ended. How many nights had I crept from my bed and peered warily out our windows? It was hard to see the yard in the dead of night and even harder to see the woods behind it, but I was convinced that one night soon my father would slip into them unnoticed to watch us from the shadows. The wind would rustle a branch, and I would freeze, sure I saw him lurking in the trees, ready to strike.

Sometimes I felt like I couldn't survive one more day. But my kids . . . what would happen to them if I gave up? They were the reason I kept going, steeling myself, expecting at every moment to hear my father pounding on the front door and shouting my name, to see him burst in wielding his wooden dowel over us as my children cowered in fear behind me.

BAM!

The silence of the night was broken by the sudden slam of a door. My heart took off like a thoroughbred out of the starting gate. My body stiffened, bracing for the figure from my nightmares to come striding into my dining room. A moment later, relief swept through me as I heard light footsteps run down the hallway, away from the bathroom. One of the kids was headed back to bed, blissfully unaware of the danger surrounding all of us.

I closed my eyes and tried to think through the hours ahead. Had I overlooked anything? Forgotten any documents or essentials for the children? Was that a footstep I heard outside? I had been operating on no more than five fitful, nightmare-filled hours of sleep for months. No doubt chronic sleep deprivation was fueling my delusions and paranoia. But even in my addled state, I was clear on one point: The IFB was a cult, and getting our children away from it was essential. We had to break free.

Was the devil behind us or up ahead? I didn't know.

2

MY CHILDHOOD IN WISCONSIN (1975–1985)

> You see all these husbands doing dishes, cleaning,
> vacuuming, dusting—it's not their job, it's ours [as
> wives]. You know there might be a time when they
> help, when we're sick or in difficult circumstances, but
> that is not his job and we should not rely on that man
> to do our job that God has given to us to do.
> —*Diane Olson, President's Wife's Address,*
> *Northland Baptist Bible College, 2004*

I smoothed my little red dress down to hide my knees and hugged
Emily, my favorite baby doll. With her chestnut hair and her big brown
eyes, I thought she looked just like me. I spent all my time during the
summer months in rural Wisconsin cuddling her soft beaded body and
dreaming of the day when I would be a real mom. My favorite pastime was
to put her in my ladybug buggy and stroll her up and down our driveway.
When I was six it seemed to stretch on for miles, though looking back
now it was no longer than five hundred yards.

On that particular breezy summer afternoon, I was seated in the grass
in our yard tucking a blanket around Emily and getting her ready to be
put down for her "afternoon nap" when I was jarred out of my reverie by
deep guttural yells emanating from the small barn my father had built
on our property to house a few chickens and pigeons.

I sensed danger instinctively and my whole body tensed. My father's footsteps thundered up the wooden planks that led into the back of the barn. "Get him!" he bellowed. "Don't let him get through that door! Close it NOW!"

I looked up and saw Rob, my sister Meagan's cat, leap into the air in a frantic attempt to escape through the open barn door. But my brother Jason slammed it, catching the animal in midair and pinning him between the door and the frame. Rob screeched and clawed, struggling wildly to break free from the heavy wood that was crushing him. A second later, a jolt of terror surged through me as three sharp metal points burst out of Rob's rib cage. Blood splattered everywhere and Rob let out an agonized, high-pitched squeal. The cat squirmed, thrashed, and mewed pitifully on the end of the pitchfork my father had thrust through his body. Eventually Rob went limp and I knew he was dead.

Too shocked to cry and too petrified to run away, I stayed rooted to the grass, staring at the barn as if transfixed. Slowly I became aware that I was shaking. My entire body felt tight and hot, as if I had been standing too close to a heat lamp.

And, as was so often the case in my childhood, just when I thought the terror was over, it got worse. My father lit out after Moses, my sister Melissa's cat, chasing the terrified animal around and around our backyard. He soon managed to trap the little black cat in a gunnysack. He tied the sack to a fencepost, grabbed a BB gun, and fired into it again and again until the sack was motionless and soaked in blood.

It was too much for a six-year-old to process. My brain numb and my motions mechanical, I turned my attention back to Emily, silently praying my father's wrath wouldn't fall on me next.

Rob had lived with us for more than a year. Meagan was so crazy about the little brown and white tabby that she had named him in honor of her favorite babysitter and secret crush. He had always been a beloved family pet. Moses had too. Or so I thought.

I found out later that Rob had scratched Meagan's neck when she tried to pick him up, an act that apparently warranted a death sentence in my father's mind. Moses, he conceded, hadn't technically done anything wrong. But after Rob's misdeed, he was through with cats. They didn't deserve to live.

For years my father recounted the event to anyone who would listen, reenacting the most dramatic moments and rounding out his tale with deep, hearty guffaws as if it was all uproariously funny. He was part braggart, part self-styled comedian on these occasions and, though I cringed internally, we were all expected to laugh at his antics or risk a beating.

I have only recently begun to fully understand the effects of incidents like this on my psyche. For many years, my father was my hero. I convinced myself that there was a good reason for every decision he made.

In fact, if you had asked me at the age of twenty what my childhood was like, I would have said it was wonderful. I would have told you how loving and kind my parents were. I would have said they were some of the godliest people I knew and that they had endured great heartache and trial. And I would have assured you that the Lord had seen them through all of it. But by then I had become a master at blocking out the more unbearable aspects of the truth.

My Parents' Background

My parents, Bart and Sandy Janz, grew up in conservative Catholic households. My mother was the oldest of three girls, a straight-A student and homecoming queen at West De Pere High School in the small town of De Pere, Wisconsin. My grandfather, Jim McCabe, was a mill worker and a war veteran. He and my grandmother, Marilyn, provided a loving and stable, albeit strict, home for Sandy and her sisters, Sally and Debbie.

My father was a stark contrast. He had once been an altar boy, but by the time he reached high school, he was notorious as a hard-drinking rabble-rouser, the prototypical bad boy, prone to benders and bar fights. He was raised on a farm as one of eight kids, and he harbored a lot of anger about his upbringing. He used to tell us tales about how rough his childhood was because he had to get up early every morning to milk the cows before school. Apparently the rigors of farm life prevented him from playing sports in high school, and he was deeply resentful about it. He also claimed that his five sisters tormented him unmercifully when he was little, and, perhaps because of this, he had a tremendous hostility toward women. He condemned the entire gender as manipulative and conniving, and would sometimes launch into long, loud misogynistic rants, all of which ended with his vowing, "No woman will ever run my life!" as he slammed his fist down on whatever hard surface was nearby.

My mother met Bart in high school. My grandfather's protective instincts must have been aroused instantly, because he did his best to stop the relationship as soon as they started dating. But my mother always said that she would have spent the rest of her life wondering what he was up to, so she married him to find out. From the perspective of a studious, strait-laced high school girl, Bart Janz must have seemed wildly exciting.

They married when they were twenty, and by the time my mother was twenty-one she had given birth to her first child, my brother Jeremy. In the next four years, she would have four more babies—my older brother Jason, me, and my twin younger sisters Meagan and Melissa.

My father was relentlessly critical of all of us, even when we were tiny. One of his favorite pastimes was rattling off our many faults and vowing to correct everything he deemed a character flaw. Jeremy got upbraided for his fiery temperament. We used to say he was full of life, but in truth he was a loose cannon, flying high on happiness one moment and teeming with rage the next. You never knew which Jeremy would surface.

Jason was full of strength and passion, but my father accused him of having a devious, manipulative streak. He often predicted that Jason was destined to be a "great man of God," but would figure out how to control people and use his power against them.

I was born January 1, 1975. As the middle child and the first girl, I ended up squarely in my father's crosshairs. According to him, I was in serious need of taming. I was too talkative, too emotional, too dramatic, too eager to please. And my will was too strong for a female child. My father was determined to break it to make sure I became a godly wife and mother, even if he had to beat it out of me. I did ultimately bend to my parents' wishes, but I nearly lost my soul in the process.

He chastised Meagan incessantly for being too soft-spoken. He was convinced that she couldn't make decisions for herself and, if not "corrected," she would grow into a manipulative woman.

Melissa, on the other hand, was too strong-willed and independent. Like me, she needed to be reined in and subdued. But my sister was smart. She figured out early how to fly under the radar and escape my father's fury. As a little kid, even though she received her fair show of beatings, she became strategic about avoiding conflict and punishment. I wasn't as skillful, and I tended to let my emotions guide me, so I fell victim to many more of his physical assaults than she did over the years.

Converting to the IFB

Before he joined the IFB, my father was still in unbridled party mode. He worked as a carpet layer and as soon as he got off work, he would hit the bars, drinking hard and staying out late. This left my mother caring for us alone in those early years, and she became depressed and distraught. The low point for her every year was the annual ten-day deer-hunting trip to northern Wisconsin he took with his buddies. She dreaded being left with us for such an extended period of time.

She used to tell us a story about the one time she tried to take the five of us grocery shopping when we were all under the age of five and the twins were still babies. She loaded her cart with canned goods and was waiting in the checkout line when Jason clambered up on the side of the cart, overbalanced it, and sent the whole thing toppling over with a crash. Canned goods rolled everywhere, under other shoppers' feet and out the front doors of the store. Kids were tangled in the overturned cart, piled on top of each other, lying on the floor wide-eyed in surprise or bawling among the dented cans. Sympathetic grocery workers picked us up, packed us into our car, put the groceries in the trunk, and told her to come back and pay later. The clerks assured her it was no big deal, and when she recounted the story to us as teenagers we laughed uproariously. But my mother was humiliated. She cried all the way home. And she never took all of us out together again.

When my parents married, they were both disdainful of religion. They had experienced enough of Catholicism to know they didn't want to raise their children as Catholics, and church played no part in my infancy. But one fateful weekend when I was two, a friend of my mother's invited her to come to church with her on Sunday morning. My mother agreed but backed out at the last minute. Undaunted, her friend invited her again and this time she went, leaving us home with my father.

First Bible Baptist Church was housed in a small building on Libal Street in nearby Green Bay, Wisconsin. It was one of thousands of Independent Fundamental Baptist congregations across the country. Almost all IFB churches share certain rituals and practices, including what is known as an altar call—a period following the sermon when attendees are invited to come to the front of the church, kneel, pray, and confess their sins. Altar calls can last anywhere from five minutes to two hours, usually with a single hymn playing over and over. If you want to take part, you approach the altar during the "invitation" and ask to pray with a deacon. You can also choose to become "born again," which means you pray for Jesus to come into your heart and save you, calling you to a life of obedience to Him and the Holy Bible. You follow this with a prayer of conversion and participate in believers' baptism.

An IFB pastor named Harley Keck led the service that Sunday at First Bible Baptist, and something he said must have inspired my mother because during the altar call she stood up, walked down the aisle, and became "born again."

A few weeks later, she let herself be submerged in a baptismal tank filled with water near the choir loft. "I baptize you now in the name of the Father, the Son, and the Holy Spirit," Keck proclaimed.

"And all God's people said?" he demanded.

"Amen!" the congregation responded enthusiastically.

My mother said she was flooded with an immediate sense of peace, joy, and contentment. She went home soaked but elated, filled with a happiness she had never felt before.

My father happened to be gearing up for one of his yearly hunting trips at the time, so she proposed a deal: If he was going to leave her alone for another ten days with the five of us, he had to promise to go to First Bible Baptist at least once when he returned. He agreed. When he got home, he did his best to back out of it, but she was determined.

Finally, he caved in and let himself be dragged to a service at her new church. As always, an altar call followed the sermon. The way my father told it, he leapt out of his seat and bolted for the exit, assuming the service was over. But several deacons blocked the doors, refusing to let him leave and doggedly attempting to engage him in conversation. A man named Dave Dunbar asked him to go downstairs with him to spend some time in prayer. My father felt trapped, so he acquiesced. During the meeting he prayed with Dunbar to become "born again."

Later, he swore he had faked the repentance act just to get the deacons off his back and that it wasn't until a year later that he became "born again for real." But from that day on, our family attended First Bible and my parents soon committed their entire lives to the IFB. I was so young that I can barely recall a time before the cult's strict dogma controlled every aspect of my childhood.

The Schoolhouse Years

My earliest memories begin in a small, renovated schoolhouse, a home my parents rented on an isolated country road in De Pere. It had been converted into a three-bedroom home, with all of us girls packed into one room and the boys into another. They had a trundle bed and we loved to play "shark" on it. We would pull out the bottom bed, then one child would crawl into the space under the top bed and the rest of us would jump from mattress to mattress. The child under the bed would reach out and try to grab our legs and arms as we squealed with laughter. The boys were always much better at catching an arm or a leg than we were and whenever they got one they would pretend to chew it to pieces.

Another of our favorite activities was running through the sprinkler in the front yard on hot summer days. There was a kindly elderly lady named Mrs. Deitrich who lived across the street, and she used to tell us that Popsicles had come in the mail so she needed children to eat them. We would make as much noise as we could in the sprinkler every afternoon, hoping she would hear us and come out to offer us one of the frozen treats. If she didn't, we would feel disappointed, but we always tried again the next day. We managed to land about one Popsicle per kid every week.

There was a cornfield behind our house and we spent countless hours running through it, playing hide-and-seek among the seemingly endless tall green rows in the summer, though I always secretly worried a tractor would crush me if I strayed too far from home. We also had an apple tree in our yard, and one of my brothers' favorite games was having apple fights against us girls. It was much more fun for them than it was for us because the apples could leave welts that stung for days. My father soon found out about the game and, far from reprimanding them, he got in on the action, pummeling us all so hard with apples that my brothers would end up huddling on the ground, covered in bruises and begging him to stop. Like all of Bart's "games," it was cruelty masquerading as fun. His other favorite was pouncing on us and tickling us until we were literally sobbing and sick to our stomachs. He called the game "tickle torture," and the emphasis was definitely on torture.

My mother realized the apple wars were getting so aggressive that somebody was going to lose an eye sooner or later if the game wasn't stopped. But telling Bart to take it easy on his kids was like telling a fox to leave the chickens alone. She finally got him to stop by convincing him she needed the apples for pies and if he smashed them all it would be like pouring money down the drain.

Since finances were tight, my father was always looking for ways to cut costs. One of his schemes was to build what he called a "pet barn" at the back of our property, a one-room model no larger than a storage shed. Inside, he built small coops for chickens, with the hopes that we could collect fresh eggs. Outside, he erected a fence, creating a pen to hold a few goats and one cow, which would provide fresh free milk for us. He also caged a few pigeons that were supposed to be pets. I was fond of animals and at first I found the barn a source of great interest. But after watching poor Rob pinned in its door and impaled on a pitchfork, the barn became a source of nightmares for me.

That wasn't my only sinister memory of the schoolhouse years. My brothers often caught live frogs and played tug-of-war with them. They would literally tear the frogs into pieces, ripping them limb from limb and determining the winner based on who was left holding the largest part of the frog's body. It was sickening to watch, but Jeremy and Jason would laugh hilariously at the sight of the mangled frogs. They also experimented with putting firecrackers in the frogs' mouths to see if they could blow them up. I thought it was gross and mean. I used to cover my eyes so I wouldn't have to see what they were doing. But my father, who always fanned the flames of violence in his boys, thought the "game" was a laugh riot. My mother, who came increasingly under my father's influence, not only tolerated but at times facilitated my father's abuse, and chuckled about it too.

Isolation from Extended Family

Even as a small child, I knew money was scarce. My father had a hard time finding work, and my mother never attempted to get a job, largely because our IFB community was adamant that mothers of young children should stay at home. I remember times when we had to use newspaper as toilet paper, and my mother sometimes told a story about the morning when she only had one can of peas left in the cupboard to feed all of us for breakfast. My father was a proud man. He would never ask for help, especially from my mother's dad, who already disliked him. And since we spent less and less time with our relatives after my parents' conversion to the IFB, they knew too little about our family's financial problems to offer help.

My parents never had anything good to say about my aunts and uncles. According to IFB doctrine, even though they were devout Catholics, they were going to hell because they hadn't converted to the IFB and become born again in the IFB way, by praying the "sinner's prayer." I could never reconcile that notion with the devout and goodhearted relatives I knew and loved, particularly when it came to my Aunt Sal, who was so unfailingly kind and loving toward us when we were little that she seemed like a living saint.

But my parents deemed them bad influences and warned us repeatedly to be careful about what we said in their presence. The fact that they drank wine at family gatherings, an act condemned as pure evil by the IFB, was the best proof to my young mind that my parents' fears were justified: These were not people of God. I remember seeing their priest drinking with them at a family party once when I was little and thinking the man was destined for Hell and sure to drag all my aunts, uncles, and cousins there with him.

Demonizing every other religious group—even mainstream Baptists—was a favorite tactic of the IFB to separate its members from outsiders and to instill distrust and fear. They're hardly the only sect to use the technique, or to believe that they alone are God's elite "chosen" people, but they are particularly vigorous in condemning all outsiders. There is no tolerance for different beliefs or viewpoints.

Gatherings with my mother's side of the family came to an abrupt halt during one ill-fated visit when I was eight. I remember it vividly. I had spent the afternoon cuddled up next to my grandfather, who was one of the kindest men I ever met. He always told me I was special to him and I can remember him whispering, "If you ever have anything to fear, you can tell me all about it." I knew intuitively that he wanted me to be safe. Brutal spanking sessions had long since become a fixture in our lives, and I'm convinced that he suspected we were being abused. But our parents had drilled us never to breathe a word about our corporal punishments, so my grandfather had never had any evidence, until now.

We had all taken a walk in the woods near their house earlier in the day and now adults and children were talking, playing, and laughing while my grandfather and I watched. The mood was jovial as the summer sun shone down on us, and soon the kids started chasing each other around the yard with water balloons. I ran to the side of the house to join in, but before I reached the balloons, I heard the familiar harsh, strident yells of my father. This time, instead of freezing as I normally did, I followed everyone else in the direction of the commotion.

My grandparents had a decorative water pump in their yard, under which was a large wooden water bucket painted red to match their house. Standing over it, his voice booming and his face a mask of fury, was my father, holding Jeremy upside down with one arm wrapped around his back and another wound around his feet. As I watched, he slammed Jeremy's head into the bucket of well water and held it under while Jeremy struggled, helpless and panicked just as Rob the cat had done, desperate to get away.

My father loved to frighten us, flooring the accelerator as we drove around dangerous curves and laughing when we shrieked. Right now, his eyes glinted in malicious delight at the eruption of terrified cries all around him.

"He's drowning him!" I screamed as my grandfather sprinted toward the struggling pair.

"Get him out of there, now!" he bellowed at my father.

Before my grandfather could intervene, my father yanked Jeremy's head out of the bucket and stood him upright on the ground. Drenched and terrified, Jeremy started gasping and vomiting water everywhere. "What's the matter with you!" my grandfather screamed at my father. Then he bent down to examine Jeremy, wiping the water off his face and trying to comfort him.

Without bothering to justify his actions or explain what had triggered them, my father glared at the rest of us. "Get in the car!" he ordered. As always, we obeyed unquestioningly. I huddled in the backseat of our rusted-out station wagon and told my sisters between huge shuddering sobs, "I want to stay with Grandma and Grandpa!" They were sobbing too and holding hands, trying to comfort each other. My mother sat in the front seat, crying as hard as any of us. Jeremy and Jason just sat there, bug-eyed and silent.

I turned and peered over the passenger seat at my grandfather in the driveway, his tall, lanky body towering over my short, beer-bellied father, as he waved a bony finger in his face. "Don't you ever come back here again!" he cried. "Do you hear me?" My aunt and uncle were shouting too, but I can't remember any of their words.

My father turned his back on them and marched to the car. He slammed the door and said, "Children, that's how you act when you do not have the Lord in your life. Those people are lost and in sin. They are going to Hell when they die. We are never coming back here. You will never see them again. I don't want an ounce of their negative, godless influence on you." Although my mother did not directly participate in his sadistic behavior, she remained silent then and throughout all the years of his abuse.

An immediate sense of loneliness overwhelmed me. When we got home I pulled out a porcelain elf that my grandmother had made. She had her own kiln in the basement of their house and she made a lot of beautiful things over the years, from flowerpots to figurines. But this elf was special because my grandfather had given him to me. He became my new Emily, my favorite doll. For the longest time afterward, I slept with him by my side. I talked to him and played with him and pretended he was my baby, just as I had done with her.

Dedication to All Things IFB

Though no dramatic incidents drove us away from my father's side of the family, we seldom saw them and they played no significant role in my childhood. My clearest childhood memory of my father's mother is of her being so distressed over the news that we had joined some "cuckoo cult" that she baptized me with tap water in her kitchen sink when I was a toddler, to wash away my sins, according to Catholic doctrine.

With our extended family shut out of our lives, the drama in our home intensified. Perhaps the worst consequence of this was that, because men hold the reins of power in the IFB and their authority is absolute, my father's temper went unchecked.

Our family sank deeper into the IFB subculture with every passing year. Our home life and the Christian school we attended, in the basement of our church, were steeped in IFB philosophy and rhetoric. The cult breeds paranoia in its members, about society, law enforcement, and the government so we became more and more isolated.

The more immersed my parents became in IFB ideology, the more abnormal and confusing things got in our home. The combination of dire financial struggles with the IFB's draconian rules and isolationist culture sometimes made me feel as if I was losing my mind. My parents fought constantly about money, and the strain of poverty stoked their belief that the U.S. government was the enemy. Most of the other IFB families we knew were as dirt poor as we were, and the church leaders exploited the emotional instability engendered by poverty. Police officers too were bad guys, according my parents—the only "good guys" were members of our own church.

It was a frightening way to grow up. Instead of reassuring us that the monsters from our nightmares were figments of our imagination, our pastors seemed to assure us that the monsters were real and that they were everywhere, waiting to pounce. Our parents and our fellow IFB members were the only ones who could protect us, they preached. Yet this was hard to reconcile with my father's cruelty, which kept escalating. Essentially, the IFB ideology inculcated children in sadomasochistic thinking. It taught that love and pain were interconnected and that by hurting you, your father—or your teacher or your pastor—was expressing his love for you. A shrink could have a field day with this.

So, steeped in IFB thinking as I was and removed from objective, caring adults like my grandfather, who might have given me some real perspective, I developed a sort of blind allegiance to my father, despite his faults and his uncontrolled rages. I looked up to him. He called me his "special little girl." He gave all three of his daughters nicknames. I was his Little Ladybug. Meagan was Mag-pie. And Melissa was Muff or Muffy. The term of endearment softened her enough toward him that at least she stopped running to hide behind the living room chair whenever he came home from work. It wasn't until we were adults and she had left the IFB and started working as a nurse that she learned the term "muff" was slang for a woman's pubic hair. She was humiliated, but perhaps not surprised that what seemed like affection from our father was a demeaning sexual double entendre.

My Father's Escalating Violence

My father's murderous tendency toward animals pervades my childhood memories. One day I was putting my shoes on in the bedroom that I shared with my sisters, when what looked like a long rat ran across my leg and scratched me. I hurried out to the living room and told my father about it.

"Mike!" he shouted to his work buddy. "That weasel is back again. We need to catch that sucker and do away with him."

My mother ushered us all into the kitchen while he and Mike started banging the walls in our room and scooting beds around. "There he is! Get him!" I heard my father cry, then came more banging and shuffling. Finally, both men emerged from the bedroom grinning victoriously and announced proudly that they had beaten the weasel to death. In a sick attempt at humor, my father propped its bloody, mangled body up on the front lawn against some large stones and placed an open copy of the New Testament under its paws. "Look, the weasel's preaching," he said and bent over laughing. I was happy the rodent could no longer run up my leg to scare me, but I was still disturbed by what my father had done.

Not only did my father consider animals disposable, he seemed to relish killing them and he taught my brothers to do the same. He even put a picture of my brother Jason strangling a pigeon in our living room and tried to convince us it was funny. He loved to boast about his ghoulish boyhood hijinks, like the time he tied up a bunch of his family's chickens in nooses and suspended them over a bar in the barn. He would let out a hearty guffaw when he described how they flapped helplessly as they strangled to death. His father, he said, had gone ballistic when he found the birds and rammed his head through a plaster wall to punish him. I'm not sure whether my grandfather was mad about the senseless savagery of the act or its damage to the family's livelihood, but his son certainly didn't get the message that killing birds was wrong.

Studies show that sociopaths, rapists, and serial killers often start out abusing animals and graduate to harming humans. That's what Ted Bundy did. So did Jeffrey Dahmer. You can imagine how fearful I became in later years for my own children's safety and how much danger I now believe we were all in as children in my father's house. But at the time we had no idea how bizarre his behavior was. Animals had no immortal soul, he said, so what did it matter? Not only did he encourage cruelty toward them, he forbade sympathy for their suffering.

The only time I remember crying over what happened to four-legged creatures at my father's hands was when he beat Exes, our Lhasa apso puppy, with the same wooden dowel he used on us. Exes had been scratching the back patio door when he wanted to go in and out, and my father caught him in the act. He grabbed Exes by the scruff of his neck, hoisted him into the air, thrust his face into the puppy's and roared "BAD DOG!" then slammed him back to the floor. Next, he started bashing his front paws with the dowel, stopping between blows to rub the puppy's nose hard against the glass while Exes yelped and whimpered piteously. He beat the dog so severely that he broke both of his front legs. Exes had to scoot around the yard on his hind legs and use his head to propel himself to his food and water dishes. Naturally, no one took him to see a veterinarian, and even after his legs eventually healed, he walked with a limp.

I loved Exes dearly and I can remember standing nearby, quivering and crying silently as I watched him cower under my father's blows. My father caught sight of me and shouted, "Get in your room! No one in this house is going to cry over a *stupid* dog!" Then he beat me bloody with the wooden dowel too.

Breaking the Will of the Child

The IFB teaches that a child's will must be broken, just like a horse's before it can be ridden. It is one of the most dangerous tenets of the cult. How do you break a child's will? You spank her until she is docile, broken emotionally, and wholeheartedly repentant for whatever transgression you think she committed. The key to spiritual maturity, the IFB claims, is reaching the place where one has no internal will. IFB parents are fond of advising each other to "break the will of the child, but not the spirit." But in my experience, no one knew how to distinguish between the two. It was ambiguous messaging, to say the least. And it dovetailed beautifully with my father's penchant for brutality. It gave him carte blanche to beat us whenever the mood struck him. He could vent his frustration, disappointment, and rage on us and then blame us because we "asked for" a beating by displeasing him. Better yet, he got to feel righteous about it; he was being a "good father" by bloodying his own children.

Convinced as my parents were that the five of us had strong wills, they decided we needed *severe* correction even by IFB standards. My father was always the disciplinarian. We could be beaten for anything: Sloppy handwriting, a misplaced backpack, crying too hard during a spanking session, or a simple sigh on our way to do a chore was enough to incite rage in my father. I can still hear the familiar words, "If you ever do *that* again, I'll kill you! Do you understand me, girl? You better!"

Though many IFB mothers I knew beat their children as mercilessly as their husbands did, my mother left it to him. I can only recall one time when I was thirteen that he insisted she spank me, but she barely touched me with the dowel. Knowing her personality, I think her actions stemmed less from compassion than from a desire to keep a physical distance from me. It seems ironic now that I spent my childhood dreaming about having a baby to cuddle when my own mother was so relentlessly disapproving and cold with us. She seemed to have a specific disdain for me and would often exaggerate claims of my "disobedience" to my father, which would result in one more horrific beating. At times, it appeared as if she were even smirking at me when my father flew into another rage— outlining all my wrongdoings. I can remember trying desperately to coax a smile out of her and getting only a raised eyebrow. Our preachers told parents to be stern and my mother was exemplary in that regard.

When it comes to spanking, IFB parents use all kinds of instruments. The most popular is a rod of some sort. My father favored one-inch-in-diameter dowels of a heavy wood, usually oak, from Menards home improvement stores. They typically came in eight-foot lengths, so he would buy one and cut it in half. He was so proud of his "spanking instrument" that he engraved Bible verses in the wood. One read, "The blueness [bruising] of the wound drives away evil." He stained and lacquered the dowel and drilled a hole in the top through which he looped a leather strap. Throughout my childhood, it hung on the kitchen wall, prominently displayed as a constant reminder of the harsh consequences my siblings and I would face if we ever disobeyed. He was exceedingly proud of his spanking instruments and he made use of them on us almost daily.

Even if they genuinely believed they were saving our souls by beating us, my parents must have been aware that most of society would beg to differ. At least they took great pains to ensure that no one found out what my father was doing to us. They went so far as to stage Child Protective Services training sessions with us. I'll never forget them. My father would call us all into the living room and tell us that we needed to have a family meeting. He would line us all up on the sofa, then my mother would come in wearing a gray wig and horn-rimmed glasses, clutching a clipboard.

"Children, my name is Myrtle and I'm from Child Protective Services," she would say in a high-pitched, whiny voice. "I'm here today to talk to you about what goes on in your home." The two of them would instruct us on what to say or not say if we were ever questioned about their method of discipline. They made us rehearse over and over. *"Where did you get that bruise?" "I fell." "What about that one?" "I bumped into something."* They even recorded the sessions on audiotape and replayed them as we were playing with our dolls and toys in our basement. I still have vivid memories of looking down at my doll and hearing my father's recorded voice in the background saying, "Does your dad spank you?" and all five of us children responding in unison, "No. We've never been spanked." Looking back now, it sends chills down my spine.

As the spanking sessions in our home became more aggressive, my father created what he called the "spanking position." When he decided we were in need of a beating, we were to lie facedown on our beds and put our hands under our stomachs and our faces in our pillow. This ensured that he wouldn't break any of our fingers or hands. Plus, if we ever cried out, our pillows would muffle our screams so the neighbors wouldn't hear.

It's difficult to convey the deep-seated confusion and insecurity you feel as a child growing up in an environment like ours. Irrational and sadistic behavior was often considered normal, even admirable, in our culture, so discerning between right and wrong in my father's actions got muddled in my mind. Nothing speaks to this more than the morning of my tenth birthday.

I woke up early, excited about being in the double digits, even though we had all been up late the night before, ringing in the New Year. My birthday celebration was planned for the afternoon of New Year's Day. My parents didn't make a big deal out of birthdays since money was so tight, and celebrations usually consisted of a cake, a song, and a gift or two. Still, it was a big deal for a child. That day, my father came down the stairs waving the spanking rod over his head.

"It's Jocelyn's tenth birthday today and I want you all to know that she's had a bad attitude lately," he said in a low, menacing voice. "This year for her birthday, I'm taking her upstairs and she is getting ten swats. Let's go, young lady. To your room!"

My heart started thumping wildly. Was he kidding? My father was a prankster and sometimes played tricks like this, so I sat for a moment, waiting for him to burst into laughter. Instead, he shouted, "MOVE!"

I leapt up and took the steps two at a time. Though I assumed my father's wrath was justified, I had no idea what I had done wrong and no time to think it through. I felt no sense of anger, resentment, or injustice. My only emotion was terror. And it was well founded. He gave me a birthday spanking I'll never forget. Welts, blood, and bruises were my only gifts that year. He never elaborated on what I had done to constitute a "bad attitude" and I never asked. I wouldn't have dared.

3

INSIDE THE WORLD OF THE IFB

Any believer who wants to be God's mouthpiece in the world must be a separatist.

—*Bob Jones III, 1985*

"Thank you, Meredith. This is WGRE on location tonight in Green Bay, Wisconsin, where five young children were removed from the home of a Baptist children's pastor after nursery workers at the church they attended discovered bruises, welts, and other signs of physical abuse on the youngsters and called local authorities. When police arrived at the pastor's home, they found a number of wooden rods he had evidently been using to beat his children with on a regular basis. A police spokesperson stated that there was evidence the pastor had also tortured and killed several kittens the family had been keeping as pets. The children were placed in protective custody and are undergoing counseling. Extended family members are working with the state and hope to assume responsibility for all five siblings shortly."

Had that imaginary scenario unfolded, it would have changed the course of my life. Unfortunately, it didn't happen for me. Or for seven-year-old Lydia Schatz, beaten to death in 2010 by her adoptive parents, who claimed they were following the advice of Michael Pearl in his book *To Train Up a Child,* a favorite IFB homeschooling discipline manual, when they held her down and hit her with a plumbing supply line for seven hours, pausing only for short "prayer breaks."

No one stepped in to rescue Esther Combs, the homeschooled daughter of an IFB pastor in Tennessee, during the decade she spent being beaten with whips, chains, bats, ropes, and umbrellas by her adoptive mother, who also pinched the skin off her arms with pliers, and her adoptive father, who sexually abused her, assuring her that King David had concubines too, so the Bible condoned it. When she finally turned up in an emergency room in 1997 after a nearly successful suicide attempt, hospital staff found scars covering nearly every inch of her body. They counted more than four hundred of them. Esther had to swallow almost enough antifreeze to kill herself to kick-start the process that would eventually lead to prison terms for the people who tortured her.

Nor did anyone protect thirteen-year-old Hana Grace-Rose Williams, a Washington girl who was adopted from Ethiopia in 2008. She was beaten, locked in a closet, deprived of food, and forced to sleep naked outside by her new parents, which led to her death from hypothermia in 2011.

The sad truth is, thousands of children just like Lydia, Esther, and Hana are victimized at the hands of Independent Fundamental Baptist churches members every year. And no one comes to their aid.

Like me, they have nowhere to run. Raised in a clandestine subculture that breeds fear and suspicion, they've been taught from birth to distrust outsiders. Most have no idea that charitable organizations and government authorities exist that could offer them counseling and protection. Even if they did know, the majority wouldn't dream of seeking their help.

They are trapped—and invisible to the people outside the IFB who might be able to rescue them. After all, when your teachers, preachers, neighbors, and doctors all embrace the same sadistic childrearing mentality as your parents, who is going to report your injuries? The cashier at the grocery store? The attendant at the gas station? Even if they did, your parents would hide behind the First Amendment, and odds are good nobody from the outside would meddle. It's tragic, but abusers in the IFB know they can use the "religious freedom" argument to do the same kinds of things that would bring Child Protective Services banging down the door in other circumstances.

How the IFB Started

The Independent Fundamentalist Baptist Church movement grew out of a concept called the Doctrine of Separation. This teaching was touted by "Dr." Bob Jones Sr. in the 1950s and then "Dr." Bob Jones Jr. in the 1970s, and it held that all churches and Christians not associated with their ideology were "compromising" and "liberal" and needed to be completely shunned by the Joneses' followers. (I use quotes here and elsewhere to indicate that many leaders of the IFB who refer to themselves as "Dr." only have honorary doctorates.)

"Dr." Bob Jones Sr. was the founder and first president of Bob Jones University. Born Robert Davis Reynolds Jones in 1883 in Alabama, Bob was the eleventh of twelve children and grew up working on his family's farm. The family attended the local Methodist church, and Bob's father encouraged him to memorize and recite Bible verses. Though he was initially shy about public speaking, he turned out to have a remarkable natural talent for it. When he was twelve, he held his first revival meeting. A year later, he organized his own congregation of fifty-four members. By the time he was fifteen he was a licensed preacher for the Alabama Methodist Conference, traversing the state to give sermons. He graduated from high school and attended Southern College, continuing to preach when he wasn't studying. He soon found his fiery sermons in such great demand that he decided to leave college and devote himself to preaching full-time to help support his family. By the 1920s, Jones had become one of the country's best-known evangelists and among its first to broadcast over the radio.

The Roaring Twenties, however, were tumultuous years in American Christianity. Theologians, clergy members, and ordinary churchgoers were clashing bitterly over whether a liberal or a conservative approach to Christianity was right. Everything from the virgin birth of Jesus to the role religion should play in American culture was hotly debated. Of course, philosophical differences still exist among Christians today and probably always will, but the rift of the 1920s and 1930s was significant enough that religious leaders were hired and fired, churches split, and new denominations formed. Scholars call the schism the Fundamentalist-Modernist Controversy. "Dr." Bob Jones Sr. and other leaders in his movement have described his ideology as "militant fundamentalism," founded for the purpose of doing "battle royal for the Christian faith."

This was also the era of the famous Scopes Monkey Trial, when the state of Tennessee prosecuted public school teacher John Scopes for teaching Darwin's theory of evolution. The national furor the trial sparked in 1925 showed just how deep the divide was between Americans who believed in a "biblical" approach to education and those who favored an exclusively "scientific" one. There were plenty of churchgoers in the latter camp even then.

"Dr." Bob Jones Sr. deemed Darwin's theory an abomination, and was dismayed by what he saw as the secularization of higher education in the United States. So he decided to fight back. In the fall of 1925, he created a college of his own, where faith would be honored in every aspect of the curriculum. Its first location was near Lynn Haven, Florida, though the school moved to Cleveland, Tennessee, in 1933. It eventually outgrew its space there and the Jones family broke ground on the current campus in Greenville, South Carolina, in 1947.

Jones founded his namesake college on a thorough rejection of secular humanism and on the creed that the Bible was divinely inspired and not open to modernistic-liberal interpretation. As Jones put it: *If the Bible says so, it is so.*

The Furor over Billy Graham

Jones's hallmark Doctrine of Separation emerged a few decades later, and the catalyst for it was prominent evangelist Billy Graham. Graham gained a national following in the late 1940s and early 1950s through his sermons, which were first broadcast on radio, like Jones's, and then on TV.

Before his rise to fame, Graham spent a semester at Bob Jones College in Tennessee in the fall of 1936 and Jones became a mentor to him. He was among the first to encourage Graham to use his voice to help people find God, and his college even conferred an honorary doctorate on Graham in 1948.

But Graham gradually started distancing himself from fundamentalism and advocating a greater degree of unity among Christians everywhere, rejecting the Doctrine of Separation. Jones was as opposed to this idea as he was to teaching evolution. He thought if conservative and liberal Christians joined forces in any way this would compromise the word of the Lord. He warned his followers that Graham was "muddying the gospel" by including "liberal mainline" clergy from Catholic, Lutheran, Methodist, and other churches in his crusades. He urged them to warn others about the dangers of Graham's "watered-down" message and to oppose the man's nationwide crusades in the late 1950s. Thousands of IFB pastors took his advice and condemned Graham.

Jones's harsher critics speculate that his hatred of Graham stemmed from jealousy. Graham had amassed a huge following. He was on a first-name basis with presidents including Dwight Eisenhower and Richard Nixon. In many ways, his fame had eclipsed Jones's.

The fact that Graham advocated integration and shared the pulpit with Martin Luther King Jr. probably further antagonized Jones, who was no civil rights activist. In a 1960 radio broadcast, Jones told his listeners that God was the author of segregation and opposing it was tantamount to opposing Him. (Bob Jones University later came under fire about the segregation issue and began admitting African American students in 1970. However, the school lost its tax-exempt status in 1983 because it refused to allow interracial dating among its students. Finally, BJU dropped this ban on interracial dating in 2000, though students were still told at that time that they had to get signed permission from their parents to date a student of another race.)

Whatever the real motivation for their animosity, Jones and Graham were both prominent religious leaders, and their battle split believers into two groups: the evangelicals, who supported Graham and his message of cooperation among all conservative Christians, and the fundamentalists, who embraced Jones's Doctrine of Separation from such compromisers.

The last straw for the fundamentalists was Graham's famous 1957 crusade in New York, where he included both Martin Luther King and the prominent liberal Christian leader Norman Vincent Peale. From then on, Bob Jones University drew clear lines of separation from Graham, and shortly thereafter any pastor or congregation associated with him. The school drafted a long list of "acceptable churches" and students were barred from attending any that weren't on the list. Those who got caught worshipping at forbidden evangelical churches received demerits and even risked expulsion if they continued.

All this separatism paved the way for the emergence of the IFB, with its isolationist philosophy and its condemnation of all other Christian churches. Today the cult has even codified the degrees of separation it deems necessary. First-degree separation is from liberals. Second-degree separation is from evangelical leaders like Graham who refuse to separate from liberals. Third-degree separation is from Christians who refuse to separate from leaders like Graham. And fourth-degree separation is from Christians who refuse to separate from fellow Christians who refuse to separate from Graham and his ilk.

As proof of the enduring animosity the Jones family harbors toward Graham, when my husband was on staff at BJU from 1993 to 1995, "Dr." Bob Jones III told a thousand employees, "Billy Graham has done more damage to Christianity than any other person in the twentieth century."

Tightening the Reins

By the 1970s, the IFB was urging its members toward even stricter separation. The sect's rules for living grew more rigid. Christian Contemporary Music was on the rise in America at the time, and churches across the country were embracing artists like Michael W. Smith, Amy Grant, Sandi Patty, and Bill Gaither. "Dr." Bob Jones Jr. and his associates seized on this as proof that American churches were growing more liberal. No IFB pastor who was true to the gospel would allow a rock beat into his music, they warned. Such tunes were of the devil, and it was a perversion of the gospel to mix good, godly words with melodies so demonic.

BJU students were forbidden to attend churches where "worldly" Christian rock bands performed. Friends of mine were expelled from the university for sneaking off to see a local Christian contemporary music concert. Frank Garlock, founder of a company called Majesty Music, traveled around the country warning IFB audiences that the syncopated beat in rock music originated in séances held by African witch doctors. He said laboratory tests had proven that the rock beat killed plants and that long-term exposure to it would damage the human heart. We were all scared to death of the stuff after hearing him talk.

The 1980s and 1990s cemented the rift between the IFB and the rest of the Christian world. At this point, the argument erupted over what version of the Bible believers should read. Hard-line IFBers even claimed a person could only be "saved" after having read the King James Version (KJV), specifically the edition published in 1611. Naturally, churches that let their members read other versions of the Good Book were on the path to damnation.

More moderate thinkers in the IFB (though this is an oxymoron) said they preferred the KJV but the Bible version used didn't matter; the only thing that did was to truly mean it when you prayed to have Jesus come into your heart. Even today, there is fierce debate over the issue, and mentioning it still roils IFBers, who are more or less split down the middle. One evangelist even wrote a song about the Bible version debate (non-rock, of course) called "The Bible Bookstore," commenting ironically on the multiplicity of competing Bibles:

> *Well, I went down to the bookstore, just the other day.*
> *I went to buy a Bible, for I had just got saved,*
> *When I asked to see a Bible, I could not understand,*
> *They had a shelf-full ten feet long, each one a different*
> *   brand.*

After noting many of the different Bibles:

> *They had the ASV, RSV, Good News for Modern Man,*
> *They seemed to have a Bible, for every cult and clan.*

The song humorously blames the devil and Satan for the conflict, concluding that "all of this was part of Satan's plan."

Thanks to the KJV controversy and clashes over other minor religious points, infighting became rampant in the IFB and battle lines that still exist today were drawn between prominent IFB colleges. It's grown into a sort of religious Hatfield and McCoy feud. IFB members align themselves with the prominent IFB leader whose personality or point of view they like best. Some follow "Dr." Bob Jones III or "Dr." Bill Gothard, while others are loyal to men like "Dr." Jack Schaap, who pastored the country's largest IFB church (fifteen thousand in attendance weekly) until he was caught having a sexual relationship with a sixteen-year-old church member in July of 2012.

Prominent IFB leaders run Bible colleges, seminaries, or institutes, which often enables them to indoctrinate young adult followers and keep them loyal for life. IFB colleges and universities bring in millions annually in the form of tuition, grants, and endowments from wealthy alums. Many receive significant funding from the federal government too, while disparaging it at the same time.

Every IFB college has its own pet issue, whether it's the right Bible version to use, the right style of music to play, or the correct definition of "modest" dress for women, or "short hair" for men. Its leaders harp on the issue repeatedly to disparage rival IFB leaders who preach contradictory messages. The goal is to make students wary of the competition so they won't dare explore other viewpoints and get tempted to stray from the flock.

Technically speaking, there are some members of the group today who are not part of any Baptist denomination. In fact, "Dr." Bob Jones Sr. himself was a Methodist until his death in 1968. However, at present, the overwhelming majority of churches that support BJU's Doctrine of Separation are Baptist and the acronym "IFB" is commonly accepted by those inside and outside the group to refer to this belief system. Page 36 of the 2011 BJU faculty handbook sums up the Doctrine of Separation for their employees as follows:

> *Employees may not be members or regular attenders of churches affiliated denominationally with the National Council of Churches or the National Association of Evangelicals. Employees or their dependent children may not attend churches which are liberal or affiliated with or sympathetic to the new evangelical, charismatic, contemporary, liturgical or emergent church movements. This prohibition includes churches affiliated with the Southern Baptist Convention and the Presbyterian Church in*

> *America. While we respect the efforts of conservatives to*
> *rescue Christian organizations from within, our teaching*
> *practice is to separate from false teaching and teachers*
> *rather than to tolerate and cooperate with them....For*
> *your reference, a list of partner churches that students*
> *may attend is available on the intranet under "Life at*
> *BJU."*

Everyone raised in the IFB knows "the rules"—to remain in the good graces of the unofficial, but universally recognized, pope of the cult ("Dr." Bob Jones III), you must follow the guidelines of the Doctrine of Separation above or risk being permanently shunned. Here are some specific examples of current conservative evangelical leaders with whom IFB members are strictly forbidden to associate or cooperate in any way: Rick Warren, Pat Robertson, Jerry Falwell Jr., John Piper, John MacArthur, James Dobson, and Mark Driscoll. These men would be deemed "compromising Christians" by BJU.

My parents were unusual by IFB standards because they bought into the views of nearly every IFB faction at one time or another. As a result, I was exposed to the whole spectrum of its patriarchal ideology. Until I was ten, we followed "Dr." Jack Hyles and "Dr." Peter Ruckman, and we attended "Dr." Bill Gothard's seminars whenever he was in town. When I turned eleven, we joined a BJU church, and "Dr." Bob Jones III became our new "man of God." After we were married and needed marital counseling, my husband and I turned to "Dr." Jim Van Gelderen (vice president of Baptist College of Ministry in Wisconsin). Jim and his family were all BJU grads and his late father was a former board member at the university. After my own children reached school age—or, rather, homeschool age—I started listening to men like Michael Pearl, Doug Wilson, Doug Phillips, Michael Farris, Reb Bradley, S. M. Davis, and Richard Fugate. Beneth Jones (wife of "Dr." Bob Jones III), Mary Pride, Nancy Campbell, and Debi Pearl, wife of IFB spanking guru Michael Pearl, became my heroines.

Conservative politics and IFB membership went hand in hand, so the only news we watched came from Fox. My father was a huge fan of Rush Limbaugh and Bill O'Reilly, and he used to rave about how wonderful both men were for exposing the government's wrongs. After listening to him, I started delving into the conspiracy theories of an extremist named Alex Jones, who advocated building bunkers and stockpiling food. I had friends at Northland Baptist Bible College, when my husband was on faculty there, who actually did those things. They also refused to get Social Security numbers or birth certificates for their children to protect them for the future, convinced that all Christians would be herded off to concentration camps.

Many members of the IFB gravitate toward conspiracy theories and doomsday thinking, and their pastors encourage it. Despite their rivalry, all the IFB leaders embrace Jones's Doctrine of Separation and they all know the best way to keep their congregants separate is to keep them frightened, uninformed, and isolated. It certainly worked on me when I was growing up. You name it, I was afraid of it.

4

THE INNER WORKINGS OF THE IFB CHURCH

God is looking for an army. The greatest threat to Satan in this world is godly parents who understand God's intentions and who will bring forth and train a godly seed to fulfill His eternal plans. God's people have unwittingly decreased God's army in this hour. The womb is a powerful weapon against Satan!

—*Nancy Campbell, Above Rubies blog*

The Church and Sermons

When my childhood pastor, Harley Keck, at First Bible Baptist Church wasn't describing the eternal torment awaiting sinners, he could lapse into long diatribes that were nearly impossible for us to understand as little kids. We sat through them Sunday mornings, Sunday evenings, and Wednesday evenings each week without fail. To a seven-year-old, an hour-long talk dragged on for an eternity, and we were expected to sit perfectly still the entire time. I joke now that if those sermons were an accurate depiction of what's waiting for us in Heaven, I might prefer Hell.

One morning, I remember hearing a noise and glancing down the church aisle to find its source. I caught sight of my sister Melissa with the spine of the church hymnal wedged between her legs. She was moving rhythmically and breathing heavily. I suddenly realized she was using the book to masturbate. Curious, I picked up my own hymnal and tried it too. But it hurt, so I gave up. Eventually, my mother spotted my sister and realized what she was doing. "Stop it!" she whispered in disgust. "Put that down."

My sister did this so often; my mother was mortified and she eventually stocked all the hymnals under her chair and made Melissa sit next to her. But I had to give my sister credit, at least she had found a way to relieve the monotony of Harley Keck's sermons.

An even more bizarre event took place during one Sunday night service. Pastor Keck was in the middle of one of his usual rants, shouting, pointing his finger at us, and banging his fist on the pulpit. All of a sudden a dark-haired man leapt to his feet and started racing in circles around the church, yelling and chanting at the top of his lungs.

"Quick! Get under the chairs!" my mother barked. As always, we did exactly as we were told.

Maybe Pastor Keck's endless descriptions of Hell had gotten to the guy and pushed him over the edge. I peered curiously over the seat of the chair I was huddling under and saw the man grab a potted plant from the front of the church. He resumed his maniacal sprint around the chairs, this time with the pot hoisted above his head, the plant's leaves waving like some bizarre headpiece.

At last the deacons wrestled him into submission and hustled him out the back of the church. Pastor Keck instructed us to take our seats again and, to our astonishment, he resumed his sermon as if nothing had happened. He merely raised his voice to make sure he could be heard over the still audible din in the lobby.

The explanation we heard later was that the stranger was possessed by a demon and the deacons had to exorcise it out of him. Apparently, whatever they did worked because the crazy man became a regular at the church. My siblings and I gave him a wide berth after that.

Although things inside the church were traumatizing, our pastors warned us constantly about the evils that lay just beyond our church doors to reinforce the psychology of suspicion, fear, and alienation. They said plastic toy trolls, like Smurfs, would bring evil spirits into our homes and Cabbage Patch dolls would lead us into witchcraft.

IFB pastors also preached entire sermons on the evils of the television set. In the 1970s and 1980s, television-smashing sessions came into vogue. The pastor would tell the church members who wanted to rid their homes of evil to come to worship prepared to destroy their television sets. I can still remember watching fathers, many of whom had worked long and hard to save up for a television, lugging their sets out of their cars after Sunday services and hurling them onto the pavement behind the church. Then they would use baseball bats to smash the TVs to pieces. I can still hear the splintering, shattering sounds and our pastor's voice above it all, a smirk on his face, crying, "And all God's people said?"

"Amen!" we responded on cue.

BOOM! CRACK!

"And all God's people said?" he demanded again, to which we would blurt out another resounding, "Amen!"

Many of the adults we knew said they felt relieved knowing they were no longer allowing Satan into their homes through those evil machines. Eventually some IFB pastors relaxed their standards regarding owning a TV and—though many still ban most of the programs on it—it's now perfectly normal and acceptable to see homes with one, two, or even three television sets. Even the blessing of their preacher hasn't convinced some die-hard conservatives, though. They still say TVs in the home will be the "slippery slope" down to compromise.

The Church and Biblical Authority

IFB churches deny adamantly that their ministers wield absolute power because almost all of them have church constitutions mandating congregational government. However, corrupt pastors skilled in control have little trouble stacking their deck of deacons with men who will do as they are told, especially if these sycophants have skeletons in their closets that can be used as blackmail. As in secular politics, these IFB leaders live by the adage, "Never trust anyone who doesn't have as much to lose as you do." With the undying loyalty of his deacons in hand, an IFB minister can easily marginalize or drive out any church member who becomes a problem.

After listening to IFB sermons for over twenty-five years, I can hardly remember one where God's command to submit to authority was not mentioned (to one's pastor, husband, or father). As a result, healthy and discerning adults who visit these ministries for the first time typically do not return after a few weeks or are intentionally driven out by the pastor. Yes, IFB churches are governed by the congregation—precisely as the preacher desires. But not every IFB minister is corrupt. Many of them are as brainwashed by the top-tier bosses as their followers, especially those men who lead smaller churches. However, it's very difficult to make it to the upper echelons of the nationwide community without mastering the art of using these spiritually abusive control tactics.

A Man's Authority

The IFB church maintains a strict patriarchal hierarchy, with the pastor at the top, answering to no man. He is considered God's anointed, the mouthpiece of the Lord to His people. Each man in an IFB church answers to the pastor and to "godly counselors," other IFB men who are considered ahead of him on his spiritual journey and act as his mentors.

The powerful men who run the IFB believe that the only way to maintain members' fear of the Lord (and, by extension, effective control over them) is by, first, convincing them to fear and respect the pastor in each IFB church, and, second, convincing them to fear and respect the father or husband in each home.

A Woman's Submission

Wives are taught that they must always remain under their husband, the head of the home, who is God's representative on Earth and their "Umbrella of Protection." Women are never allowed to teach or have any leadership over men in IFB churches. Women often get reprimanded for everything from the meals they cook to the clothes they wear to the extra weight they carry (even after giving birth, an IFB woman is expected to be slim and attractive, to look pleasing to her husband in the eyes of God).

Women are told they are made for the man, as his helpmeet. When it comes to sex, a wife is taught her body belongs to her husband and she is encouraged and expected to provide sex on demand.

A woman's life in the IFB is one of subservience. At the age of three or four, many girls receive their first aprons and start learning to cook, sew, clean, and manage the home to perfection. They're told that their holiest calling is to be obedient daughters who grow into exceptional wives and mothers with a humble and quiet spirit so that their husbands will rise up and call them blessed.

From the time we could speak, my sisters and I learned that our place was below the boys'—and we accepted it. Starting in preschool, we had to adorn ourselves in "modest apparel" (ankle-length dresses and floral jumpers) and keep our hair neatly combed to maintain a godly, Christ-like appearance. My father gave us what he called Christian femininity classes. During them, he made us walk with books on our heads to develop proper posture and "sit like ladies" with our legs crossed, our hands folded in our laps, and our dresses smoothed over our knees so that we showed no skin. He warned us that one of the gravest sins any young girl could commit was to cause a brother in the church to stumble with impure thoughts.

Until they marry, IFB women are expected to obey their fathers with a sweet spirit. After that, they must obey their husbands with the same blind humility. Ideologically speaking, they are striving to live devoutly, but in truth they are utterly powerless.

A Child's Surrender

IFB children fare even worse. They must obey *all* adults in the church. Our Sunday school teachers were dogmatic about the importance of what they called first-time obedience. We were consistently reminded to obey "immediately, completely, reverently, and sweetly." We were never to question adults, whether they were teachers, pastors, fathers, mothers, or other grown-ups in the church.

The running theme of submission to authority is most often impressed upon the children first. The IFB had its own music, which our Sunday school teachers used as a tool to reinforce their authority. The lyrics were set to light, childish tunes that kept us oblivious to the message of enslavement hidden in each phrase. We would smile as we sang, "I will obey the first time I'm told. I will obey right away. Never asking why, never with a sigh, I will obey right away." There was also a strong emphasis on being "warriors for Christ." Our children's songs were wrought with militaristic lyrics, saying, "I'm in the Lord's army, yes sir!" We were continually reminded that one day we may need to rally together and "take up arms" to go to war to "defend our faith" against an evil U.S. government regime and we never questioned any of it.

The IFB church's most effective tool for keeping children obedient was—and is—corporal punishment. It is a cornerstone of the sect's approach to childrearing. Even at the age of seven, when I spanked my doll, I believed wholeheartedly that I had to discipline her to keep her soul out of Hell. I was "rearing" her the same way that my mother and father were rearing me, to be a holy and humble servant.

The adults in the church were all authorities in our lives, and refusing to follow any command they gave would most often result in a beating at home, at church, or in school. My father promoted his wooden dowel at First Bible Baptist Church and was so proud of his innovative "spanking position" that he started teaching other parents in the church how to do the same thing with their kids.

IFB parents were urged repeatedly *not* to spare the rod—a message my father embraced with unabashed zeal. As a pastor, he taught his fellow church members that when the Bible said to beat children with a rod, it meant they should literally use a wooden stick.

Some of my friends' fathers used one-inch-thick paddles with holes drilled through the wood to cut the wind resistance and make the blows harder. Other IFB families used thick belts, leather whips, PVC pipes, and even wooden two-by-fours. Fathers chose their favorite weapons, and we were all ordered to keep quiet about the details of our punishments.

I was playing with my sisters at church one day when my father strode up to us and ordered us to go to the church basement immediately. Terror surged through me. When we got to the bottom of the steps, we saw several parents standing in a circle. "Girls, lay on the floor, in the spanking position," my father ordered.

I was quaking and scared out of my wits, sure we were all about to get a beating for some mystery transgression right there in front of our friends' parents. But we did as we were told, dropping to the floor without hesitation or protest. I have a distinct memory of the cold cement against my nose. Relief flooded through me as, instead of the usual searing pain across the backs of my legs and buttocks, I heard him talking casually with the other adults over our heads. I realized he was doing a spanking demonstration. For my sisters and me it was another exercise in degradation, but he reveled in the power he held over us. I wouldn't have put it past him to spank us just to show off for his audience.

The wooden dowel caught on so well that soon enough, our Sunday

School teachers placed one above each doorway—ready on a moment's notice to administer discipline if need be. You can imagine the culture of submission, silence, and secrecy this engendered.

Along with strict authoritarian methods of parenting, the pastors also preached that our eyes should "glow with the light of the Lord" during worship services, so His joy would radiate in our countenance. This command, they claimed, came straight from God through the instructions in the King James Bible. Only by adhering rigidly to the rules laid out in it could we rest assured that we would meet the Lord unashamed after we died or when we were caught up with Jesus in the Rapture at His Second Coming. As a result, I was continually filled with anxiety about my soul's eternal destiny.

Clandestine stories inevitably circulated in whispers and hisses about the latest discipline sessions. Dr. Ralph Roland, our OB/GYN, a member of our church and a graduate of Bob Jones University, was a staunch supporter of corporal punishment, and my father knew that whenever he beat one of us severely enough that he thought we might need medical attention, Dr. Roland would patch us up without batting an eye—or alerting the authorities. This same man had no qualms about beating his child who suffered from Down Syndrome. Few IFB parents recognize Attention Deficit Hyperactivity Disorder (ADD or ADHD) as a medical condition; most IFB families see it as a sin issue, and are generally even more zealous about beating children with the disorder, in the misguided belief that enough discipline will "correct" their behavior.

Knowing that our friends were getting beaten too gave us some small consolation as kids. But the real driving force behind our passive acceptance of the violence in our lives was that we genuinely believed what we heard in our Sunday School lessons: that only a father who loved his family as much as our fathers did would watch so carefully and work so hard to ensure that our behavior was well pleasing to God.

The Church and the Apocalypse

As a child, I was obsessed with the fear of being left behind when the Rapture came. So were all my friends. This obsession undoubtedly came from the countless sermons we heard from Pastor Keck. Every one of them was filled with hellfire and brimstone. The Apocalypse and eternal damnation were his favorite topics.

"Will you be sent to the dark horror of Hell where the worm [the human spirit] dies not and the torment of hellfire continues for eternity?" he would thunder in his booming voice from the pulpit.

I got a vivid idea of the anguish I would feel in eternity every time my father beat me bloody in the name of God. Our abject terror of the Lord's vengeance kept us all awake at night as kids and, when we finally succumbed to exhaustion, made our imaginations fertile ground for gruesome nightmares.

To reinforce our terror, the church offered Friday Movie Nights—with titles like *Left Behind, Mark of the Beast,* and *A Thief in the Night,* and all with plots involving the imminent doom and destruction of the world. It strikes me as more than a little ironic now that we were warned so frequently about the evils of watching TV while the church was filling our heads with some of the most hideous ideas and images imaginable.

Children in the world outside the IFB were being brainwashed by a "bunch of homosexuals" who ran Disney and hid the word "sex" in the animated twinkling stars of *The Lion King,* our preachers said. Children on the outside of the IFB were blithely unaware that the name of the cat on *The Smurfs* cartoon—Azrael—was the name of one of Satan's top demons, and that anyone who brought a Smurf doll into their home was inviting demon possession. Nor did they know that the "worldly" culture they were submerged in was being seduced by the Antichrist in the form of Barney the purple dinosaur, according to more extreme conservatives in the cult, who preached that the Book of Revelation had warned us of the dinosaur's prophesied coming. "And there appeared another wonder in heaven . . . a great red dragon," pastors would shout from the pulpit. "And they worshipped the *dragon* which gave power unto the beast . . . the dragon, that old serpent, which is the Devil, and Satan . . ."

Lucky us. We were spared from the evil influence of Barney. Instead, we sat in frozen horror watching actors refuse the Mark of the Beast (the number 666 on their foreheads) and then get led by U.S. government officials to the guillotine.

I had vivid, agonizing nightmares after every Movie Night at church.

I can't count the number of times I lay awake too petrified to move. Would the government start beheading everyone who believed in God during my lifetime? If it happened, would I have the courage to die for my faith instead of giving in to Satan? I pictured myself marching solemnly up to the guillotine. Would it be gleaming silver or already gory and bloodstained?

I thanked God that we lived in small-town Wisconsin then and not New York, San Francisco, or Las Vegas. Pastor Keck told horrible stories about the wicked atrocities there. I knew those modern-day Sodoms and Gomorrahs would be destroyed first when God poured out his wrath on the "infidels." Maybe that would give our family time to prepare for our escape. Then again, maybe the Rapture would happen in the blink of an eye—that's what the Bible said. But what if it happened before I had a chance to get married and have kids? Here was another fear to add to the list. If I was raptured so young, I'd miss out on the most wonderful thing to come in my future.

There was a particularly disturbing song we heard in one of the movies about the Apocalypse. Unfortunately, it had a catchy tune, the kind that appeals to us kids much more than a standard hymn and it used to get stuck in my head, playing over and over. I can still recite the lyrics, which focused on the terrible fate of nonbelievers at the time of the Second Coming when: *Life was filled with guns and war/And everyone was trampled on the floor."* The song mercillessly depicts how *"The children died"* and *"the days grew cold,"* lamenting for those who were not ready when there would be *"no time to change your mind/The Son has come and you've been left behind."*

In retrospect it seems downright cruel to expose children to such lyrics, while being taught that if we were "left behind" we'd be facing the guillotine. And there was more than a little hypocrisy in church leaders who bombarded us with dire warnings about the evil words in rock and roll while leading us in songs about dead children and demons. But it took me a long time to see that. It wasn't until years after leaving the IFB that I heard other survivors confess that they too had grown up in abject terror of the end times. I had chastised myself relentlessly, convinced I was only afraid because my faith was weak. Now I know I was afraid because our pastors and parents deliberately instilled fear in us and it made us putty in their hands to control.

We were consumed with visions of death by beheading and fire. We thought all that and more was waiting for us if we so much as questioned a word our pastors said. It was a powerful disincentive to leaving the IFB, the one true church of God on earth.

The Church and Country

Another ingenious method the IFB uses to manipulate its members is to intertwine the theme of American pride with the theme of loyalty to the church. Patriotism was a prevalent topic in every IFB church I attended growing up. American flags and red, white, and, blue color schemes were everywhere. Church leaders told us, "You must pledge your allegiance to God, country, and family in that order."

"America is the greatest nation," they said, "because America puts God first. You should feel proud to be living the greatest lives in the greatest nation on earth." The IFB constantly disparaged and belittled other countries. It proselytized xenophobia, so it's no surprise to me that I heard so many IFB families over the years express a callous attitude toward immigrants within our own borders. Nor did the IFB members I knew seem to feel concern for the poor, the starving, or the wounded in war-torn countries. "What they really need is the gospel," our pastors would say, disparaging the compromising evangelicals for emphasizing social justice issues.

Rather than urge the flock to help the downtrodden of the world, our preachers warned us to ensure that the government didn't give "our money" away to people who didn't deserve it. So much for the Judeo-Christian ethic.

My pastor never acknowledged America's dependence on foreign oil or the importance of maintaining good relationships with other countries. The attitude was simple: It's us versus them. If we need to go to war to get what "we deserve," so be it. We were told that American lives are more important than foreigners' lives. So when a political rival called the president a "traitor" for "buddying up" to foreign dictators, it was easy for me to buy into it wholeheartedly. The cult mind is so filled with misinformation, so deluded, that it's easy to dupe, and extremists in the political sphere have played on this weakness successfully for decades now.

Almost every IFB church I ever set foot in had an American flag on one side and a Christian flag on the other, with its trademark red cross in a blue square on a white background. Between them stands the pulpit because, we learned, God's Word is most important.

Patriotism was woven into many aspects of our schooling too. Our uniforms were red, white, and blue. The boys wore navy pants, white-collared dress shirts, and American flag clip ties. As girls, we wore royal blue skirts that fell several inches below our knees, white blouses, and red ribbons tied in a bow around the buttonhole at our necks. Our uniforms were expected to stay neat and clean at all times. I lost my red ribbon one day and got a memorable spanking for having been so careless.

We began every school day by pledging allegiance to the USA, the Bible, and the Christian flag. Most people know the standard Pledge of Allegiance, but at our school it led into these two variations.

> *"I pledge allegiance to the Bible, God's Holy Word. I will make it a lamp unto my feet and a light unto my path and will hide its words in my heart that I might not sin against God."*

> *"I pledge allegiance to the Christian Flag and to the Savior for whose Kingdom it stands. One Savior, crucified, risen, and coming again with life and liberty to all who believe."*

Mixed-messaging is part and parcel of the IFB, however, and despite all the proud-to-be-an-American propaganda, our pastors often warned us that the country was headed for destruction. The proof? The government was banning the Bible and prayer from public schools and godless feminists were taking over, they said. Women were leaving their homes to go to work and using birth control because they wanted to dominate men, when we all knew it was God's plan that men dominate women.

Listening to them, I could never quite figure out if I was really supposed to love America or despise it. On one hand, ours was the best country, and we were the best people. On the other, God was going to destroy the U.S. for its wickedness—and that destruction could happen any day now. Our pastors continually contradicted themselves, which made it impossible to figure out what was truly "right" and "wrong."

Like so much of the teaching I received as a child, it was a recipe for emotional imbalance. Our cult leaders knew exactly what they were doing; they knew that confused, unstable people were more likely to cling blindly to them for support.

The Church and Outreach to the Community

When I was a child, the IFB ran programs called Bus Ministries to draw disadvantaged children to the church, a concept pioneered by the IFB icon, "Dr." Jack Hyles. Pastor Keck's mentor and the guiding force for our little IFB church in Wisconsin, Hyles was a controversial and hugely influential figure in the cult until his death in 2001. He founded his own Bible college (Hyles-Anderson in Indiana) in 1972, eschewing accreditation. And like others, he found himself embroiled in financial and sexual scandals.

But Hyles is best remembered for building First Baptist Church in Hammond, Indiana, to a staggering fifty thousand members in its heyday, largely through his innovative Bus Ministries program. *Time* magazine featured him in 1975, dubbing Hammond's First Baptist a "superchurch" and noting that attendance at Sunday services had been known to exceed thirty thousand even at that early date. At one point, Hyles had more than a thousand workers on 230 buses, bringing as many as fifteen thousand believers to Hammond to hear him preach. Every Saturday church members went door-to-door throughout the neighborhoods "soul-winning," in an attempt to keep the church growing. "Dr." Jack Hyles's son-in-law, "Dr." Jack Schaap, took over when Hyles died, but as I mentioned, lost his pastoring job in the wake of a recent scandal.

My father eventually became a deacon at First Bible Baptist Church in Wisconsin and was appointed bus captain and pastor to the "bus kids." He held a painting party to deck the outside of the buses out in red, white, and blue and then spent Sunday mornings coaxing kids he found hanging out on the streets to climb aboard and take a ride to our church. He coordinated bus routes through the projects of Green Bay to recruit youngsters. He and the other drivers sang songs, played games, gave out tons of candy, and told the kids how much fun they'd have at church, if they would only give it a try.

Once they arrived at the services, the adults kept the "church kids" and the "bus kids" separated. Remember, we weren't allowed to associate with worldly children who might lead us astray with their devilish ways. I had little contact with these underprivileged youths, but I remember seeing them trudge into church with dirty pants and matted hair and thinking about how much they needed Jesus. I was convinced that if He came into their lives, they would don pretty dresses like the ones I owned, wear their hair in beautiful braids, and be filled with joy. Not that I was particularly joyful myself. But I mention this to show how little I understood about poverty. Kids in the IFB had a Victorian mind-set; we thought poverty was a direct result of laziness or bad morals. We assumed the bus kids were a tarnished group because their parents had chosen the wages of sin.

I suspect one incentive for the adults in our church to expose us to impoverished inner-city kids was to reinforce our appreciation for our own parents. Weren't they wonderful? They taught us about God and the appropriate way to live. Every time I saw another bus kid, I felt flooded with pride and gratitude that *my* parents had chosen the path of purity and righteousness.

The Church and Holidays

When I was a child, the IFB condemned most mainstream Christmas holiday traditions. In my church, Santa was strictly forbidden (I grew up believing the name was an anagram for "Satan"). Halloween was the worst of all. It was the devil's own holiday, so we called it "Harvestfest," instead. Most IFB kids weren't allowed to dress up or go trick-or-treating. Instead, we filled Ziploc bags with candy and slipped an IFB comic book called a Chick Tract into each one to give out to worldly kids who knocked on our door. Chick Tracts told sinister stories about kids who made the wrong decisions and got cast into the lake of fire, but we loved them. We even had a "Tract rack" filled with them in our church. We figured the kids who knocked on our door would love them too and accept Jesus into their hearts after seeing pictures of people burning in Hell.

The books probably gave those unfortunate trick-or-treaters quite a scare, but my memories of Halloween are even more macabre. My father had a talent for taking even the most twisted IFB tradition to new extremes. On one unforgettable October 31, my father staged a Haunted Woods Walk for all the kids in our church. Though he had no training and was not ordained, he was the children's pastor by that point, and he was given free rein to design the activities. Knowing him all too well, I was terrified as our group gathered at the edge of the woods at 9 P.M. We shuffled along a path, pressed close together for safety, as adults from the church jumped out from behind the trees to spook us. My father had also rounded up a huge number of live pigeons and set them loose so they scuttled around our feet and took flight suddenly, flapping past our ears in a cluster when we got too close. It heightened the drama delightfully and I remember squealing from both fear and excitement.

But as we pressed deeper into the woods, the scenery became more grisly. My father had hung dead mutilated deer, rabbits, squirrels, and raccoons from nooses in the trees, and the kills were fresh enough that blood dripped from their torsos as we passed. Sickened, I averted my eyes. Then I heard a noise that snatched my voice away and chilled my blood. Somewhere ahead in the darkness, my father was laughing. But it wasn't a normal laugh. It sounded warped, sadistic. I was keenly attuned to his moods and every instinct told me to bolt the other away. But I was swept along in a tide of kids blithely unaware of the danger.

"Quick! Grab him," I heard my father hiss. "Good job! Do it just like this."

We came to a clearing in the trees and there stood my father, demonstrating to a group of enthralled, horrified boys how to snap the neck of a pigeon. As the bird's body went limp, he let out a demented howl of laughter and contorted his face into a hideous expression mimicking the bugged-out eyes of the animal he had just murdered. Several of the men from church were leaning against tree trunks nearby watching the show, and they chortled approvingly, spurring him on. "Now do this," my father said, showing the boys how to tear the legs off the pigeon's body. Even in the dim light of the moon, I could see blood spattered everywhere.

The boys giggled and raced off in all directions, chasing pigeons. Several of them rolled on the ground laughing hysterically, whether from nervous shock or genuine enjoyment I had no idea. One came barreling toward me, waving a mangled bird in my face. I bolted past them and pounded down the path as fast as my legs would carry me, gasping for breath, not caring that I was alone in the woods at night. I wanted nothing more than to get as far away from that walk as possible, to get as far away as I could from my father.

The Church and Private School

It's quite common for IFB churches to run their own private Christian schools, usually housed in the same building as the church and headed by the local pastor. Classes generally range from one to twenty-five students, and total enrollment can be anywhere from thirty to four hundred students in a K–12. You don't need any formal training to teach in most IFB schools; you just have to belong to the church running it and buy into its views. The vast majority of these schools have no state accreditation or curriculum checks and no oversight. In fact, they have no outside involvement whatsoever.

When we weren't hearing about the imminent dangers of watching Saturday morning cartoons like *The Smurfs* during Sunday sermons, we were treated to a description of the litany of horrors in the public school system. It was run by the dreaded "secular humanists," whose primary agenda was to ensure that the American people would accept the gay and lesbian community. Homosexuals, we were assured, were the worst of all sinners. They wanted to take over our country and destroy every shred of morality left in it. By the time I was seven years old I could rattle off a complicated definition of a secular humanist. I don't mean to imply that I was well educated. I had no idea who Martin Luther King Jr. was. But I was steeped in IFB ideology. I was sure that "they" were the bad guys and we were the good ones.

In nearly every service we heard another tirade against public school. My father vowed that he would never subject his children to such a godless system. "When you have kids of your own someday, you'd better put them in Christian schools," he warned. "If you don't, they'll lose their souls to the devil!"

In my mind, public school was a place where you got drugged, raped, and murdered. It sounded as terrifying as the impending Apocalypse.

It's no surprise that the IFB leaders fear public schools. Concepts like progressive education and experiential learning encourage kids to question accepted ideas, think independently, and draw their own conclusions. Those are dangerous concepts when you're trying to keep the sheep in the pen.

Worse, public school teachers taught scientific subjects like the theory of human evolution. True to the spirit of "Dr." Bob Jones Sr., our IFB schoolteachers assured us that evolution was nonsense. They made fun of it. An IFB evangelist even wrote a catchy little song called "I'm No Kin to the Monkey," that became a favorite in our Sunday services. I liked it so much I sang it while I played with my toys at home. This song decries and makes fun of the teaching of evolution, and concludes:

> *Oooo, I'm no kin to the monkey,*
> *The monkey's no kin to me,*
> *I don't know much about his ancestors,*
> *But mine didn't swing from a tree....*

Our Christian school in Wisconsin was a tiny operation, owned and run by our church, with classes in First Bible's basement. Our elementary curriculum was a self-directed program called Accelerated Christian Education, ACE for short. We had to complete workbooks every day. Whenever we finished one, we were supposed to go to the "score table" to correct our work. To indicate that we were ready, instead of raising a hand, we put a small American flag in a hole at the top of our desks that were painted red, white, and blue. When the teacher saw the flag, she'd say, "You may go to the score table."

All our parents signed waivers stating that school personnel could spank us whenever necessary. Based on my experience, school "spankings" ran the gamut of abuses from physical to sexual, just as "spankings" did in many IFB homes.

When I was in second grade, I had a hard time scoring my work thoroughly. I compared what I had written to the answer key, but I was always missing little errors like misspelled words. Whenever I failed to correct one of my mistakes, my teacher deemed it cheating. She thought I was trying to make it look like I'd done a better job on the work than I really had. And every time I "cheated," she led me to the bathroom upstairs for a spanking. The school's policy was to emulate your parents' discipline sessions, and I remember her putting a paper towel under my nose as I lay on the cold tile floor with my hands under my stomach while she whipped me with the familiar wooden dowel. The pain in my wrist bones as they were compressed against the hard floor was excruciating.

With every spanking, I grew more riddled with anxiety—and more prone to errors. To add insult to injury, the school told our parents whenever they had disciplined us, and my father's rule was that if you were spanked at school, you would get a repeat performance at home that night—with double the number of "swats" received at school—to reinforce the point.

I tried diligently to correct every booklet perfectly, but inevitably I'd miss something and get dragged upstairs for another beating. Then I would stumble home filled with dread, knowing an equally vicious session lay ahead.

Looking back, I realize how ludicrous it was to expect a seven-year-old to be so precise in her schoolwork. The correction process became so distracting and traumatic for me that I couldn't focus on reading or writing and it was a struggle to learn anything. No wonder. Research shows that high levels of the stress hormone cortisol can actually decrease the size of a child's hippocampus, the part of the brain you need for processing information properly.

The Church and Home: The Gospel According to Bill Gothard

While I was spending my mornings facedown on the bathroom floor at First Bible, my father was growing more and more enamored with an IFB icon named "Dr." Bill Gothard. He started attending parenting and family seminars led by Gothard, a minister and founder of an organization called the Institute in Basic Life Principles. While I was growing up, I can't remember an IFB home that didn't contain at least one of the distinctive red notebooks handed out at Gothard's Basic Life Seminars.

Though he has never been married, Gothard instructs men and women all over the country on the biblical model for the husband-wife relationship. He tells them women should not use any form of birth control and that a wife must submit completely to her husband's every wish (provided he doesn't command her to disobey a clear biblical teaching like stealing, murdering, or becoming a prostitute) in order to stay under the "Umbrella of Protection," a term he popularized. If a wife stepped out from underneath her Umbrella, he warned, God would punish her Himself or use the devil to chastise her. Either way, it was a grave sin.

Gothard was also a big proponent of keeping unmarried women under their fathers' Umbrella of Protection for life. After my sister Melissa graduated from college with her nursing degree and was working to support herself, my father tried to insist that she move home and live in the basement until "God brought the right man along." She told him no in no uncertain terms. She was truly the independent one. That's the reason she left the IFB four years before my husband and I did.

Gothard runs seminars on childrearing too, and his instructions for children are essentially identical to his orders for women: They are to obey unconditionally. Those who fail lose the blessing of God on their lives, he warned in the seminars my father attended.

He also advocated another bizarre behavior for children called "making an appeal." My father loved it and implemented it in our home immediately. We were never to ask for anything directly. Instead, we had to make an appeal to him. So rather than say, "I'd like a piece of candy," we would say, "Dad, would it be possible for me to have a piece of candy? I don't need one and if you don't think it's best, that's okay. But I would really enjoy one. Please?" This was so drilled into our psyches that I would lie in bed, silently crafting statements to my father for hours. I knew that if I phrased one sentence wrong I might well get a beating for making an inappropriate appeal. With my father, it was always better to say too much to qualify an appeal than to say too little and leave room for doubt in his mind. To this day, I use too many words to express my feelings because I was so conditioned to "make an appeal."

It had had horrible ramifications in certain situations. For instance, in 2007 Matthew Murray, a former student enrolled in Bill Gothard's program, shot and killed four people at two Christian Centers in Colorado before turning the gun on himself. Murray, had stated in blog posts, "[we] were raised on home school and we both went through some insane stuff growing up in The Nightmare that outsiders just do not understand." He went on to say, "Me, I remember the beatings and the fighting and the yelling and the insane rules and all the Bill Gothard [expletive] and the trancing out [expletive]. I'm still tranced out."

Another issue to consider is the IFB's culture of abject submission of daughters to their fathers, and the disturbing sexual undercurrent that ran through it. Thousands of IFB survivors are speaking out publicly now about abuse and have confirmed the rampant sexual abuse within IFB homes, which is perhaps not surprising considering how many fathers in the cult were ordering their daughters as old as seventeen to lift up their dresses and bend over the bed so they could be spanked.

The IFB song that seems to me to epitomize this subliminal sexualizing of father-daughter relationships is "I Want to Marry Daddy When I Grow Up." Little girls in the IFB sing it most often on Father's Day and it makes my hair stand on end because of its fantasized approval of an imagined, physically incestuous relationship ("I love for him to hold my hand and cuddle up with me") between father and daughter. ("If I could marry Daddy when I grow up, I'd be as good as any girl could be.") You can find videos on YouTube of them in their little dresses in Fundamentalist churches like the ones I attended, looking out at their dads adoringly and singing the lyrics.

The phenomenon of Purity Balls is equally unsettling. Conceptualized more than a decade ago by a Colorado couple named Randy and Lisa Wilson, Purity Balls are formal dances fathers attend with their daughters of all ages, in which the daughter signs a contract agreeing to stay a virgin until marriage and the father makes a pledge to protect the girl's purity. The Wilsons, founders of their own ministry called Generations of Light, have grown the concept into a huge enterprise. Nearly five thousand dances have been held in forty-eight states and tickets often cost upward of $100. If they had existed when I was a kid, I have no doubt my father would have dragged us to them. Mothers can attend similar balls with their sons, which are sometimes called A Knight to Remember, though they're far less popular.

Purity Balls strike me as yet another sugarcoated means of subjugating young girls. Not only does the ritual minimize a mother's role in her daughter's life, but it asks girls to relinquish control of their own bodies and put their sexuality into the hands of a man. Here's the pledge itself for fathers:

> *I choose before God to cover my daughter as her author-*
> *ity and protection in the area of purity. I will be pure in*
> *my own life as a man, husband, and father. I will be a*
> *man of integrity and accountability as I lead, guide, and*
> *pray over my daughter and my family as the high priest*
> *in my home. This covering will be used by God to influ-*
> *ence generations to come.*

After a lifetime under the patriarchal thumb of the IFB, words like "authority" and "covering" send up red flags the moment I hear them because they smack of Gothard's Umbrella of Protection approach. From an IFB husband's viewpoint, a wife and a daughter are equals on many levels. If the IFB fosters a father-daughter relationship between men and their wives, is it sending confusing ancillary messages about the relationship between fathers and their daughters? It certainly did in my home when I was growing up.

I find even more cause for concern in the fact that extremists like Doug Wilson are loud proponents of Purity Balls. Wilson, one of my idols in my cult days but no relation to the Purity Ball movement founders, is an IFB homeschooling advocate and founder of a ministry called Vision Forum. He is also unabashedly medieval in his views on sex, claiming that the Bible commands a woman to be no more than a passive recipient, a vessel. With male chauvinists like that as its champions, it's hard to believe the Purity Ball movement really has young women's best interests at heart.

The Church and a Woman's Reproduction: Quiverfull

Arguably, the nation's best-known window into the world of the IFB these days is the Duggar family. Arkansas couple Jim Bob and Michelle Duggar and their now nineteen children have been featured on five Discovery Health and TLC documentaries and spotlighted by countless TV and radio shows, including the *Today* show, CNN, MSNBC, NPR, AP Radio, CBS Radio, and Fox Radio, not to mention international outlets. They've been the subject of articles everywhere from *The New York*

Times to *Parents* magazine to *Ladies' Home Journal* about their astonishing number of kids (all of whom are homeschooled and all of whose names begin with the letter "J") and their conservative Christian lifestyle. Most people know them as the stars of TLC's hit show *19 Kids and Counting*.

Judging from blog comments, American audiences find something appealing in TLC's portrayal of the clan's lifestyle as a wholesome *Leave It to Beaver*–esque throwback to simpler times. For viewers who've grown up in modern America and have no experience with oppression or patriarchy, I can see how the network's depiction of the Duggars might seem like heaven on earth. But, speaking as a survivor of that subculture, the reality is far different.

For months, I couldn't bring myself to watch the show. Even reading articles about the family sent me spiraling back into the darkness of my own childhood. Though the Duggars don't use the term "IFB," the telltale signs are everywhere from the language they use to the homeschooling curriculum they recommend (the same ones all of us IFB moms used when we were homeschooling our kids).

When I finally steeled myself to sit through a few episodes, I wasn't surprised to see scenes shot in an IFB church (the family's oldest son was married in one during an episode) or to see footage of a music conference at one of the largest IFB churches, Bethel Baptist, in Schaumburg, Illinois. My husband had actually spoken at a Fundamental Baptist Fellowship conference at Bethel Baptist and I hosted a ladies seminar for homemakers there—so it was a flashback to my past. Hearing ads for "Dr." Bill Gothard's unaccredited Advanced Training Institute (ATI) was another telltale sign that they were loyalists of his teachings. Gothard is a big proponent of living debt-free, as are Michelle and Jim Bob Duggar. It might be an admirable principle—and the Duggars seem to manage their finances successfully—but avoiding debt entirely is unrealistic for many Americans, and it can have dangerous consequences for less business-savvy families. You get a glimpse of this when the TLC show focuses on son Josh Duggar's in-laws, who raised their six daughters in a trailer. Untold difficulties arise when you're not only living but homeschooling children in such cramped quarters.

Based on my years of experience, the Duggars' success is the exception, not the rule. No story illustrates the dire potential consequences of following this model more than that of Andrea Yates, a homeschooling mother of five who lived in a few hundred square feet, though her husband worked for NASA, because the family wanted to embrace the "simple lifestyle." Ultimately, Andrea lost her mind and drowned all five of her young children in the bathtub. I spent a year with four kids and a fifth on the way living in a doublewide trailer and I, too, thought I was going to lose my mind with so little space.

A wave of anger flashed over me when I heard Michelle Duggar mention a "jurisdiction." To an average viewer, it would just sound like odd phraseology, but it left no doubt in my mind that she was a Gothard disciple. "Jurisdiction" is a term he coined to replace the more familiar "chores." The theory is that using it gives children a sense of ownership for certain responsibilities. But in reality it's just more cult lingo, and you'll hear a lot of IFB lingo if you watch the Duggars. The men who run the IFB are masters at using language to reinforce their followers' sense of separation from everyone else. As children, my siblings and schoolmates and I were forever being reminded that the IFB was better than the rest of society; others weren't enlightened enough to understand terms like "jurisdiction" when it came to parenting.

People on the TLC show sometimes ask Michelle Duggar if she wants more children. Invariably, she replies with an enthusiastic, "Yes! We want all that God will give us." No one explains to viewers that as a Gothard follower, she'll undoubtedly believe it's a sin to use birth control and that to balk at the idea of pregnancy would displease God. In IFB circles, this is known as a "Quiverfull ideology." It comes from Psalm 127: "Like arrows in the hands of a warrior are sons born in one's youth. Blessed is the man whose quiver is full of them [children]."

My own father became so enamored with the Quiverfull concept when we were in Wisconsin that he decided to form us into a family nursing home ministry. He made us practice songs like "Amazing Grace," "Just as I Am," and "I Surrender All." Then he dressed us up in our matching Sunday best clothes and dragged us to every assisted-living facility for the elderly he could find, billing us as the group "Quiverfull." Whenever we sang, we held a small American flag in one hand and a Christian flag in the other. Afterward, we would talk with the residents, presumably spreading Christian warmth and cheer to lonely old folks. My love for the elderly was seriously shaken one day when a lady named Kora suddenly slapped me across the face as I was chatting politely with her. I had been so trained to control negative emotions that I simply stood there in stunned silence. My father walked over, checked my cheek to see that no serious damage had been done, and soon he turned it into another funny anecdote he could recount to friends in the years to come.

Not all IFBers take a no birth control stance, but the Quiverfull lifestyle has thoroughly permeated the movement. My dear friend Vyckie Garrison escaped it after giving birth to seven children and has started a blog called No Longer Qivering (minus the letter "u" because "there is no 'you' in quivering"), dedicated to exposing the domineering, patriarchal practices within the IFB. On her blog, she explains how dangerous the Gothard viewpoint is for women and how stressful it can be to feel that God expects you to give birth to another baby every year. Of course I can relate to that anxiety well, having had eight babies in nine years. It took an incredible toll on my young body, which would have been obvious to anyone. The psychological effects are much harder to see, but so many pregnancies combined with having to care for so many small children on what's often a tight budget can set IFB women up for incredible depression and anxiety. That's exactly what it did to me.

Giving birth year after year obviously can be dangerous. You run the risk of everything from gestational diabetes to preeclampsia. If you're prone to morning sickness, you're consigned to years on end spent bolting to the nearest ladies' room to vomit. Repeated weight gain and loss puts great stress on your joints. Childbirth comes with even more risks. IFB women who have endured a problematic labor but feel forced to have another baby every year constantly face the possibility that they might not make it this time. But, as Vyckie has explained in interviews, we were always told that a woman shouldn't shrink from dangers. We should honor God with our bodies. After all, Jesus died for us. We should be willing to die for him, argued Quiverfull proponents like writers Mary Pride, Nancy Campbell, and Debi Pearl.

Many IFB homeschoolers were firm opponents of pain relief during labor too. God intended women to suffer during childbirth to remind us of our original fall from grace in the Garden of Eden, they said. But having a beautiful baby placed on our chest afterward was supposed to compensate for all this because it reminded us of God's redemptive plan for us.

Gothard would have you believe mental illness is just a manifestation of sin, so if you are a woman suffering from postpartum depression, you are sorely out of luck in the cult. Those in power will tell you all you need to do is succumb to the will of God and read the KJV and you'll be fine.

Vyckie has done an admirable job raising awareness about the dangers of the Quiverfull lifestyle. A number of survivors have also come forward to share stories of the abuse they suffered at the hands of overstressed fathers and mothers in Quiverfull homes, some in the throes of untreated mental disorders. To date, Vyckie has shared hundreds of their accounts and has had 1.9 million visitors to her blog, demonstrating the prevalence of these oppressive beliefs still in our society today.

I find it astonishing that anyone could present the patriarchal lifestyle as if it's as sweet and wholesome as apple pie. Yet the Duggars come across as modern-day Waltons. The truth is, if you're a Gothardite, Campbellite, Pearlite, or Prideite, as IFB survivors call people who follow those icons' teachings, you not only buy into the notion of complete subjugation of women but you also subscribe to the idea that every child's will must be broken.

It's a demand—not a suggestion—that "you beat him to save his soul from Hell," as Proverbs 23:14 instructs. Nobody talks about it on TLC, but those of us raised in homes like the Duggars' know full well that you can't be deemed "a godly family" if you spare the rod. One can only wonder how Bob and Michelle get nineteen kids—most of them under age twelve—to stand still, fold their hands, and smile into the camera?

After spending most of my life immersed in the darker, more sinister underside of the IFB ideology—the side that led to Lydia Schatz's and Hana Grace-Rose Williams's death—I feel it's important for Americans to see more than the sanitized utopian version reality TV presents. That's my motivation, painful as it is to relive my past, for sharing my story.

5

EARLY YEARS IN COLORADO (1985–1988)

I spanked my daughter when she was seventeen . . .
and she'll tell you, she needed it.
—Matt Olson, Lecture to Pastors,
President of Northland Baptist Bible College/
International University, 2006

Growing Anxiety and Restlessness

I could feel my body switching into fight-or-flight mode. Adrenaline surged through me, making every muscle tense and reducing my breath to quick shallow gasps. But I had no way to escape. I was seven years old. I wasn't allowed outside without permission and I was too little to think of running away. So I crawled under my bed and curled into a ball, covering my ears to muffle the awful sounds coming from the next room.

My brother Jason, who was now eight, had gotten into the habit of lying and my father swore that every time he caught him doing it he would double the number of blows he gave him with the wooden dowel. I knew it was going to be a bad night when Jason blundered into another obvious fib a few minutes after we all sat down to dinner in our converted schoolhouse home. My father exploded. He'd already given Jason thirty blows with the wooden dowel. This time it would be sixty.

As I huddled in the darkness under the box springs, I sang softly to my doll, trying to drown out the barbarity that was only too audible through the wall.

"Jesus loves me, this I know, for the Bible tells me so . . ."

"Roll over!"

My father's harsh shout was followed immediately by the ominous whistle of the rod and a sharp *smack* as it made contact with my brother's skin. Jason let out an anguished cry. I could tell by the muffled tone of it that his face was buried in his pillow.

"Do you think you can lie to ME and get away with it?" my father boomed. "Who do you think you are? You little punk! Now, roll back over!"

My stomach muscles clenched at the fury I heard in his tone and at the low, pitiful sobs of my brother. I tried again to tune it all out.

"This little light of mine, I'm gonna let it shine. This little light of mine, I'm gonna let it shine, let it shine, let it shine, let it shine . . ."

I ran my fingers through my doll's hair and whispered gently into her ear, "Everything's going to be okay." Being her mommy, I knew it was my job to make her feel safe. I repeated the words like a mantra, as much to quell my real fears as her imaginary ones.

Sometimes the blows came in furious succession. Sometimes my father paused to rant or preach at Jason, and anywhere from two to eight minutes elapsed before I heard another *smack*. At last the whistle of the rod stopped. "Stay put," my father ordered tersely. I heard him stomp out of the bedroom and head for the bathroom. I knew Jason was covered in bloody welts and my father had gone to retrieve the first-aid supplies he always used to treat the wounds he inflicted on us.

It was over. Still, I remained pressed against the wall in my hiding place, cringing as I thought about the pain Jason must be feeling. I knew that pain all too well myself.

Jason's brief stint as a compulsive liar would soon become one of my father's favorite jokes. Through some irresistible urge to tempt fate, Jason lied to him one more time after getting sixty lashes. He was now facing 120 blows with the rod. Maybe my father didn't want to bother with a marathon spanking session. Maybe he was afraid he'd do real damage. Or maybe he was seized with a rare fit of compassion. Whatever the reason, he reduced Jason's sentence to a single blow. When he announced his decision, Jason was dumbfounded.

"You mean, you're only going to give me one?" he asked. "Not two? Not three? Not four? Just one?"

This struck my father as comical and he doubled over laughing. We never heard the end of it. He told the story countless times, even to our teenage friends when they came over to our house years later.

Looking back now, I can't find any humor in the incident. It strikes me as yet more evidence of the psychological manipulation that was so typical in the IFB. The fact that Jason received unexpected mercy from my father when he had deliberately defied him threw us off balance just as much as my getting a beating on my tenth birthday when I'd done nothing wrong. Somehow, trivializing Jason's misbehavior after having beaten him so savagely a few days earlier made my father even more menacing. He doled out punishment all the time, but he was utterly unpredictable about it. He might fly into a rage. He might burst into laughter. We never knew what to expect. But we were groomed to accept whatever he did to us from the time we were toddlers.

It's a classic move in power politics, and Bart knew how to use it instinctively. "Be deliberately unpredictable," advises Robert Greene in his bestselling book *The 48 Laws of Power*, analyzing the most effective tactics of ruthless leaders from Machiavelli to Mao. "Behavior that seems to have no consistency or purpose will keep them off-balance, and they will wear themselves out trying to explain your moves. Taken to an extreme, this strategy can intimidate and terrorize." Many victims leave a cult only to join another. Reading the "laws of power" highlighted in Greene's book is highly beneficial for former cult members, to help them understand what they have been through and protect themselves from being exploited, once again, by the tactics cult leaders use instinctively to control people.

The Way West

By the time Jason had his legendary run-in with my father, our family was in desperate financial straits. The tension in our home was reaching a crescendo. Carpet-laying jobs were scarce in our part of Wisconsin and my parents were in debt up to their ears. There was barely enough money to buy food, so we were living from one can of peas to the next. When my father discovered that my brothers' winter boots were full of holes, he made them secure plastic bags over the toes with rubber bands to keep the snow out. We heated our home with a wood stove, so Jeremy and Jason had to tromp out in those ruined boots even in blizzard conditions to cut wood for the fire. When she could scrape together the ingredients, my mother would bake because it was cheaper than buying bread, and one of my few happy memory of those dark times is the sweet smell of freshly made dinner rolls filling the air of the shabby little schoolhouse.

Bart knew we were headed for disaster. He needed to take drastic action. He and my mother had honeymooned in Colorado and they must have had pleasant memories of it because they decided the road to financial freedom led to the Rockies. My father always said he was a cowboy at heart, and he had had enough of Wisconsin's long bitter winters to last a lifetime. So one night after we finished our evening prayers (we called them family devotions), Bible study, and one of "Dr." Bill Gothard's read-aloud Character Sketchbook lessons, he pulled out a U.S. map and pointed to Colorado.

"Would you like to move away from Wisconsin?" he asked. In a rare pretense of democracy, he took a vote. All five of us raised our hands. I remember hesitating, unsure which answer he wanted and worrying that I would provoke him by getting it wrong. We were wide-eyed, tingling with fear and excitement at the thought of going on an adventure, starting a new life in the mountains.

Over the next few days, we told everyone at church we were leaving. My four best friends and I all cried and hugged each other, realizing our days of playing house with our dolls together in the church nursery at recess were ending. We loved each other dearly and I knew I'd miss them. First Bible only had about thirty students, and in a school as small as that, you get very close. Our IFB friends were not only our confidants but also our only social contacts.

The congregation threw us a going-away party, but Pastor Keck was livid when he found out we were leaving. My father had been a pillar of Keck's church—children's pastor, deacon, and de facto PR man for First Bible through his Sunday bus routes. Vicious as he often was to us, Bart could be extraordinarily charismatic when he wanted to win someone over. Almost everybody loved him when they first met him. Not surprisingly, he had increased Keck's flock considerably through his weekly Bus Ministry. He and Keck also had attended "Dr." Jack Hyles's annual Pastors'

School in Hammond, Indiana, and Keck had come to regard my father as a close friend during those retreats.

"You're stepping out of the will of God," he warned my father. He told the church members God wanted the Janz family to stay in Wisconsin, and we were ignoring His wishes for us. But Bart was not a man to be intimidated, even by his own pastor. He reminded Keck that the church had done nothing to help our family monetarily. "There's no way I can stay here and keep a roof over our heads," he said.

Our fellow church members empathized with our decision and didn't hold it against us. They cried, hugged us, and passed pictures around the food tables, reminding us of all the fun times we had shared. There were photos of our family wearing cowboy hats and riding horses during the week we spent at family camp at Bill Rice Ranch (an IFB summer camp in Tennessee named for the evangelist who founded it in 1953), and snapshots from Northland Camp and Conference Center in Dunbar, Wisconsin, where our entire church went every summer and where my future husband, Joseph, would eventually work. More pictures passed hands, followed by tearful goodbyes. But, as sad as I was to leave my friends, I was brimming with excitement about our new adventure.

From Small Town to Big Time

Several days later we were packed like sardines into our old station wagon with my mother at the wheel, ready to make the long trip to Colorado. My father led the way, driving ahead of us in a U Haul truck. We had no money for fast food restaurants, so my mother had packed homemade snacks to eat along the way. When we finally arrived in Denver, we drove straight to the house of a couple my parents knew. Though they were strangers to my siblings and me, they had generously agreed to let us stay with them for a few months while my father jump-started his carpet business.

We did our best to be unobtrusive, but living in another family's home is always a little uncomfortable. Still, I remember feeling less afraid in the weeks we spent under their roof than I had in my life. I knew that as long as my father was around other people, he'd never act out the way he did in private with our family.

My parents practically gushed with enthusiasm as they told us about the new church we would be attending. The pastor was "Dr." Ed Nelson, a graduate and board member of Bob Jones University. "Wait until you see the church," they said, their eyes shining. "It's huge!"

To me, bigger was always better, and from the moment I set foot in South Sheridan Baptist Church's two-thousand-seat auditorium, I loved it. It was all perfect—the beautiful music the choir sang, the gorgeous foyer, the women's sophisticated long floral dresses with their crisp white collars and hose to match, the men's sleek suits and ties, the pastors' elevated platform, reminding everyone that they were in charge. At first I felt intimidated by the church's sheer size. But as I grew accustomed to it, it shrank, as things tend to do in a child's eyes, until it had almost the same dimensions as our old Wisconsin church and everyone inside it seemed like extended family.

From an IFB family's viewpoint, the transition from Wisconsin to Colorado was momentous not just geographically but philosophically. We were switching from a small church loyal to "Dr." Jack Hyles, to a big church, whose loyalty was with Bob Jones III. Both men were formidable forces in the IFB, and intense rivals. Each demanded absolute loyalty of all his followers and they could make or break a man's ministry career. Every IFB insider knew that the way to climb the church ladder was to be asked to speak at the cult's prestigious annual leadership conferences, and a word from Hyles or Jones could get you an invitation—or ensure that you *never* got one. IFB pastors lived under the sword of Damocles: They could be blackballed at any moment by their respective IFB godfathers for doing or saying anything that wasn't approved by the top brass. In moving to South Sheridan, my father had essentially switched "mob" families (Hyles to Jones—to put it colloquially).

Shortly after we arrived in Colorado, Bart met with "Dr." Nelson to find out whether South Sheridan would be right for our family. He was floored when, on hearing about our financial hardship, Nelson wrote him a check from the church for $200 for groceries. He said the man won his heart on the spot. Pastor Keck had known how desperate we were for years, yet he had never offered us a penny.

Practically speaking, most IFB pastors have complete control over how their church's money is used. If that control isn't codified by the church's own bylaws, then it's often secured through the pastor's selection of yes-men deacons who rubber-stamp their decisions. In addition to using money to create lifelong loyalty in down-and-outers like my father, many IFB pastors regularly invite fellow ministers from other states to their churches as special guest speakers. Afterward, they send them home with a "love offering" of thousands of dollars, expecting the men to return the favor in the future. "Dr." Bob Jones III most likely received record love offerings since he was on the road for a large portion of every year ministering to his international IFB flock, flying from place to place in his private jet, then back home to his mansion on the BJU campus.

Nelson's generosity to Bart set the trajectory of my life. From that moment on, the man could do no wrong in my parents' eyes. Not only was he a BJU alumnus, he was also a long-standing university board member, pastoring one of the country's largest BJU megachurches. He and "Dr." Bob Jones Jr. seemed to be bosom buddies. Later "Dr." Bob Jones III would visit annually. "He's the godliest man alive," they told us in hushed and reverent tones. We were forbidden to speak a word against either "Dr." Nelson or "Dr." Bob Jones III, though the rebellious kids called him "triple sticks" under their breath. On the rare occasions when one of these two icons walked into our Sunday School classes or a classroom in our IFB school, our teachers ordered us to leap to our feet to show respect. It was like having the president of the United States pay you a visit.

Actually, it was better. We thought much more of "Dr." Ed Nelson and "Dr." Bob Jones III than we did of the president, no matter who was in the White House. Growing up, whenever a Democrat was elected we heard that America was "in big trouble." When a Republican took office, we were "in a time-sensitive situation" and needed to act quickly to run the liberals out before they could ready us for the guillotines.

Our overriding concern was always our religious freedom. We were terrified some godless liberal would restrict our ability to worship and bring God's wrath down on us. Given our belief in the impending Apocalypse, we thought one misguided decision in the White House could put our immortal souls in danger.

A Curriculum Change

My parents soon found a house for us to rent and enrolled us in Silver State Baptist School, the local private IFB K–12. I was ten and starting fifth grade that fall. Our first year in Denver was particularly traumatic. My father was still struggling to get his business up and running, so my mother took a job at United Airlines out of desperation. They were both still staunch believers that mothers should stay home, but there was no other way they could pay for tuition and necessities for five growing kids.

One reason our IFB education cost more in Colorado was that Silver State used different teaching materials. "Dr." Jack Hyles churches most often used "Dr." Bill Gothard's Advanced Training Institute (ATI) and the Accelerated Christian Education (ACE) curriculum favored by TLC's Duggars, which were relatively inexpensive. Bob Jones University churches, on the other hand, used Bob Jones Press materials and A Beka Books from Pensacola Christian College, the two largest IFB curriculum distributors in the country. Both programs were considered top notch in the IFB, and they were, not surprisingly, considerably more expensive. IFB home-schoolers often use a mix of all of these programs.

It didn't matter which "curriculum" they favored, Christian schools and textbooks typically taught nothing but memorization and obedience. We were drilled in reading, writing, and math, but we learned almost no legitimate science or history. Our critical thinking skills were virtually nonexistent. We were told exactly how to think on just about everything.

The ACE textbooks we used were always red, white, and blue to underscore the IFB-patriotism link and they featured Christian character-building lessons at the bottom of every page, even in math. BJU's books contained blatant inaccuracies. For example, according to one Bob Jones Press fourth-grade science textbook:

> Electricity is a mystery. No one has ever observed it or heard it or felt it. We can see and hear and feel only what electricity does. We know that it makes light bulbs shine and irons heat up and telephones ring. But we cannot say what electricity itself is like. We cannot even say where electricity comes from. Some scientists think that the sun may be the source of most electricity. Others think that the movement of the earth produces some of it. All anyone knows is that electricity

seems to be everywhere and that there are many ways
to bring it forth.

Another passage from a seventh-grade Bob Jones Press textbook instructs students that, "Since the Bible is always accurate, we can use it to
judge scientific observations and any conclusions based on observations.
Any observation or conclusion will fit one of three categories. It will
1. contradict the Bible and be wrong, 2. agree with the Bible and be accurate, or 3. not be discussed in the Bible and may or may not be accurate."

And one passage from an ACE textbook notes, "Biblical and scientific evidence seems to indicate that men and dinosaurs lived at the same
time. . . . Fossilized human footprints and three-toed dinosaur tracks occur in the same rock stratum. . . . That dinosaurs existed with humans is
an important discovery disproving the evolutionists' theory that dinosaurs lived 70 million years before man. God created dinosaurs on the
sixth day. He created man later the same day."

It appalls me that after enduring years of such mis-education myself,
which contradicts modern science, and finally getting our own children
away from it, my husband's and my tax dollars—and yours—are being
used to underwrite the same misinformation for a new generation. School
voucher programs were designed to help low-income and special-needs
students obtain a better education. But the reality is that vouchers allow
states to use public funds to pay for private education in religious schools,
many of which teach some of the same nonsensical IFB rhetoric my classmates and I learned. According to recent data from the U.S. Department
of Education, 80 percent of students who participate in Washington,
D.C.'s, voucher program attend a faith-based school. The number is even
higher in Florida, which has the country's highest number of tax-subsidized
school vouchers.

A 2012 report presented to the House Committee on Education and
the Workforce by the National Coalition for Public Education noted that,
"Private schools are not subject to the same transparency as public schools—
there are no elected school boards, rights to review records, or other accountability measures. . . . Students attending private schools with vouchers
are stripped of their First Amendment, due process, and other constitutional and statutory rights offered to them and guaranteed in public schools."

In Colorado the Bullies Rule

Academic issues aside, our move to Silver State Baptist school caused great upheaval in our family. My mother was no longer around to keep an eye on us at a time when my brothers were adolescents, going through all the biological shifts that age entails, and we were all struggling mightily to make friends in a school where it wasn't easy.

Cliques were well established at Silver State and there was a distinct division between the "cool" church kids and the "losers." The "losers" were children whose parents had unimpressive minimum-wage jobs and held no leadership positions in the church. The "cool" kids' parents were professionals who earned good salaries and played influential roles in the church. It was easy to spot their offspring. They all hung out together. They played sports. And even though the standard IFB regulations applied to clothing, hair, music, and television, these kids knew how to look more fashionable than everyone else.

Most IFB girls weren't allowed to wear pants, except on very specific occasions. For instance, if we were at home with the family or doing something athletic like horseback riding, my parents deemed pants acceptable. But the sartorial goal for IFB girls' clothing was "lots, loose, and long." (Needless to say, we weren't allowed to color our hair. Boys had strict guidelines as well and weren't allowed to wear theirs longer than their ears or spike it with gel.) Most IFB moms made their children's clothes and many were accomplished seamstresses. My mom had spent hours at the sewing machine when we lived in Wisconsin making us culottes, which were essentially big skirts split down the middle—cotton ones for youth group activities and snow-pants-style ones that could be worn in the winter for sledding, hiking, skating, and skiing. Mixed swimming was generally banned in the IFB, but on rare occasions when we were permitted in the water with boys present, we had to wear dark T-shirts and culottes, which ballooned out awkwardly and tangled around our legs, creating a drowning hazard. Girls were always worried the water would "take them away." It was no surprise to me when the Bates family, the newest Quiverfull family with a reality show on TLC, made their teenage daughters wear full-length skirts while whitewater rafting during one episode and their teenage sons swim in jeans at their hotel swimming pool.

During our first years in Colorado, my mother broke the IFB pattern and stopped sewing altogether and most of our clothes came from Goodwill. I was petite and rail-thin, so I managed to scrounge a few decent size 0s and 2s, but my sisters were stockier. It was almost impossible to find anything flattering that fit IFB standards and so their self-esteem plummeted.

While the "cool" girls all wore long khaki skirts with polo shirts, a number of the "uncool" kids at school wore tattered, disheveled clothing. Some of the girls hung their heads and their eyes had a vacant look. I remember being struck by how hopeless they seemed. The homeschooled kids who showed up for our Sunday School classes exuded the same morose, downtrodden aura. My heart went out to them. We weren't segregated from them like we had been from the bus kids in Wisconsin, so I tried to be friendly, but they barely talked and we never became close. Looking back, I'm struck by how similar their demeanor and body language were to that of many victims of abuse I've met since leaving the IFB. Now I would recognize the telltale signs, and I would have a better understanding of how to reach out to them. Back then I had no clue.

There is one boy who stands out in my memory. His hair was greasy, his clothes were too small and filthy, and he smelled. Every time I saw him at school or church, he was wearing the same pair of pants. He was sullen and distant, with a pained sort of expression. It never dawned on me that he could be being abused to extremes even we couldn't have imagined—extremes like those in the Esther Combs case. As a kid, I just thought he was slovenly and apathetic. After all, one of our favorite Sunday School songs, sung by our favorite Christian music artist, Patch the Pirate (Ron "Patch" Hamilton), included these lines:

> *Pigs don't live in houses and pigs don't make their*
>   *beds.*
> *Pigs don't wash their faces. They love the dirt*
>   *instead.*
> *So, if you're not a piglet, make the difference clearly*
>   *seen,*
> *Pick up that messy bedroom and show you're Christian*
>   *clean.*

On and on that song went, listing different childhood scenarios and making the point that a messy family was not a God-honoring family. Dirty boys and girls were lazy. They needed discipline. Is it any wonder I concluded that the boy was a little piglet who lacked the godly character to keep himself clean? My heart breaks when I think back on that now. But the IFB didn't advocate state intervention even when they suspected severe child abuse. Nobody seemed worried about the boy's welfare. The pristine, well-dressed kids in the IFB just wrinkled their noses whenever he passed.

There was a little girl in my fifth-grade class who didn't seem much better off than the boy. But rather than ignore her as they did him, the boys targeted her mercilessly. Their favorite game was to pass her "cooties" around. I distinctly remember the teacher, a graduate of Bob Jones University, as virtually all of them were, rolling her eyes and chuckling at their cruelty. "Hey, now. Stop it. Don't say that about her," she chided, but her tone was light and her manner implied that it was all in good fun. With no consequence, the boys redoubled their attacks. One day I glanced over and saw tears streaming down the girl's face, cutting a clear line through the dirt and revealing bright, white skin. I remember being shocked at the amount of grime on her cheeks and feeling sorry for her. Eventually they got bored tormenting her. By the time we reached junior high school, they treated her as if she didn't exist—just like they did the little boy in the grubby outgrown pants.

You could make the case that bullying is endemic in schools, but our school seemed worse, given the fact that the people running it professed to be teaching us to follow Jesus's example. Not only did the instructors at Silver State habitually ignore bullying, some of them fostered it. They seemed as immature as the students, giggling along sycophantically at the bullies' antics.

My Father: The Biggest Bully

My father was a natural when it came to bullying, and it didn't take him long to figure out that our new IFB church was on the same page as the old one when it came to discipline sessions. Pastor Ed Nelson was a proud proponent of "breaking the will of the child" and he proclaimed it vociferously from the pulpit. He even told stories of the many times he had needed to break his own children's wills.

Like many other members in our congregation, we soon became patients of Dr. Roland, a general practitioner who was a fellow member of our church. Dr. Roland was so passionately anti–birth control that he refused to prescribe contraceptives for any of the women in the church. He and his wife had nine children and when he found out my mother was working outside the home, he launched into a lecture about how they were doomed to lose all of us to the wicked world outside the IFB.

Christy, the Rolands' third child, became my best friend. We both loved practical jokes and we spent hours laughing over the silliest things. But the best fringe benefit of befriending the Rolands, from my parents' point of view, was that the good doctor was always ready and willing to patch us up without blanching if my father went too far during a discipline session.

I remember one beating in particular that my younger sister Melissa got in third grade for not completing her chores, always a sure way to infuriate my father. He beat her so severely that she couldn't sit down. Fortunately (from Bart's perspective), Melissa's teacher was a BJU graduate, and instead of calling the police or Child Protective Services, she simply stacked cardboard boxes up in the back of the classroom to form a makeshift desk. My sister stood behind them and did her school work for three days, until she was able to gingerly rest enough weight on her thighs and buttocks to stay seated at her desk through the day again.

I knew Melissa was in agony and that standing for so long made her shaky and weak, but even I applauded her teacher's solution at the time. Everyone in the cult would have considered her "crazy" if she had arranged for a state investigation of our household because bringing ungodly people into our lives would cause us to lose our souls to Hell. In my mind, Melissa's teacher had done exactly as God would want her to do.

I wish that was my worst memory of abuse, but those were some of the darkest days of my life. Dealing with a working wife and a houseful of preteens while trying to build a new business was getting to my father, and his violent temper manifested itself in new and terrifying ways.

He started beating us for things as simple as not emptying the dishwasher, forgetting to put in a load of laundry, or failing to dust his desk. I was responsible for pulling what he called "fuzzies" off his dress socks. He was obsessive about little details like that and if he discovered a stray hair or piece of string had somehow attached itself to one of them, he would fly off the handle and beat me. I was desperate to perfect my work, spending from two to three hours at night meticulously picking tiny lint balls off the socks, but it felt like second-grade workbook scoring all over again: No matter how hard I tried, I could never get it right. I would always end up in the spanking position, facedown with my hands tucked under my pelvic bones, getting battered with a rod.

Over time, the endless beatings took a toll on our emotional stability. We were crumbling inside. But you would have never guessed it as an outsider looking at us. We were well mannered and flawlessly groomed. We were also "cultured" enough to play musical instruments. I sang, as well as played piano and violin, and loved doing all three. We were the model perfect family on the outside, which seemed to matter most to the IFB.

Melissa fared even worse than I did back then when it came to punishment on one memorable occasion. She was a born rebel and, one night when she was eleven, she decided to express her independence. She had vacuumed the entire house, but when my father came home, he found two balled-up carpet fibers under his bedroom nightstand. To him, this proved she had been lazy. Too angry to waste time retrieving the rod, he flew down the stairs with his belt in his hands and screamed, "Get upstairs to my room NOW!"

Melissa hesitated, but stood her ground. "No," she said tentatively, as if she was testing the waters.

No Janz child had ever refused to lie down and take a beating. None of us had ever defied my father this openly and, hearing her refusal, I gasped so hard I felt light-headed.

My father seized Melissa and threw her onto the steps. She landed on her side, but scrambled to her feet, pure terror in her eyes. He lunged after her and shoved her hard. Her head slammed into the wall, but she bounced back to her feet and scrambled up the staircase. Over his yells and her shrieks, I heard thuds and crashes as he shoved her down the long upstairs hallway toward my parents' bedroom.

She told me the details later. She said he ripped her clothes off, stripping her naked, and threw her onto the bed. "You're about to get the beating of a lifetime," he growled. "Put your face in the pillow and your hands under your stomach, girl. Nobody says no to me!"

Frantic to get away, Melissa rolled off the far side of the bed. But Bart vaulted over the edge of it, swinging the belt wildly and striking her anywhere he could land a blow. He hit her legs, her hands, her back, even her face as she crawled on her hands and knees toward the door. Naturally, it was locked, but she gripped the handle and managed to pull herself to her feet and fled for the master bathroom, with him in pursuit, flogging any part of her body he could reach. There was no bathroom door, so she had no hope of protecting herself. At last she surrendered and agreed to lie on the bed to avoid any more blows to her face.

Even after that, he beat her so viciously for so long that as she lay there with her hands pinned under her abdomen, she gouged deep chunks out of her own skin in an effort to cope with the pain. She thought she was going to die. More than a half hour later, he finally decided she'd had enough. He told her to put her clothes back on and marched her out of the bedroom.

He called all of us into the living room to make sure we got a good look at Melissa and assured us that if we ever refused to lie down for a spanking, the same or worse would happen to us. Every part of my sister's body bore the marks of the beating. There were wide angry red lines across her face. She could easily have been blinded if the belt had caught her a few inches higher or lower.

My father ordered me to go upstairs and get the thickest foundation and face powder I could find on my mother's dressing table and bring it to him. Without a word, I did as he instructed. We all watched him cake layer after layer of makeup and powder on Melissa's face to conceal her wounds.

We were supposed to attend a U.F.O. (Unusual Fellowship Opportunity) that included a movie at church that night and we were forty-five minutes late. When we finally arrived, Melissa couldn't sit in the pews. She stood in the back of the church next to the ushers, just as she had done in third grade. Eventually my father spotted her and told her if she didn't take a seat, he would take her home and give her a second beating to rival the first. She hobbled over to her friends and lay on her side next to them in a pew.

"What happened?" they whispered.

"I got a bad beating," she rasped. Her stomach ached, she was running a fever, and she could barely sit up. When we got home from church that night, she went straight to bed.

Melissa was never the same after that. She became brooding and introverted. Whenever she could, she would escape to her room and vanish into drawing, which resulted in her developing unusual artistic skill. Even now, so many years later, she's still an amazing artist.

The Price of Playing the Devil's Tunes

Melissa wasn't the only one chafing under the harsh rules of my parents and the IFB. My brother Jeremy, however, was more covert. When he was fifteen, my parents caught him masturbating and listening to rock music. To an IFB father, those are sins as grievous as doing drugs or running away would be to the average American parent.

On one occasion, my father found a tape by the rock band Bon Jovi hidden in Jeremy's bedroom. He flew into a blind rage. "GET THE ROD!" he shouted at me. "Bring it here!"

Petrified, I ran downstairs for the dowel, wondering if I was about to get a beating too. I knew when he became this livid, he could turn on any one of us. Sometimes three or four Janz kids would be lined up for discipline sessions.

Bart dragged Jeremy into his bedroom and locked the door. We heard him yell, "Get those clothes off!" Jeremy was blubbering the way you would expect a five-year-old child to cry. As usual, I stumbled numbly into my own bedroom and sat like a statue, trying not to listen to the hideous clap of the wooden dowel as it hit Jeremy. Between blows, my father paused long enough to upbraid my brother for his disgraceful behavior and to bellow the familiar, "ROLL BACK OVER!"

When the beating had dragged on for more than thirty minutes, longer than Melissa's terrible session with the belt, my whole body started to sweat. I couldn't take any more. I dropped to my knees beside my bed and begged God to save Jeremy.

"Please don't let him die!" I prayed. "Please, God. I love my brother. Let him live through this."

I started telling God about all of Jeremy's wonderful qualities. I told him how empty our lives would be if my father killed him. "I know he sinned, but I'm sure he learned his lesson. He'll choose to walk uprightly now. Please, God, make my father stop," I implored.

At last the door opened and my father shouted, "All of you, get in here NOW!"

I can still see it in my mind's eye, as if it were a movie playing. Terrified I was about to find Jeremy's bloody, lifeless body sprawled across the bed, I stepped tremulously into the room. My sisters followed, cowering behind me. My father lined us up shoulder to shoulder at the edge of the bed. Jason stopped in the doorway, so petrified his eyes seemed to be bulging out of his head.

"Take a good look at Jeremy," my father ordered.

There was a long pause as we all looked down. Jeremy lay naked, facedown in the spanking position with his hands hidden under his stomach and his head buried in the pillow weeping. The pose was familiar, but he was shaking so violently from head to toe that it was obvious he had no control. Blood covered the entire backside of his body. It was splattered all over the sheets and pillows.

We stood transfixed until my father broke the silence, his voice shooting through us like a jolt of electricity. "If you EVER listen to rock music, this will happen to you too!" He shook the bloody rod in each of our faces, then he threw it at Jason. "Take that to the kitchen and wash the blood off of it! Now get out of here!" he told us, reaching for the salve to treat Jeremy's wounds.

Bad Attitudes and Homeschooling

Not long after this, Jeremy got caught stealing equipment from the science lab at Silver State Baptist High School, where he and Jason were students. My father met with the principal at the school, which was adjacent to our church, and told him to expel his son. He would homeschool him instead. That would be Jeremy's wake-up call, Bart predicted.

A short time later, Jason got caught stealing candy from the gas station across the street from school. My father was so angry he not only beat them, but he pulled all five of us out of school and forced us to do a year of homeschooling together. My brothers were football players in the school sports program and they were devastated to be off the team. (The

IFB places tremendous importance on boys' sports—not surprising, given its male-dominant culture.) Jeremy was on the small side, and he was painfully self-conscious about it. A year without football practice would set him back so much he might never get to play a starting position. But that didn't matter to my father, despite the fact that he had spent our whole childhood brooding over the fact that his own dad never let him play high school sports.

He vowed to correct our bad attitudes and teach us to be grateful. Naturally, no one at school ever brought up the subject of abuse with my father. Nobody dared suggest that Bart's children might be acting out because there were problems in the Janz home. There are no licensed school counselors on staff at IFB schools, so there was no one to intervene on our behalf, though we would have been ripe for a state intervention. Private IFB schools like ours are, to this day, utterly autocratic. They operate with complete disregard for traditional educational norms. And in all my years attending them, no one outside ever intervened.

Children like us were, and still are, left alone in isolated religious settings, without even one responsible, caring adult to turn to when they are in danger. We were at the mercy of my father in every way, and school personnel backed him unconditionally. They gave full support to his idea of removing us from school at the end of the year. They asked no questions about how our homeschooling would be handled, who would be in charge of teaching us, or what academic materials my parents planned to use.

Nobody warned my parents that homeschooling without supervision was illegal in Colorado, though every member of the administration and faculty knew that both of my parents worked full-time. They never suggested that we come in periodically so they could evaluate our academic progress. My father was the head of our home. He made the decisions. They believed that no one inside the IFB or out should question his authority.

Curtains Drawn, No One Watching

The year that followed my brothers' expulsion was a travesty. Both of my parents left for work around 8 A.M. Neither one got home before 5 or 6 P.M. Before they left, they drew all the curtains in the house and warned us to keep them closed to make sure no passersby glanced in and saw five unsupervised teens at home. They told us to be perfectly quiet and never to answer the door or the phone. We were to sit at our desks in the front room for the entire day and do our ACE and Alpha Omega booklets, then score the work ourselves. Of course, while my parents were gone we just filled in all the answers from the score keys in our booklets. We received no education whatsoever that year.

Instead, my brothers and sisters would sneak off to watch MTV, while I went to my parents' room and settled down in front of their small black-and-white television set. My favorite shows were *I Love Lucy*, *Leave It to Beaver*, and *The Brady Bunch*. *The Brady Bunch* was strictly forbidden because my parents thought the characters had bad attitudes and wore feminist clothes, but I loved it.

My job was to listen for the garage door. When I heard it go up, I would run down the hallway and call, "They're here!" The kids downstairs would switch off the TV and race back to their desks, while I flipped off the set upstairs and pounded down to mine. By the time my parents walked in, we were seated like perfect angels, diligently bent over our schoolwork. My brothers affectionately called our homeschool, "Party Hearty Christian School."

Unfortunately, it wasn't much of a party for me. I had just turned thirteen and I was going through significant hormonal changes. I felt exhausted all the time. I had put on thirty pounds, and the extra weight was taxing my small frame. Maybe it was inevitable that my changing body would draw the attention of two hormone-fueled teenage boys who were keeping close quarters with me and had no healthy outlets for their pent-up sexual urges.

During those long terrible months with no one around to watch us, my brother Jeremy molested me more times than I can count. He had been groping me about once a week ever since I'd turned eleven. Now, finding himself in an unsupervised environment, his attentions grew more frequent and more intense. He was extremely violent. I became hyper-vigilant whenever I walked past bathrooms and closets, because he would hide behind doors then leap out and grab my arm with incredible force, yanking me in and slamming the door behind us. I had deep bruises in the shape of fingerprints all over my upper arms. As soon as he got me alone, he would start to kiss me aggressively and grab my breasts until they throbbed. The harder I pushed against him to get away, the more threatening he grew. He never looked me in the eye, but kept his eyes fixed on my breasts and lower body as he took off my clothes piece by piece until we were both naked. He would then jam his penis between my legs and rub against me until he ejaculated against my vagina.

This happened several times every week. And even though Jason had also kissed me and ejaculated against me while groping my breasts, I remember he and my sisters banging on the bathroom door and yelling, "Stop! Disgusting! Get out of there!"

Jeremy would bang back on the door from the other side and scream, "Leave me alone!"

I was appalled and deeply ashamed, but I had no idea how to get out of the situation. I was frightened of Jeremy's violent temper, but I was equally afraid my father would chop him into pieces and bury him in the backyard if he ever found out, assuring IFB church members and friends that Jeremy had run away. Then he would chain me in my room for the rest of my life, blaming me for having somehow enticed my own brother.

Sometimes Jeremy dragged one of my sisters off and did the same thing to her. I remember feeling sorry for them, but utterly powerless. The molestation continued until I was fifteen when Jeremy left for college. Years later, after going to therapy, I realized what a miracle it was that I never got pregnant.

Being molested by my brothers was only one of many violations I suffered. I've had to find a way to come to grips with much more than that.

6

STRUGGLING THROUGH THE TEEN
YEARS (1988–1993)

Listen, mom and dad, do you know many times your daughter sneaks out in the wee hours of the morning to have sex with her boyfriend? . . . I'll take pictures for ya.
—*"Dr." Pastor Jack Schaap, sermon,*
First Baptist Church, 2012.

I knew punishment and fury would always be inextricably linked in our home. No matter how immersed he was in IFB philosophy, my father never mastered the concept of administering "biblical discipline" without wrath. He raged through every beating, crimson-faced and roaring at the top of his lungs about our shortcomings, our selfishness, and our failure to please both God and him. Year after year, his anger seemed to intensify, as did his unpredictability. Sometimes he seemed bent on finding any excuse to punish us, as if he was searching for a reason to unleash his hair-trigger temper and vent pent-up hostility.

I've always suspected that this was what brought on the terrible beating I got when I was thirteen for the crumbs on the dishwasher. Under his orders, I had spent an entire weekend day exhaustively cleaning the house. I had dusted and vacuumed, polished and scrubbed, straightened and tidied until the place was immaculate. I had been beaten for minuscule oversights like wiping around canisters on the kitchen counter rather than under them and failing to line up the cans in the cupboard neatly with all the labels facing front, so this time I had paid scrupulous attention to detail. Or so I thought.

Before my father left for the day, he commanded, "I want this kitchen spotless when I get home!" I knew what that meant: The smallest infraction would merit a beating. So I was taking no chances. I devoted hours to working my way through every drawer, the pantry, and each appliance in the kitchen.

As soon as he got home, he began his usual white-glove test, combing over every inch of counter and cupboard. I held my breath as he lifted each object, inspecting the spaces under them for dust and crumbs. Then he opened the cabinets and scrutinized every shelf of dry goods for disorder. I was just tentatively starting to exhale when he opened the dishwasher. I felt a surge of panic, but I reminded myself that I had emptied it hours earlier, taking care to make sure every dish was perfectly dry and neatly stacked in the cabinets. I had even double-checked to make sure no silverware had slipped into the space at the bottom.

There was a moment of silence as he peered inside the machine. Then his back went rigid and my heart stopped.

"WHAT IS THIS?" he bellowed. "COME HERE AND LOOK AT THIS!"

Timidly, I approached. To my horror, I saw a fine line of golden crumbs along the ridge at the top of the machine's door. It must have been slightly ajar when I wiped down the counter, and I had knocked a few crumbs onto the lid without noticing.

"YOU THINK YOU CAN GET AWAY WITH SLOPPY, CARELESS WORK LIKE THAT?" he roared. "GO TO YOUR ROOM! NOW!"

Terrified, exhausted, and fighting back tears as usual, I did as I was told. A few minutes later, he barged into the room, slammed the door behind him, and locked it.

"Take off your clothes and lie down!" he yelled. "Face in your pillow!"

I did as I was told, tucking my hands into the familiar position under my stomach. The motions were so ingrained I didn't need to hear the words. Soon enough, I heard the whistle of the rod, followed by the sudden shocking force and the intense, agonizing pain. I flipped onto my back as I always did, fully exposed to my father. It's a testament to the abject terror we all felt that, even as teenagers, my siblings and I gave no thought to modesty during our beatings and instinctively rolled over naked on our backs to protect our thighs and buttocks, which he always targeted.

For some reason, I specifically remember counting in my mind during this particular beating: "34 . . . 35 . . . 36 . . ." I lost track after 37 hits, overwhelmed by the intense pain and the knowledge that there was more to come. When it was over, I could barely stand, but I managed to maneuver my way to the linen closet, where I used an old towel to wipe up the blood. Lying awake that night—I didn't move much—as I was racked with fever and chills.

Years later, after my departure from the IFB, I saw the Julia Roberts thriller *Sleeping with the Enemy*, about a woman who escapes a cruel, sadistic husband. There's a scene in the movie where the main character opens a cupboard and finds all the cans aligned perfectly—a chilling warning that her abuser has returned to her home after discovering her whereabouts and is stalking her. Seeing it hurtled me back through time to that terrible day in the kitchen in my parents' home in Colorado and triggered a full-blown panic attack. The cans were aligned identically to the ones I had arranged in the cabinet when I was a teenager.

It strikes me as odd now that never once did it occur to me that there was anything sexual about the beatings my father gave me. We were almost always at least partially naked during our beatings, and it was totally acceptable behavior in our home. He had disciplined all of us this way since our toddler years, so I thought his demand that I take off my clothes was just part of the discipline process.

I knew what my brothers had done to me was wrong, but I believed my father was spanking us for our spiritual benefit. So what if our developing bodies were fully exposed to him on a regular basis? I had never heard of BDSM (bondage, dominance/discipline, sadism, and masochism). I was still laboring under the delusion that his only motivation was to save our souls. How naive I was. In retrospect, it's a wonder I didn't realize he had been sexually abusing us in many different ways for years—and not just during our spanking sessions.

Back to High School

After our year of homeschooling, my siblings and I returned to Silver State as if nothing had happened. Jeremy and Jason rejoined the football team, which made them big men on campus. Meanwhile, I became a basketball and football cheerleader. In keeping with IFB modesty standards, we wore split skirts that fell below our knees, harking back to the culottes my mother used to make. Dancing was forbidden in the IFB, unless it was with family members (yet another rule that drained the joy out of life) and we weren't allowed to perform any cheers that involved moving our hips in an "ungodly" way, so our routines were grossly lacking. We became acutely aware of this whenever we played public schools, because their squads' impressive flips and drills made us cringe in embarrassment. Our moves could have been choreographed by the Three Stooges in comparison.

My parents' financial situation had improved considerably by this time, thanks to my father's now booming carpet business. IFB children are drilled from a young age to have the strong work ethic required of "disciplined servants of the Lord," and as teenagers we spent long hours working alongside Bart, providing free labor for him. My brothers cut the tile and laid the carpet, mastering tasks that are typically done by adult men, while my sisters and I went along to do the cleanup on each job.

Making the most of their newfound affluence, my mother drove a convertible, and my father bought a new super-cab pickup truck every few years. Bart and Sandy became well known for throwing ribeye-grilling parties in our backyard for all their friends from church. "The steak is on us," they'd proclaim with magnanimous grins. But no matter how much they spent on the things they wanted, they were relentlessly tightfisted when it came to their kids. They thought nothing of dropping $200 dining out, but they "couldn't afford" braces for us. When school started, we were given $50 each for new clothes, so we were still forced to shop at Goodwill. When I needed money for my cheerleading uniform, my parents humiliated me in front of the entire squad with their theatrics. "You want *how* much?" they demanded. I'll never forget the decorative throw pillow that lay for years on our living room couch with the embroidered words, "If you don't fly first class, your children will."

Years later, when Melissa and I went to counseling after breaking free of the IFB, we realized their miserly behavior had been yet another form of manipulation. My father used money, just as he used physical violence, to keep us dependent and helpless. He refused to let us get jobs, assuring us that he would pay for our college tuition. But, as was so often the case with Bart, he fell through on his promise when the time came. Melissa took a year off school to work to help pay for Meagan's school expenses and then used student loans to get her own degree. I too depended on student loans to cover the costs of college, and the first check Joseph wrote each month after we were married was to repay my unpaid school bills, a hefty blow to our meager budget.

Road Trips from Hell

One of my mother's perks as a United Airlines employee was that we could all fly standby for almost nothing, and when I was in high school we traveled extensively. We went to Disneyland, Walt Disney World, Hawaii, Chile, and even took a cruise to the Bahamas. By the time I was eighteen, I had visited almost all fifty states. My brother Jeremy wanted to take his senior trip to London before graduating from college, so we all went. After I left home, my parents and brothers went to Russia, Africa, India, Ireland, Australia, and the Cayman Islands.

Despite the cult's reclusiveness, traveling wasn't as uncommon as you might think. Many IFB kids I knew in Colorado had been all over America. But often the only places they visited on their trips were IFB churches and IFB colleges. The Bob Jones network was extensive, so you could travel from an IFB stronghold in the West to one in the Deep South and still feel right at home. This allowed members to have the illusion of seeing the world without actually getting exposed to any new subcultures or viewpoints. As insular and isolationist as they were, the cult maintained a number of missions that preached hard-line IFB ideology around the world, and teenagers were sometimes sent to places like Mexico and Africa to help build and paint IFB churches. To protect them from the corrupting influence of the locals, they were cloistered in the mission churches, with the girls cooking and cleaning for the work crews and the boys doing manual labor and preaching in the evening.

Our travel itineraries sounded enviable, and I felt very lucky to have the opportunity to go places, but my father made every trip nerve-racking. He never budgeted correctly, so we were always precariously short on funds. We would pack suitcases full of dry cereal to take to London or end up with $15 spending money per person in Hawaii for the whole family. To cut down on expenses, my parents often booked two small hotel rooms, assuring the front desk staff there were three people per room, then packed us all into one room while they took the other. My maternal grandfather had passed away by that point, and, after my father reconciled with his mother-in-law, he got into the habit of inviting her along, which made us even more crowded, though she was able to defray some of the expenses. When our flights were delayed or we got bumped from a full flight, we usually slept at the airport rather than spring for another night's accommodations.

My mother and father could never seem to get anywhere on time. The two of them would scream at each other all through the drive to the airport, glare at us as we rushed through security, and then yell at us to "Run!" to our gate. In the late 1980s and early 1990s, United employees flying standby were expected to dress up. For my parents, that meant making my sisters and me wear full-length Sunday dresses, and we were always sprinting through O'Hare International Airport, desperate to catch a connecting flight without tripping and sprawling flat on our faces. Nowadays, I'm habitually early when I travel. I get to the airport three or four hours before every flight because having to rush brings back memories of all those miserable, stress-filled trips.

Flying standby meant we had to wait for everyone else to board and then squeeze onto packed planes, splitting up and grabbing any seat available. After all that, the eight of us would have to de-board whenever a latecomer with a paid ticket showed up. We would cringe when we heard the familiar "Janz party of eight, please return to the gate," and then we'd all stand up, maneuver awkwardly out of our middle seats, and slink off the plane under the baleful glares of the legitimate fliers. As a self-conscious teenager, I already felt like a freak in my ankle-length floral dress, and this was almost more humiliation than I could bear. On the flip side, once in a great while we would find ourselves on an empty flight and slump blissfully into the luxurious oversized leather seats of first class.

It didn't take a genius to deduce that my father's real incentive for the vacations was to bolster his reputation as a man of means in the IFB, not to expand his kids' cultural horizons. The itinerary was always suited to my parents, not to us, and the minute we got home, he and my mother would start regaling everyone in the congregation with tales of their latest trip, reveling in the status it gave them in the church. But for my siblings and me, every trip bred anxiety. We knew the bills wouldn't be paid for months after we got home. Would we have money for food? Would we get our paltry $50 for school clothes in the fall?

Even on vacation we couldn't escape my father's goading. If we went to the beach, he would grab us as we swam and shove us out into the deep part of the ocean, laughing as we struggled against the undercurrent, frantic to get back to shore. And if he thought we set a toe out of line, he would whip off his belt for a makeshift spanking session. Even more menacing were the times he would growl, "When we get back home..." Those words could ruin the rest of a trip.

The Creep Factor

My father's dominant personality trait was his predilection for violence, but his obsession with sex came in a close second. Although the IFB leaders typically forbade discussing any details about reproduction or physical relationships between men and women (we weren't even allowed to watch most PG movies), Bart talked candidly about sex, even with our friends, when we were teenagers. He used to boast about having had sex with my mother seven times on their honeymoon night and said it stressed her body so much that she broke out in hives the next day. He told that story to every teenage boy who set foot in our house, even with girls around, and the boys all called him "Superman." My mom would laugh and say, "Bart, stop that!" But she attested that it was true.

Such lewd conversation seems starkly out of place in a subculture where college kids weren't even allowed to hold hands with members of the opposite sex. But in spite of—or perhaps because of—all that priggish repression, many of the males in the IFB reveled in crude locker room talk.

Unfortunately for my sisters and me, we sometimes bore the brunt of my father's overactive sex drive. By the time I was in high school we had our own in-ground pool and, in the privacy of our backyard with our own family, we were allowed to wear bathing suits rather than culottes and T-shirts. Melissa was quite large for her age and developed breasts early. One afternoon when she was about fourteen, she was swimming with my father when he suddenly ducked underwater and yanked her swimsuit straps down to her waist. She was standing in the shallow end, and the water only reached her belly button, so she ended up with her breasts fully exposed. She was devastated. She turned crimson, pulled her swimsuit up hurriedly, and bolted from the pool sobbing.

My father just laughed. "Oh, don't be such a baby, Muffy," he called. "I was just playing around!"

But he wasn't. I remember him pressing against me underwater frequently, deliberately rubbing his erect penis against my back. I felt deeply embarrassed and I wanted him to stop, but I couldn't put the correct label on his behavior. And getting mad was not the way to handle my father unless you were up for a beating, so I had long since learned to laugh my way out of uncomfortable situations. Trying not to panic, I would giggle and wrestle my way out of his arms pretending it was a game, but scrambling out of the pool as fast as I could.

When I was around fifteen or sixteen, he often wanted me to lie next to him on the couch in our living room, while he watched Fox News. He would always position my rear end against his groin. Before long, he would start making ejaculatory movements against my body. I could feel his erection rubbing against me, but I pretended not to. What else could I do?

Unable to escape, I retreated into my imagination just as Melissa did with her art. I used to pretend I was Anne Frank. The IFB has always been enthralled with Jewish culture and, despite the fact that our textbooks often omitted women's suffrage and black history entirely, we learned a lot about the Holocaust. Maybe it's because we were forever envisioning ourselves being persecuted by our government the way the Jews were by the Germans in World War II. Maybe that sense of "kinship" explains why the IFB encouraged support of the Jews for Jesus conversion effort in the 1970s. Repulsed by what my father was doing but pinned against him and unable to wriggle free, I slipped away to an attic room in my mind, listening for the pounding of German soldiers at the door, waiting for them to drag my family off to a concentration camp. If Anne could endure all that, surely I could get through this. She became one of my heroes. I even carved out a place in my closet where I would sit with my books "in hiding" imagining the Nazis were coming soon to take me away. I developed a vivid imagination, creating an alternate universe for myself as a way to escape the pain of my immediate surroundings.

Once, when I was fifteen, my father came into my bedroom, lay down next to me on my bed, and began kissing my neck. Soon he was groping every part of my body. I squirmed my way out of his tight grip, feigning a fit of giggles, then rolled off the bed to escape. As I've said, any display of negative emotions would have been an invitation for a beating, so making light of these excruciating situations with him became my coping mechanism.

First Dates

Despite the rampant sexual abuse in my own home, my father subscribed to the IFB's strict old-fashioned mores when it came to dating. My sisters and I had our share of crushes on boys in our classes, but we weren't allowed to date in high school. My brothers, on the other hand, could take girls out on double dates. On rare occasions during my junior and senior year, Bart allowed me to tag along with one of my brothers on a double date, presuming they would act as chaperones.

My first serious crush was on a man I met at one of our high school football games. He was much older than I was and in the Navy. Greg Patterson was an alumnus of Silver State and a former football star at the school who often came to watch the games when he was home, and apparently I caught his eye while I was cheerleading in front of the stands. I was only sixteen and he was twenty-five, but the age difference didn't faze my friends, who gushed over him and whispered about what a "hunk" he was.

At first my father allowed us to talk to each other and write letters, and eventually he allowed me to go on one date with Greg, without either of my brothers present. We simply went to dinner and he never touched me, but he gave me his gold chain to wear while he was away. I wore it with great pride, glowing when the other girls admired it or eyed it jealously. I find it odd now that, though I wasn't officially allowed to date, my father allowed me to flirt with a man so much older. Even more disturbing is the fact that, though my own parents and all the adults in my school and church seemed to be aware of my budding romance, no one ever explained that a physical relationship between us would have been illegal.

My father eventually told me I had to cut off all contact with my crush. I was heartbroken. I had envisioned a long-term relationship with this man after I got out of high school. I even dreamed of marrying him. But my father was the decision maker, not me, so there was little I could do.

Shortly after that "breakup," Jason introduced me to his new best friend from Northland Baptist Bible College, a boy named Will Galkin, who had come home with Jason on a college break. We went on a few double dates with Jason, but our long-distance "relationship" was far from serious and it ended within a matter of months. I was still sixteen and he was a college freshman, but again no one mentioned our age difference or the fact that, under Colorado law, a physical relationship would have been illegal.

Camping with God

The highlight of my teen years was the annual week-long trip my siblings and I took after school ended in June to The Wilds of the Rockies in Steamboat Springs, Colorado. It was an IFB camp run by Bob Jones University graduates, and most of the camp counselors were students at one of the four most prominent IFB colleges in the Jones Camp (BJU, Pensacola Christian College, Maranatha Baptist Bible College, and Northland Baptist Bible College/International University).

Of course, we got more cult indoctrination there, but we didn't care. The cheers, competitions, camp food, and new friends from IFB churches all around the country were enough fun to counterbalance the endless hellfire and brimstone sermons.

"Dr." Tom Farrell, a BJU graduate, was the fieriest of all our camp preachers, but also the most loved by the teenagers. He would work himself into a frenzy, yelling until he turned beet red and spraying spit on anyone seated in the front row. Fire seemed to blaze from his eyes and his skintight polo shirts strained against his huge bulging biceps. He looked like he could snap you in two if you crossed him. If anyone dared to yawn, slump in his chair, or look bored, Farrell would pounce.

"Young man in the back row!" he would scream, pointing a damning finger. "Yes, I'm talking to you, big boy! Sit up! You may sit that way in your youth group at your church, and your youth pastor may let you get away with it, but when I'm up here preaching, you will respect my God! Do you understand me?" The culprits snapped to attention like recruits at boot camp every time.

One of Farrell's favorite bits of showmanship was to play music samples from popular rock bands and performers like Bon Jovi, Madonna, Michael Jackson, and Def Leppard to highlight their "satanic" lyrics. Sometimes he even played the songs backward so we could hear the *hidden* satanic messages. By the end of his sermons, I was thoroughly convinced that nearly every artist in the Billboard Top 100 practiced black magic and the beat of their music conjured up demons.

We worked hard all week to get our hearts "right with God." Many campers, myself included, decided they weren't living for the Lord sufficiently and were "born again" *again* at camp and opted to be rebaptized when they got back to their home churches. "Dr." Tom Farrell had a talent for making even the purest, most obedient teenager feel like a deviant. Everyone at camp went for "spiritual counseling," whether it was to overcome our sinful desire to date or to find the strength to obey our parents more reverently and sweetly. When I was in eighth grade, I wanted so much to shed my excess weight that I would slip off to the basement and do aerobics to "worldly" Christian pop artists like Steve Green and Sandi Patty because their bouncy music made it easier to exercise. But after Farrell's camp sermons, I repented of my "sin" and headed to a clearing behind the chapel to drop my CDs into the Burn Barrel. (Burn Barrels were common in the IFB, a practice inspired by the Book of Acts, in which converts of the Apostle Paul threw all their occult materials into a huge bonfire in the city of Ephesus.) Into the Wilds' Burn Barrel went all sorts of worldly entertainments discarded by penitent teens, from romance novels to teen magazines. At the end of the week, we each threw a stick into a bonfire near the lake as a sign of our renewed surrender to God.

Farrell ran through a menu of sins so exhaustive that, looking back, I'm sure he must have consulted a thesaurus for synonyms. There was bound to be at least one we had committed. If you didn't think you'd been guilty of pride, he might catch you when he mentioned a "spirit of worldliness" and you'd feel obliged to atone and seek spiritual counseling. "Anger,

bitterness, frustration, laziness, sloth, deceit, a lack of forgiveness . . ." On
and on Farrell went until he reached one of the worst, listening to rock
and roll music.

The IFB leaders often gauged a camp speaker's success on the number of kids who responded to invitations for counseling, and "Dr." Tom
Farrell basically guaranteed that almost all 250 of us junior high and
high school kids would file out of his sermons having found *something* to
confess to a camp counselor.

Every time we confessed a sin to one of our counselors, they filled out
a corresponding "confession card" or "decision slip." I didn't know it at the
time, but IFB camps often kept all our slips on file for future reference.
They also shared them with any parents who asked.

I was foolishly candid with the camp director, "Dr." Robert Allamon,
and his wife, Janie, both BJU graduates, about struggling to forgive my
father for his bouts of rage. I had been warned by IFB leaders more times
than I could count that the Bible said we must honor our father and mother,
and that God might cut my life short if I failed to do so. (My father had
told us from a young age that he prayed God would kill us if we ever
strayed from the path of righteousness.) But, as I told the Allamons, I also
knew that anger for its own sake was strictly forbidden by the IFB, and I
felt my father disciplined me with unrighteous anger. One of my friends
told me her parents never raised their voices during their discipline sessions. I understood that my father needed to beat me for my sinful actions,
but I couldn't understand why he couldn't try to control his rage.

Did my father find out everything I confided in the Allamons? I can't
say for sure, but it would have been par for the course in the IFB. It would
also explain why my father's violence toward me always seemed to esca-
late after camp, despite the fact that I came home repentant and worked
harder than ever to please him.

I should have learned my lesson, but I was still naive enough to buy
into the IFB's rhetoric. Between my junior and senior year, I attended
counselor-in-training sessions at camp. The program was designed to give
high school students a glimpse into what being a summer counselor was
like and to see if we had the spiritual fortitude to lead a group of teenagers. In every private session I attended, I was treated to a diatribe on the
attributes of the various IFB colleges and the importance of Christian

higher education. I now realize it was a strategic marketing ploy to boost enrollment in IFB colleges. Our IFB Christian schools were feeders for IFB colleges, and they all took their students on annual tours of whichever IFB colleges their school was affiliated with—BJU, Hyles-Anderson College, "Dr." Bill Gothard's Advanced Training Institute, Pensacola Christian College, and so on.

Once you were in training, you were required to meet with "Dr." Tom Farrell in one-on-one sessions to discuss the areas of your life in which you wrestled with sin and needed spiritual guidance. In all my innocence, I repeated what I had told the Allamons about struggling to forgive my father for beating me in a rage until I bled. Farrell gave the pat response you almost always hear from IFB authority figures. "You need to forgive and not get bitter," he said. "In fact, you should apologize to your father for any signs of bitterness you may have manifested." IFB leaders always preached that, "You need to apologize for your ten percent wrong behavior even if the other person is ninety percent wrong." But, the men in power never apologized for anything to their subordinates—ever. I knew I could expect nothing different from my father, but I wouldn't have dreamed of questioning Farrell's counsel. I thought the man "walked with God." (It's worth noting that Farrell went on to receive numerous invitations to speak at my father's church, where he later received love offerings worth thousands of dollars, and that the two of them started vacationing together.)

Despite all I knew of my father from personal experience, I followed "Dr." Tom Farrell's advice and apologized to him as soon as I got home from The Wilds.

"*You're* bitter?" he exploded. "I'm bitter at you! No one knows what I've had to put up with raising you! If you're bitter, that's your fault, girl!"

Bart Janz had found the perfect home in the IFB—a community where the child is always wrong and the adult is always right, especially if he's a man, and where he could inflict untold damage in the name of God. No wonder children have been beaten to death in the IFB in recent years. No wonder pedophiles and sadists seek out the cult and blend into its ranks. The Independent Fundamental Baptist Church offers ample opportunities to insinuate yourself into the lives of vulnerable children as a pastor, counselor, teacher, or just an abusive parent. It's easy to disguise any number of atrocities as religious dogma. Often, the only ones tending the sheep are wolves just like them and if a victim doesn't stay quiet, one of the leaders is sure to give you a heads-up in time to silence the troublemaker.

Demeaning Through Sexual Innuendos

A perfect example of the IFB's penchant for cloaking inappropriate behavior under the guise of religion—and then turning a blind eye to those it victimized—happened at the beginning of my senior year. That was when our principal imposed mandatory daily "devotions"—a time for personal prayer and Bible study—before the school day started. Our senior class of eighteen was divided into two small groups, and I was the only girl in a room filled with testosterone-fueled teenage boys overseen by the basketball coach, Matt DeVries, a graduate of Bob Jones University. It didn't take long before the sexual harassment started, and Coach DeVries was often an enthusiastic participant in the laughter. For a solid year, instead of studying the Bible, I sat in silence nearly every morning enduring a barrage of lascivious comments and getting called names like "whore" and "slut." I tried to act good-natured, but I frequently ended up in tears. I was curvy and well developed, and they scrutinized every part of my body, commenting aloud like bidders at a livestock auction sizing up a heifer. My parents hadn't decided to pay for braces yet, and I was terribly self-conscious about my prominent canine teeth. The boys in my class had called me "Jaws" and "Fangs" ever since elementary school, but now they started speculating on whether my teeth would make fellatio painful. DeVries never once tried to censor them. On the contrary, he seemed to find their comments funny.

I had spent my life in a culture where boys and girls weren't allowed to touch, yet every boy in that room knew what a blow job was and sexual innuendo was not only tolerated by school personnel, it was rampant. Years later, when a Silver State school principal and BJU graduate was standing trial for sexual assault allegations, it surfaced that the male students and school staff had played a game called "sack-tapping," where they flicked each other's testicles unexpectedly, so everyone was always on the alert. Some even wore athletic cups for protection. I was out of the cult by the time the case hit the news, but the information didn't surprise me. Why did so many of our teachers seem as immature as the kids they were supposed to be educating? The vast majority were BJU grads, and I blame the environment the university cultivates. Nobody grows up there; they go from being treated like children with bedtimes and hair checks to teaching in IFB schools. Naturally, they still act like kids.

Never Too Old for a Spanking

Teenage girls in the cult were infantilized even more severely. In our world, their only way to transition into adulthood was to marry. Until then, a girl was under her father's rule.

People unfamiliar with the IFB's patriarchal culture are often shocked that we were beaten until adulthood, though it was common in our peer group. I have one friend whose father threatened to spank her on her wedding day for having the proverbial "bad attitude." Another told me that when she got into an argument with her brother during a car ride as a sophomore in college, her father pulled the family van to the side of the road, turned her over his knee, and spanked her. He didn't say a word to her brother.

The most legendary "spanking session" inflicted on a teenage girl I knew happened when my best friend Christy Roland's big sister Shannon made the mistake of falling for a black student in her class during her senior year. The formidable Dr. Roland didn't care that the boy was a fellow IFB member. He considered interracial dating and marriage a sin. Such racism is widespread in the IFB and my father even believed all black people bear the "mark of Cain," a curse handed down from the biblical Cain, who murdered his brother, Abel. Roland forbade her from talking to the boy, let alone going out with him. But Shannon disobeyed. She even snuck over to his house after school one day. Her father caught her and gave her a beating so horrific that Christy's eyes were like saucers the next morning at school when she told me about it. She said Shannon was black-and-blue and so sick she had diarrhea. She lay in bed for three days on her stomach, barely able to move. The story got around, but it didn't dissuade any of our parents from viewing Roland as a man of great wisdom when it came to raising children in a "godly" fashion.

My own final discipline session happened right before my eighteenth birthday. I was doing some of my father's laundry when the phone rang. I tucked the basket with five pairs of his socks and three of his dress shirts in my closet to hide it from view before heading downstairs to take the call, which turned out to be from a friend who wanted me to join her family at a nearby park for a spur-of-the-moment cookout. It sounded fun, but I would have to do some quick thinking to come up with a pleasing appeal for my father.

"Is the laundry done?" he asked.

"I have to starch a few more shirts, but then I'll be done for the day," I assured him.

To my delight he said okay, and I raced upstairs to retrieve the basket from my closet. I ironed and starched his shirts, then quickly plucked the lint off his socks and tucked them in his sock drawer. I had no time to change. Still wearing my school clothes—an ankle-length khaki skirt and navy blue polo shirt, the signature "cool" look for IFB girls—I tore out of the house, in a rush to meet my friend's parents when they arrived to pick me up.

When I walked back in the door later that evening, my father was sitting at his desk in the den with his back to me. He didn't turn around to look at me. "Did you have a good time?" he asked. I sensed something amiss in his voice. Hoping I was wrong, I responded, "Sure! It was a lot of fun."

Suddenly, he swung his chair around to face me, his face flushed with rage. "Well, that's going to end right now!" he yelled. "Go to your room!"

I had no idea why he was so upset, and I racked my brain trying to think of what sin I had committed as I sat waiting on my bed. After an interminable ten minutes or so, he opened my door and said, "Come to my room!"

Panic-stricken, I followed. He led me to his dresser, pulled out the top drawer, and told me to unfold his socks. When I did, he snatched them out of my hand and put them on his bed. "What do you see?"

My heart sank. A few loose strings from the bottom of the laundry basket were clinging to them. In my rush to get out the door, I hadn't taken the usual time to pick meticulously at each pair of socks, and I had failed to meet his standards.

He told me to go back to my room and wait again. A minute later, he stormed in scowling and locked the door behind him.

"Pull up your skirt!" he ordered, reaching for the wooden dowel he

had evidently propped against the wall before I got home. How had I failed
to see it?

My skirt was getting a little too tight and I had a hard time tugging
it up over my hips and rear end. As I struggled, he watched my every move.
At last, exasperated, he stormed over and yanked it up so far that it was
bunched under my breasts.

"Take your panties off," he said.

I did as he instructed, thinking all the while, *I'm getting spanked as
a senior in high school!*

He shook the rod in my face. "You are so lazy! Always have been!
And your ungrateful attitude is really getting to me! You think you're too
old to do work in the right way in this house? Well, let me tell you something, you are never too old for my expectations! Roll back over!"

The familiar agonizing ritual repeated itself until he had given me
twenty-six blows, the rod burning and biting so cruelly into my thighs
and buttocks that I flipped onto my back instinctively after each blow to
protect them even though I was naked from the waist down. Finally, he
flung the rod against the wall, and yelled, "Now get up and pull yourself
together!" then stomped out.

Wincing, I struggled to my feet, intent on hobbling to the bathroom
to view the damage to my backside. I tugged gingerly at the bottom of
my skirt, trying to ease it down over my throbbing skin. But the second
it came in contact with my wounds, it started to soak up blood. Ankle-
length khaki skirts were a precious commodity for girls at Silver State,
and bloodstains would be hard to wash out, so I stopped what I was doing
and limped to the closet. I found an old T-shirt and used it to wipe off the
blood that was dripping down my legs. Even Christy Roland, my closest
confidante, never found out. A spanking at that age was too humiliating
for words.

The Unpardonable Sin

For some time, I thought the twenty-six-blow spanking session
would be the low point of my senior year. But then an incident occurred
that eclipsed it completely. In fact, it eclipsed almost everything about
my high school life.

To my surprise, my father told me he felt bad about having put an end to my budding romance with Greg Patterson, the military man on whom I'd had a passionate crush at sixteen. Now, apparently, Bart thought it was time I developed a love interest. He zeroed in on the star basketball player in our high school and started encouraging me to like the boy. Following his advice, I took an interest and the boy reciprocated. We were "in like" and talked at school though we were strictly forbidden from having any physical contact.

There was a problem, though. My new crush's parents didn't make him follow the school's rules. They allowed him to listen to whatever music he liked, even Metallica and Def Leppard. They were the most lenient of all the Silver State parents and he knew he could get away with more than the rest of us could. One day, he told me he had books for me at his house. I could see them during study hall, if I would leave school with him. I hesitated but ultimately agreed. It felt exciting to break the rules on purpose for once.

When we got to his house, we started kissing. One thing led to another and the next thing I knew, he was lying on top of me.

"Can we have sex?" he whispered.

My mind went into a sort of hyperdrive, a million confused thoughts crashing into each other all at once. The first one that flashed into my mind was that I was wearing embarrassing underwear. In an attempt to keep us "pure," my mother bought my sisters and me giant pairs of white granny panties that reached our navels. Next, I remembered that my pantyhose had a big run down the upper thigh. (Hose were mandatory for girls in our school.) None of that seemed very sexy.

"No," I whispered back, shaking my head.

"Please?" he coaxed.

It was the oldest cliché in the teen sex lexicon. So why did I say yes? Was it something I genuinely wanted to do? Was I flattered by his attention? Was I caught up in the thrill of doing something forbidden? Maybe it was a combination of all those things.

Whatever the reason, I let him keep kissing me. He pulled off my skirt, my hose, and eventually my panties. I had no idea what I was doing and I was a bundle of nerves. He tried to penetrate me, but I was too tight and dry. Instead, he came on top of me. We both stood up and put our clothes back on, feeling awkward. Then he went into the living room and flipped on the TV. I curled up in his lap and we cuddled, but neither one of us spoke more than two words. When we saw each other at school the next day, we pretended like it had never happened.

I told no one, but word still spread through the school like wildfire about what had happened. While I was on my senior trip it reached my brother Jason and he called me long distance.

"Is it true?" he asked, clearly distraught.

"Is *what* true?" I asked tremulously.

"Did you have sex?"

I burst into sobs and told him everything. He was furious and said the boy was telling all his friends at school. He said we would have to tell my father when I got home. For the rest of the trip I was a mess. I vomited every morning as soon as I woke up and my period was late. I was sure I was pregnant. I knew virtually nothing about my own reproductive system, so I had no idea that I was more likely to have gotten pregnant with my brother's baby than with one of this boy's.

Jason picked me up at church when the trip ended and drove me home. When we were a few blocks from our house, he pulled over to the curb and cut the ignition.

He was shaking and nearly as upset as I was. His conscience compelled him to report me to our father, he explained, but he felt torn because he knew the harsh consequence it would mean for me.

"He's going to kill me," I sobbed.

We had been agonizing over what to do for about fifteen minutes when a police car pulled up behind us and an officer startled us by knocking on the car window.

Jason rolled it down and the man asked, "Is everything okay?"

"We're fine," Jason said, perfectly mannered as always. "My sister has done something terribly wrong and we're getting ready to go home and tell my parents about it."

I ventured a glance at the officer through my tears and was surprised to see that he looked genuinely worried about me. "Is there anything I can help you with?" he asked kindly.

I had been trained never to talk to the police about "family business," or issues, but something about his compassionate expression told me instinctively that I could trust this man. I had to suppress the urge to cry out, "Can you come with us? Please! He's going to murder me!"

But I fell back on all my years of conditioning and pulled myself together. "I'll be all right," I responded mechanically. "Thank you."

When the officer left, Jason promised me he would call the police if my father got out of hand. He surprised me by saying, "I won't let him touch you," and volunteering to go into the house before I did to tell my parents what I had done.

"If he goes nuts, I'll run out and drive away with you," he assured me as we pulled up in front of our house. Then he got out of the car, ran up the steps to our front door, and disappeared.

Thirty long minutes later, he came back. "I think he's stable," he said, "but don't say any more than you have to."

I walked into the house like a convict to his execution. My mother was sitting on the couch with her head in her hands. My father had his back to me. Jason ushered me over to the love seat. I curled up in a ball and put my head between my knees, avoiding eye contact with anyone.

"Tell me what happened. Every detail," my father said, without turning to look at me.

I sobbed out the story. As I talked, he dropped his head down onto the fireplace mantel and started weeping so hard his shoulders were heaving.

When I finally talked myself out and fell silent, he came over to me and dropped to his knees. "How could you do this?" he sobbed. "How? You have tainted yourself for the rest of your life! You are ruined! Your virginity is all you have and you have given that away!"

I remember being shocked that he wasn't yelling at Jason to get the rod. The only thing I had worried about was being beaten to death. I didn't like hearing that I was pathetic and ruined, but it meant I was safe for now. If my father started losing control this time, I knew he wouldn't stop.

Suddenly, he sprang up and started pacing the living room manically, his grief hardening into anger. "I'm going to kill that boy!" he shouted.

At last, he and my mother told me to go to bed so they could call Pastor Les Heinze, another graduate and board member of BJU, who had replaced "Dr." Nelson, now senior pastor at another IFB church.

Later that night, my father lifted me out of bed and carried me downstairs as if I were six years old again. He sat me next to my mother on the couch and the two of them started grilling me.

"Did he rape you?" they demanded.

I tried to explain that I had said no initially because I was afraid to do wrong, but then I had said yes.

"But did he ask to have sex with you first?"

I was exhausted, having returned the night before from my senior trip, so it was hard to think straight, but I told them all the details. The next morning my mother drove me to a rape crisis center. My mother told me to tell the counselor all about my sexual experience. I had no idea they were hoping to build a case against the boy until the lady who counseled me met with my mother and told her, "Your daughter wasn't raped and I'm not even sure if she was penetrated."

Despite what the counselor said, I'm convinced that my parents energetically circulated the rumor that the boy had raped me. Somehow my father found out the Heinzes kept a shotgun and he called the pastor's fifteen-year-old son to demand that he bring the gun over. He swore he was going to kill the kid who had ruined his daughter. That rumor circulated back to the boy's parents and they panicked and called the police.

Terrified that members of the wicked outside world would insert themselves into our sordid little drama, Pastor Heinze jumped in and managed to calm Bart down. He spent hours on the phone with my father, convincing him that murder was not the right way to handle the situation. He also broke the news that, according to the school handbook, the loss of my virginity meant that I wouldn't be able to graduate with my senior class. He offered to come over the next day to discuss the details with my parents and me.

Instead, when he arrived, he started grilling me about my classmates' transgressions. He had a long list of the "dirty deeds" my fellow seniors had committed, from drinking alcohol to having sex. I had no idea where the list came from and no knowledge about whether the stories were true. I told him so, but he didn't care. He wanted me to verify each event—and to swear that I had witnessed them all.

I didn't want to get anyone else in trouble. All I wanted was to flee to a foreign country and escape the nightmare. I learned later that my father called Pastor Heinze and told him I had confirmed every one of his lurid accusations about my classmates. He couldn't have cared less about the truth; he was bent on proving to the IFB community that other teenagers were as bad as his own disgraced daughter. It seemed clear to me that the only thing my parents cared about was salvaging their reputation.

Those months of my life are still a blur. Things seemed to move at lightning speed and in slow motion all at once. I remember so little of it that other people have had to put some of the pieces together for me and fill me in on the details. I knew a lot of other kids were getting in trouble and refusing to speak to me, but I had no idea they thought I had ratted on them. I figured they were avoiding me because I was impure.

The worst point of the whole debacle came when my father insisted that I acknowledge my sin and ask for restoration from the church membership in public. I was made to write a letter of apology to the entire church. I wrote the letter, then he rewrote it in his own words. I had to stand next to him at the pulpit Sunday morning. He told me I needed to wear my one good white dress and hold his hand while standing in front of the entire congregation.—a sign to him of my renewed purity.

"We have here before us today both Bart and Jocelyn Janz," Pastor Heinze told the packed church. "Bart is standing as Jocelyn's representative before the Lord. She has sinned and would now like to read a letter of apology to the church."

My father's plan was to read the letter aloud himself. After all, it was *his* letter. We had even rehearsed it that way. But once we got up on the platform, the utter humiliation was too much for me. I pulled my hand out of his. He shot a withering look at me, but I turned my head toward Pastor Heinze. Then I surprised everyone, even myself, by crossing in front of my father and walking to the pulpit.

My knees were weak as I read the words, but I fumbled through them. When I had finished, Pastor Heinze said there would be a reception line at the front of the church where members were welcome to come forward and offer me forgiveness.

"Dr." Nelson and his wife were at the church service that day. He had known me for almost a decade, but he was ice cold in the reception line. He said in a mechanical tone that he forgave me and hoped I would do better in my future.

My father later chastised me for "taking control" but, to my surprise, he didn't beat me. Instead, he used the incident against me for the next decade. It was a glaring public example of my willful disobedience, he said, and irrefutable proof that I needed to be broken and "brought to a place of submission."

Nobody made the boy responsible for my "downfall" read a letter of apology, but he decided to read one anyway. In it, he made a point of stating that a lot of false rumors had been going around and he wanted to set the record straight. I realized later that he was trying to tell the congregation he wasn't a rapist.

The irony of this situation isn't lost on me now. I was made to stand in front of a church of nearly one thousand members, apologizing for what—according to every scrap of recent data available—is part of a pretty normal high school relationship in America today. The boy who took part in it with me felt the need to stand up in public, humiliated just like I was, and defend himself against a lie that he had raped me—a lie my parents started rather than accepting the truth. And all the while, my three molesters looked on from the pew and platform, weeping over the disgrace and grief I had heaped on our family through my evil deeds. Like Hester Prynne with her scarlet letter A, my shame would follow me across the country and into the next stage of my life. It was a magnificent example of the IFB's hypocritical and deceptive culture in action—where the victim is ultimately put on display to the masses as the villain.

7

MY COLLEGE YEARS (1993–1995)

[Rock music] is not fit material for a Christian to feed his soul upon. The very beat of it is sensual.

—*Bob Jones III*

No Griping, No Sex, No Walking on the Grass

Excluded from graduation ceremonies and parties, I got my diploma in June of 1993 with no fanfare and I was grateful when summer finally arrived. I kept my head down in a show of remorse for my sin and at the end of August headed off to Dunbar, Wisconsin, for my freshman year at Northland Baptist Bible College. Unfortunately, everything about a girl's personal life often reaches other IFB authorities, so my reputation preceded me.

The moment I set foot on campus, I had to meet with Wynne Kimbrough, the dean of students. He let me know I had a serious black mark on my character and told me I would be on "spiritual probation" for a year. The administration would be keeping an eagle eye on me. As my parents put it, I would be "loved into righteousness." In other words, I would be given no opportunity to sin again.

They had nothing to worry about. Not only was I getting heavily indoctrinated in the IFB's code of chastity, I was in the middle of the north woods where bears were a common sight. I couldn't get into trouble on Northland's campus, and I wasn't foolhardy enough to sneak off it. What's more, my brothers were both upperclassmen. They had promised to keep tabs on me and report to my father if I showed any sign of a rebellious spirit. They needn't have bothered. I was so broken, so defeated that I kept my mouth shut and stayed out of the action. Jeremy and Jason, on the other hand, were the class clowns, college leaders in almost every activity. Northland, like all small IFB colleges, was a glorified high school with only a few hundred students and your status was determined by who you knew. The Janz brothers knew everyone, so their antics gave me a modicum of popularity by extension.

Even though monitors prowled nearly every room to ensure that we didn't say or do anything ungodly, and I knew they were hypervigilant in my case, I still felt freer than I ever had. Sure, the rules were harsh. We couldn't listen to music with a rock beat, show up late for class, wear pants, hold a boy's hand, or be out of bed after 11 P.M. But I had escaped from my father's clutches for four whole months. I wouldn't have to see him until Christmas break. I felt like I had died and landed in Heaven. He was thousands of miles away. He couldn't touch me. I was no longer in danger of the belt or the wooden dowel. I could choose my own activities from within the guidelines of the college handbook, befriend whichever students I chose, and even sit on a couch next to a guy and "date."

Compared to life at home, nothing here bothered me. Not the palpable sense of cold and dark that seemed omnipresent in the Great Lakes winter. Not even the fierce glacial wind, sleet, and snow that lashed my legs and bit at my frozen toes through my flimsy shoes and stockings. Every muscle in my body stiffened as I plodded across the frozen field separating the classroom building from the girls' dormitory. The subzero weather made the tundra seem a mile wide. Banned from wearing slacks or jeans and too self-conscious to pair warm winter boots with our ubiquitous long khaki skirts, all of us Northland girls trudged through foot-deep snow in paper-thin dress flats. We were slaves to IFB fashion, having been warned ad infinitum by our parents and fellow coeds that we had only four short years to land a husband. If we failed to snag a man at Northland, we could end up back home living under our dads' Umbrella of Protection, destined for the singles groups at church. We called the guys there "the leftovers," the last, untouched dish in the dating potluck of IFB life. It was deemed a fate worse than death by any self-respecting woman under the age of twenty-two. Enduring minus-20-degree wind chills and risking a few frostbitten toes seemed a small price to pay for looking cute enough to catch a guy's eye.

Back at my dorm after every class, I would lift my skirt and treat my chapped and bleeding calves with hydrogen peroxide and Vaseline. I was so used to pain that I felt no emotional connection to it. Besides, these wounds were self-inflicted and mild compared to a spanking session. Internally, I felt nothing but relief.

Little Sister Chaperone

I stuck faithfully to Northland's masochistic female dress code, but my sense of urgency about looking appealing to every man around me diminished when I started dating Mark (not his real name), a BJU graduate I had met during my summer of shame. He was doing his medical residency in Iron Mountain, Michigan, about twenty-five minutes from campus, and was obviously quite a few years older. I wasn't allowed off campus with him, but we made the best of things as we sat in front of the fireplace in the snack shop and played board games, taking care not to let our hands touch.

My brother Jeremy was a senior by this time and engaged to a girl he had met at Northland named Bonnie (not her real name), who had converted from the Mormon church and had been "born again." He had been named a resident assistant, which was one of the highest spiritual leadership positions for students at IFB colleges because RAs were in charge of enforcing the dorm rules.

Seniors were allowed the special privilege of dating in off-campus settings, provided they had a third party along to chaperone. Somehow Jeremy managed to convince Dean Kimbrough to allow him to go off campus with Bonnie, taking Mark and me along to keep an eye on them. It was ironic if not absurd, given that I was on spiritual probation, but Jeremy assured Kimbrough that he would vouch for my good behavior. Kimbrough hesitated, but my brother charmed him into agreeing.

The next weekend the four of us piled into Mark's pickup truck. "Where to?" Mark asked amiably.

"Could we watch a few movies at your apartment in Iron Mountain?" Jeremy asked.

It sounded fun, so that's where we headed. But almost as soon as we walked in the door, Jeremy and Bonnie crawled under the blankets in Mark's bed and started making out.

"I thought *he* was supposed to make sure *you* didn't break any of the rules," Mark whispered, clearly uncomfortable.

"He was," I whispered back. Mark's apartment was no larger than five hundred square feet with an open floor plan, and the all too audible activity under the covers made us both blush. How could we sit and talk or watch movies with them groping each other? To make matters worse, on the drive back to campus, Bonnie leaned forward and casually switched the truck's radio station to country music.

"You know I've asked you not to listen to that junk while we're at school," Jeremy scolded her, snapping the radio off and glaring at her. They sat in stony silence for the last few miles back to campus.

We endured a few more weekends like that one before Mark said he didn't feel comfortable taking the two of them to his apartment anymore. Jeremy was taken aback, but there was nothing he could do. He knew Mark could tell the administration what he had done and get him into deep trouble.

Apology Without Consequence

Northland held mandatory chapel meetings every day at 11 A.M. on the dot. The only way you could miss one without getting demerits was to have a written note from the campus nurse stating that you were so ill you couldn't get out of bed. Many of us would have dearly loved to exchange chapel time for a little extra sleep because our schedules were round-the-clock and I was working at the library part-time to earn spending money. But the administrators used the meetings to make campus-wide announcements. Chapel was also a time when college administration often referred to us as "young people" and likened themselves to our "parents away from home"—reiterating all the rules we were overlooking in our handbooks. On Mondays, they held "Works of God" testimonies in which students stood up to expound on their recent IFB ministry experiences. Some would talk about how many people they had given pamphlets to over the weekend. Others would tell how many witnessing opportunities they'd had, sharing their love of God with the "lost" in the hopes of leading them to Christ. Sometimes it seemed like one big contest to see who was the most pious. They reminded me of fishermen swapping stories about who had caught the biggest catch.

On the other days of the week, "Dr." Les Ollila, a graduate of BJU, would preach. He was the charismatic "prophet" of the Northland culture, the mouthpiece of God, and we thought he could do no wrong. Bob Jones University had even granted him a "medal of honor" one year for refusing to get Northland accredited. They were "standing together for the truth of the gospel"—or so we were told.

Ollila had a knack for humor and would fill the first fifteen minutes of his sermons with jokes so funny we almost fell off our seats laughing. Then, in a flash, he would shift gears, browbeating us until we sank down in our chairs, crushed under the weight of our sins.

One such "Dr." Ollila sermon unleashed the floodgates of Jeremy's conscience. He felt overcome with remorse for his physical relationship with Bonnie and for having molested me, so he went to "Dr." Marty Von, the college vice president, for counseling. Von listened patiently then advised Jeremy to apologize to me for the abuse and for putting me in a position where I saw him break Northland's rules. So one Friday not long after that, my brother invited me to have dinner with him in Iron Mountain. Jeremy borrowed a friend's car, and he took me to the local McDonald's. Over burgers and fries, he told me he had gone to counseling and wanted to ask forgiveness for the bad things he had done to me. I was floored, but of course I forgave him and assured him we could move on. I promised I wouldn't discuss it with anyone.

"Just out of curiosity," I asked, "is 'Dr.' Von giving you any consequences?"

"No," he said lightly. "He just wanted me to clear my conscience."

"Wow," I told him. "You confessed to the right administrator."

"Sure did," he said with a wink.

We laughed, finished our meal, and headed back to campus. At that moment, I felt pleased with Jeremy's apology. I learned later that he had apologized to each of my sisters in turn and asked them to forgive him.

I have never struggled with anger toward Jeremy. I knew he was a tormented soul, trying to survive in a chaotic, nightmarish environment like we all were. He was literally tortured by my father and I felt deep sorrow for him. He put no blame on my sisters or me. The thought never occurred to me to try to prosecute him—law enforcement were the "bad guys"—and I knew that was something no one would encourage in the IFB. And at the age of eighteen, I'm sure I was still unconsciously trying to protect him from my father. Now, I understand that prosecuting would have been the right thing to do—to protect other kids from harm.

It never occurred to me what a double standard we were living under when I had been made to express regret for my immorality to a thousand church members and endure a year of spiritual probation, while Jeremy was simply encouraged to say "sorry" in private to atone for a sin anyone would consider far worse than mine. Had Von been a qualified counselor who knew my history, he might have put two and two together. He might have realized that girls who have been molested are more likely to engage in sexual intercourse than their peers and that this might have explained my great transgression from a few months earlier. But in the unabashedly male chauvinistic world of the IFB, Eve is the deceiver, whether she is four, fourteen, or forty-four years old. Poor Adam is simply a helpless man, wooed by her sensual charm.

A few months after Jeremy's act of contrition, Mark and I ended our relationship. He told me his parents had encouraged him to "set me free" because I was too young for him. They assured him that if it were meant to be, I would come back to him. If not, I'd move on. After the breakup, I decided I was done with relationships. I no longer wanted to marry. Instead, I set my sights on becoming a single missionary to India. I threw myself into rediscovering my passion for God, the passion I had felt before my senior year of high school and my public shaming. I idolized a woman named Amy Carmichael, a missionary who ran orphanages in India. I lay in bed at night dreaming about being just like her. I stopped wearing makeup and dressing for marriage success and embraced the "lots, loose, and long" look. My parents had finally agreed to spring for braces for me, so that accentuated my homely appearance. But I didn't care. I felt good inside. At last, I could relinquish every desire for earthly pleasure. I would give up everything and choose the road of poverty.

"The Man You're Going to Marry"

When my freshman year ended, I flew back to Colorado and took a summer job as a waitress at my beloved Wilds of the Rockies camp.

And it was here, when I least expected romance, that I met my husband. Joseph had been the president of the student council at BJU and he had even won the university's most coveted accolade in 1993, the Citizenship Medal, given to one graduating senior each year the administration considered its model student. That summer, Joseph was the camp music director, already widely hailed as one of the IFB's leading songwriters.

One day Jason pointed him out to me on the basketball court at camp. "That's the man you're going to marry," he said. In our culture, a girl's father and brothers had tremendous influence over who she courted. Girls were taught from a young age to follow the counsel of the men in their lives. If they didn't, they were no longer "in the will of God" and we all heard horror stories about what happened then—marriages filled with alcohol and drug abuse and divorce, the ultimate breakdown of God's ideal for the perfect American home. It was a sin nearly as heinous as homosexuality. Needless to say, I listened to Jason intently and, after that conversation, I started watching Joseph's every move.

Since the IFB condemns any music but its own, our songwriters had a cult following. Joseph's singles topped the Bob Jones University hymn-singing charts and his songs were always the first chosen during youth group "Singspirations" when teenagers gathered at their youth pastors' homes to worship. Two of them had even made it into the university hymnal, which put him on the level of Usher or Justin Timberlake for cult members. It certainly didn't give him their income (IFB music publishers paid only a few hundred dollars per song, assuring composers they would reap their rewards in Heaven), but Joseph was treated like a pop star at the camp bonfires. All summer I watched youth group kids stop him and ask him to autograph their Bibles and CD covers.

I wasn't impressed. In fact, Joseph's exalted status in the IFB was a turn-off for me. I knew from firsthand experience that the men revered in our church hierarchy tended to be proud, arrogant, abusive, and self-righteous. My father and Dr. Roland were prime examples, and I had no interest in spending my life with a man like that. A little of my old personality must have been struggling to break through my self-imposed humble facade because one night as I walked past Joseph I couldn't resist the urge to blurt out, "You ain't all that!"

I had never spoken a word to him before, but he decided on the spot that he wanted to get to know me. He says he liked my spunk. I suppose it made me stand out from 99 percent of my fellow cult girls, whose wills had been so broken they had no passion left.

We started spending time together after that. Joseph liked the fact that I could banter easily with him as well as discuss deeper issues. He said I stimulated his thinking, and, always enjoying more intellectual conversation, that was high on his priority list. I found him insightful and kind and I enjoyed his company a great deal, but I never felt I was falling in love with him. Joseph, on the other hand, fell deeply in love with me over the next few months and told me he was taking it as a personal challenge to win me over. He wanted to spend his life with me, but he knew I had three more years of college to complete. He said he was willing to wait as long as I needed.

I started questioning myself intensely. What was wrong with me? Here was a man of integrity—thoughtful and compassionate. He had all the marks of a godly IFB husband—someone who could be trusted to lead a home in holiness. He held an honored position in our community. Yet, no matter how hard I tried, I couldn't muster the same emotion he felt for me. When I confided this to an older female staff member at camp who had been married for almost ten years, she told me sometimes it wasn't a matter of love, but of making a choice God would be pleased with. She prayed with me. Then she advised me, "Ask God if you should marry him and then follow the heart of God on the matter." "Dying to self" was a common expression in the IFB: Our happiness wasn't important; the only thing that mattered was what God wanted. After all, He knew what we desired more than we did. "Just two choices on the shelf, pleasing God or pleasing self," we used to recite. Our leaders told us the only way to live a joy-filled life was to make decisions that pleased God. Of course the problem was that, in the IFB culture, it was hard to sort out what God might genuinely want us to do from what ordinary humans with strong wills and positions of power desired for us.

The closer Joseph and I got, the more people tried to insert themselves into our relationship. One night Craig Scott, the senior pastor of an IFB church in Denver, pulled him aside after services and grilled him about courting me. "I want to make sure you know that Jocelyn has been immoral and had to stand before the congregation to apologize for her sin," he said. Pastor Scott believed marrying a virgin was of the utmost importance, and he ingrained it in everyone who would listen, particularly through the youth group activities he led. "There are many other pure and sweet girls to choose from," he told Joseph. "You should consider one of them instead."

Joseph was taken aback by his counsel, but it didn't discourage him. He saw what I had done as a mistake, not an irredeemable act that scarred me for life. For me, Scott's actions confirmed one inescapable truth: As a woman in the IFB, a public shaming followed you forever. I lived in a world where everyone knew everyone, one sprawling Peyton Place where scandalmongers spread stories like mine from church to college to congregation until they made sure everybody knew. I would never live it down.

If I didn't choose Joseph, what kind of man would follow? How many others would be so forgiving of my tainted past? Even if I found one who stirred feelings in me beyond the deep fondness and respect I felt for Joseph, would my father and brothers give their blessing for me to marry him? Jason had already implied his approval by singling Joseph out for me, and Bart valued Jason's opinion enough by now to approve any man he handpicked. I would be a fool to reject Joseph.

Tragedy Strikes

All these troubling thoughts were churning in my mind, sending me into a fitful sleep one night in July of 1994 when I awakened in the wee hours to the sound of pounding on my door. I opened it to find the supervisor of our waitress crew standing there, looking worried. "Your father is on the phone in the lobby of the camp building," she said. "Jason is taking the call. You need to go downstairs to meet him right away."

Confused and bleary-eyed, I stumbled down to the lobby. I found Jason crying and asking a lot of questions that made no sense. He looked up at me, an agonized expression on his face.

"Jeremy was in a bad accident tonight," he said. His voice sounded thick and choked. "He's in intensive care in Utah. He may not make it through the night."

My mind went blank. Then a tidal wave of emotion swelled up inside my body and crashed over me, making my knees buckle. I started screaming, "NO! NO! NO!"

Jason pulled me onto his lap and grabbed my arms with both of his hands to steady me. "Jocelyn! We are not going to act this way!"

I struggled to subdue my sobs and tried to absorb what the news meant. I might never see my brother alive again.

I found out the details later. Jeremy had graduated from Northland Baptist Bible College in June and had taken a youth pastoring position at an IFB church in Utah that summer. He was getting married to Bonnie in forty days. He had just preached an evening service and decided to ride his bike to the small grocery store down the road for a snack before calling her. On his way back to the church, a pickup truck hit him. The impact knocked him off his bike and his head slammed into the windshield. He was airlifted to an ICU, but he was in a coma with severe brain swelling.

When we arrived at the hospital, we were horrified by the damage to his face and body. We hardly recognized him. Just twenty-three years old and his life as we knew it was ended.

We were all in shock. The doctors told us the accident had sheared his brain stem, but we didn't understand the ramifications of that. Jason couldn't bear to sit around the hospital staring at his incapacitated brother. He reacted to Jeremy's terrible accident by resolving to "win as many people to Christ" as he could. He flew into action, making a pamphlet or "tract" entitled *Why?* He filled it with Bible verses and what he considered the answers to the most important questions in life. He printed hundreds of copies and handed them out to as many people as he could find. We all did. My parents decreed that the Janzes would turn tragedy into triumph. We would set a shining example of a godly response to misfortune. Our reputation as a family depended on it.

Looking back, one of the most disturbing effects of Jeremy's catastrophe was the way my parents parlayed it into a tool to elevate their own standing in the church. They swelled up with self-righteousness in the face of their grief. We were a family specially chosen by God, entrusted to endure great sorrow and serve as a reflection of Jesus's own suffering to those around us. The IFB often taught that God gave great sorrow to the strong, not the weak. That meant we were spiritually superior to the people we knew. And there was no greater honor in the IFB than being chosen as a good soldier of Christ. God had thrust His hand down from Heaven and singled Bart and Sandy out, saying to all, "You are worthy. I entrust you with one of the harshest trials, and you will glorify me even in your pain."

I shouldn't have been surprised at their reaction. I knew that enduring adversity could be a competitive business in IFB churches. Wednesday prayer meetings could get downright ludicrous, with Sister Sue raising her hand and asking us all to pray for her, afflicted as she was with gout, diabetes, a heart condition, and a disabled pinky finger. Within seconds another hand would shoot up, and Brother Bob would rise to his feet to rattle off his woes of a distended bowel, a hernia, and bad knees. On and on it would go. After the prayer service ended, Sister Sue would assure her fellow congregants in a lofty tone, "God has entrusted me with much sorrow, but I will not fail Him." Meanwhile, Brother Bob vowed stoically to "endure with great strength all persecution from the Devil."

No one could compete with a life-altering accident on the scale of Jeremy's, though. As a result, our family's name was dropped in IFB sermons all across the country. Suddenly, my father found himself catapulted to the level of a mature spiritual leader, and he was smug enough to burst. This was his moment of glory. Finally, after having two sons kicked out of school for theft and a daughter who had disgraced him with her lewd behavior, he had become exalted as an icon of godly fortitude. He used it for all it was worth, preaching about my brother's accident for the next decade in IFB churches around the country. He manipulated people by playing on their sympathies, spinning a tale of biblical proportions and likening himself to Abraham, a hero and patriarch who had laid his son on the altar before God. As Abraham laid up Isaac, so, Bart Janz claimed, he had laid up his son Jeremy and God gave him back—just as God had given Isaac back to Abraham. The only part that didn't quite mesh with the biblical analogy was the fact that Isaac didn't need a feeding tube, and poor Jeremy did.

For months we maintained a bedside vigil, but Jeremy improved very little. Eventually he was transferred to a long-term rehabilitation facility specializing in traumatic brain injuries. His fiancée, Bonnie, moved into our home, planning to stay with us for the next year to be nearby and help with his recovery. We knew so little about brain damage that we still believed he might suddenly snap out of his comalike state and life as we once knew it would resume.

I made arrangements to transfer to Bob Jones University to be near

Joseph, who was a graduate student in his seventh year (including undergraduate studies) working toward his master's degree in counseling. I was looking forward to starting afresh and trading the merciless Wisconsin winters for South Carolina's gentler weather. As the fall semester approached, Joseph called nearly every night to talk about BJU and how wonderful our time together would be. He described all his friends and talked about nights in town bowling and eating out. It all sounded free and adventurous. Everyone in the cult considered BJU the equivalent of an Ivy League university, only better. "Dr." Bob Jones Jr. and "Dr." Bob Jones III furthered the notion, likening their school to Harvard and Yale. I was getting ready to play in the big leagues, one of several thousand elite students rather than one of a few hundred frozen souls up at Northland.

Blindsided

August rolled around and I packed my bags. The day before I was supposed to leave for school, my father called the entire family into the dining room. We had no idea what the meeting was about, but from his grim expression, we all assumed he was about to give us an update on Jeremy's condition. To my astonishment, he launched into a vitriolic tirade directed at me. "Ever since you came home from Northland, you've had a holier-than-thou attitude, leaving the room when scenes in movies bother you and acting high and mighty," he ranted.

I was flabbergasted. After a year of Bible college, I had fully embraced the strict IFB canon. Northland taught us to quietly and humbly remove ourselves from the situation whenever someone committed a sin in our presence. But my father had misread my actions as arrogance. Perhaps because of Jeremy's condition, he had recently gone into a sort of IFB rendition of midlife crisis, throwing all the rules out the window and swearing, watching pornographic scenes in movies, even listening to rock music in his pickup truck, though he still forbade us from following suit. I was reacting to his behavior the way Northland had told me to, but as far as my father was concerned, I would never get it right.

Next, he attacked my dream of doing missionary fieldwork in India. "You've got some crazy idea that you're gonna be a one-man-show on the mission field," he yelled. "You're not even grateful for what you have here at home. It's an idea built on pride and nothing more."

His speech sent me reeling. All my life, my parents had berated me for "caring too much for the things of this world." Now, envisioning a life of solitude and poverty was wrong?

"If you think you can come into this house as some highbrow, self-righteous prick, you've got another thing coming, girl!" he screamed, his face crimson and the veins on his neck bulging. "I've seen nothing in you but a bad attitude from the moment you arrived home from Northland! Well, let me tell you something . . ."

By this time he was banging his fist on the table and shaking his finger in my face. Spit hit me in each eye, but I didn't dare flinch or betray emotion. If I sighed, trembled, or glanced away, I knew he would reach for the rod. "For this reason, you will not be leaving tomorrow to go to BJU. You will be staying home and getting a job and giving your paycheck to your mother and me. In all my years, I have never seen you respond correctly—not even once! This is your final test! Do you understand me?"

I mustered a whisper. "Yes sir."

"Now go to your room!"

I skirted the back side of the table, afraid he would lunge at me. Alone in my room, I waited for him to burst through the door armed for a beating, but he stayed downstairs. Gradually, my breath began to slow down. I felt lucky to have escaped his wrath without shedding blood, but I was very confused. I didn't understand that nothing would have pleased him when it came to my behavior. It wasn't about my being holy or holier-than-thou. It was about maintaining power and control over me.

I called Joseph that night and sobbed into the phone that I wasn't coming to school.

"But you have all your boxes packed, don't you?" he asked in confused exasperation. "Aren't you supposed to fly out tomorrow?"

I repeated what my father had said, confiding that I was frustrated too because I'd been trying so hard to do right and be the antithesis of my high school self. After talking to Joseph I resolved to relinquish any will of my own for the semester. I would work even harder at stifling my outgoing personality with a serious demeanor and a contrite spirit. I took a job as a day care worker and gave every penny I earned to my father, just as he had demanded. At night I worked dutifully to make sure every piece of laundry was ironed, folded, and put away.

Despite my efforts, my father's bouts of rage worsened. He tried to keep it in check because of Jeremy's fiancée's presence, but he was a ticking time bomb, ready to explode at any second.

The Unhappiest Christmas

Finally, the holiday season came and my parents let me go to Wisconsin to visit Jason at Northland, then fly home with him for Christmas break in 1994. I welcomed the chance to get away. I visited all my old friends and had a great time. On the flight home, Jason and I were both intrigued by United's new in-seat phones. He decided to use one for fun to find out what type of reception we would get so high in the air. Jason had a job and his own credit card by this time, so he swiped it through and punched in our home number. Meagan answered, wailing hysterically. She told Jason my father had just hit her across the face and was headed to the hospital to see Jeremy. "He's losing his mind," she sobbed. "I'm afraid he'll do something to hurt him."

White-faced and shaking, Jason hung up and called the hospital from the plane. He managed to reach Melissa and Bonnie, who had been keeping a bedside vigil. They said Meagan had called them too. They were hurriedly putting on their coats, anxious to get out before Bart stormed in in a murderous rage. Both girls were panic-stricken and fighting back tears. Jason did his best to calm them down. "We land in an hour," he said. "We'll be there for you as soon as we can." They told him they would drive to a Dairy Queen nearby and hide out there until we came to get them.

The second the plane touched down, Jason and I bolted out of our seats, grabbed our bags, and sprinted through the concourse. We found my mother working at the airport, unaware of the drama at home. She gave us the keys to her convertible and told us to come back later to pick her up.

We raced to the Dairy Queen to get Melissa and Bonnie, then headed home so they could throw a few essentials in a bag while Jason called a hotel to book rooms. We were all too afraid to spend the night in the house. My mother got a ride home from a colleague, and when she walked in she found Jason feverishly pacing the floor while he waited for us. "I think he's going to come home with a gun and kill us all," he told her. "Don't you realize he's getting more and more irrational? This is a dangerous situation we're in." He pleaded with her, but she wouldn't come to the hotel with us.

The next day, my father climbed into his pickup truck and drove away, leaving behind a nine-page handwritten letter. In it, he confessed that he had been hearing voices in his head. Some told him to do evil. Others urged him to do good. "I'm in a battle with God and Satan and I'm not sure who is going to win out," he wrote. "I'm not sure I'll be coming home."

My mother spent the days that followed trying tirelessly to track his location, but with no success. Christmas Eve arrived, and we were in no mood to celebrate.

"Let's just get this over with," Jason finally said with a sigh. We never received many presents, but by this time the IFB leaders permitted Christmas trees so we had one in the living room. My father had placed packages for all the girls under it. We opened them and were astonished to discover that each one contained a Dooney & Bourke purse, day planner, wallet, and key chain.

He had done something unheard of; he had spent hundreds of dollars on us. But looking around the room in bewilderment, I saw that no one was smiling. Suddenly, Bonnie burst into tears and ran upstairs. I hurried up behind her to console her. I'll never forget her words.

"I lived in a house full of abuse, Jocelyn," she said, snatching clothes out of drawers and haphazardly stuffing them into her bag. "But this is insane. Jeremy told me all about it, but you never believe it until you see it. There's something very dark here. I don't think I can stay another day. How have you lived in this for so long?"

I had no answer for her.

A short time later, my mother discovered some credit card activity that placed my father at the bottom of the Grand Canyon, and she flew out the next day to find him. When she brought him home, he was uncharacteristically docile.

Still, he was lucid enough to rebuke Bonnie for stepping out of God's will when she left a few days after his return. She ignored him and left for good, though she wrote me a letter a year later apologizing profusely and lamenting the fact that she had strayed from God's will by refusing to stay in a terrifying, abusive situation where her life was almost certainly in danger. I keep her letter to this day as a reminder of the incredible brainwashing the IFB ideology was capable of and the power it gave the cult over us.

To Melissa, who was still living at home, the reformed version of my father was more frightening than the constant seething she was used to. She remembers the air being heavy with a sort of still, silent horror, like the calm before a storm. The ominous atmosphere escaped me, though. I felt only relief because his personality shift, however temporary, meant I would make it to BJU for the start of the second semester.

Life at BJU

After a year at tiny Northland Baptist Bible College, I envisioned Bob Jones University as an exciting and dangerous place. I saw myself like Rapunzel, falling out of her tower onto the long green grass of the outside world, overcome with wonder at her newfound freedom.

When I arrived on campus in early 1995, however, I found myself in a sea of female college students wearing ankle-length khaki skirts and colored polo shirts just like the ones I'd encountered in every other school and camp I had ever attended. It was a world of draconian rules and restrictions, just like the ones I'd left in Colorado and Wisconsin. There were BJU monitors lurking everywhere, eager to hand out demerits for simple infractions like a skirt with a slit a half inch above the knee.

No sooner did I reach campus than I was introduced to my Assistant Prayer Captain, who doubled as my Room Leader. Then I met my Prayer Captain, who led the hall meetings in my dorm. Next, I shook hands with the Dorm Counselor, who held a one-on-one meeting with every new student. After that, I went to my first hall meeting, where I met my Dorm Supervisor, and she introduced me to the Dean of Women. By the time I was through meeting all the females who would be in charge of me, I felt dizzy.

I made my first tuition payment, attended my student orientations, and registered for my classes, and then I received my student handbook. I was expected to sign it and return it within days, acknowledging that I had read every rule and agreed to abide by them all. In retrospect, it seems manipulative to distribute the handbook only after students had paid their fees and settled in, when it would be too late to decide you couldn't live with some aspect of the code.

The Anointed Handbook

Then again, at BJU the student handbook was treated as a holy book almost on the level of the Bible. No one questioned commands set by the Jones family itself. In fact, quotes by "Dr." Bob Jones Sr. were written on plaques in the classrooms to reinforce our reverence for the school's founder. His classic one (that so bothered Billy Graham it figured into his decision to leave the school) was "No Griping Tolerated." To my knowledge, it was plastered on the back of every dorm room door. It meant, for all intents and purposes, no dissent, questioning, doubt, or disagreement. It was the same message from our childhood Sunday school classes, repackaged: *Obey right away, without asking why, without a sigh—just as if you're five years old.*

Students raised in lenient IFB homes were often surprised to find themselves living under rules more stringent than they had when they were toddlers. We had mandatory prayer meetings at 10:30 P.M. followed by lights-out at 11 P.M. Talking after lights-out was punishable by demerits and no one could get out of bed (except to use the bathroom) before 5:30 A.M. and everyone had to be up, with their feet on the floor, by 7 A.M. (Monday through Friday), even if you didn't have a class that morning.

Female students were banned from wearing skirts above the knee and shirts with necklines lower than four fingers below the collarbone. Even wearing clothing from Hollister and Ambercrombie & Fitch was specifically and strictly banned. Forgetting to take out the trash in your room in the morning, walking on the grass, arriving late for class or chapel, or missing either one resulted in demerits. Our personal items were all inspected to ensure that we weren't concealing contraband such as unacceptable clothing, DVDs, romance novels, worldly magazines, Christian Contemporary Music, or, worst of all, rock and roll. The Internet wasn't a factor when I was at BJU, but now every student's laptop can be checked for inappropriate material, and the administration tells students that faculty and staff have every right to monitor their e-mails, cell phones, Facebook accounts, and any Web site they view. We were all required to report infractions we witnessed by our fellow students, just in case the administration missed one. Every student living in a dorm had to sign out to leave the campus and we always had to get written permission from a dorm leader if we went anywhere that wasn't a public place (e.g., the mall, restaurants, park), or if we would be out past 7 P.M.

Dating at BJU

Though virtually every girl on campus was working toward her "Mrs. Degree," dating opportunities were limited and fraught with risks for demerits. If a boy was interested in a girl, he could invite her to meet him in the Dating Parlor, a large room filled with sofas where courting couples could sit and talk while a parlor monitor prowled around making sure they didn't sit too close or touch. The rumor circulated around campus that throw pillows were removed from the couches, because the parlor monitors caught so many male students masturbating, trying to escape detection by using the pillows as their shields.

I was excited when Joseph asked me to meet him in the Dating Parlor for the first time. I could always look forward to good conversation with him. We selected a couch and settled in. Trying to get more comfortable, I pulled my feet up slightly under my long, full skirt and turned to face him. I was shocked when a parlor monitor swooped in and gave me a stern reprimand and a "write-up" (a precursor to a demerit, given to a newcomer still learning the rules) because my feet weren't planted firmly on the floor. That was my first and last visit to BJU's Dating Parlor. I was determined to keep a squeaky clean record, so after that Joseph and I met at one of the tables in the snack shop instead.

We weren't allowed to see movies at theaters in town, but courting couples could attend campus movie nights that showed films chaste enough to pass muster with BJU's censors. Despite the IFB's loathing for many Disney productions, *Beauty and the Beast* was a perpetual favorite, and Joseph and I decided to go when it was the featured film for university movie night. We were surprised when, partway through the movie, the lights and sound shut down. We had seen the movie at home during summer break, and we soon realized they were blocking us from seeing and hearing the animated candlestick and feather duster kissing behind a curtain. An embarrassed chuckle rippled through the room, as the same realization dawned on our fellow moviegoers. After that night, students started a trend of walking up to one another on campus and saying, "Oo la la, monsieur," the line in the movie that was censored by university personnel. Later Joseph and I joked that BJU was so extreme that it wasn't just anti-*homosexuality*, it was also anti-*"inanimasexuality"*—opposed to sexual relationships between inanimate objects. It was another reminder of the school's extremism and its tendency to treat students like toddlers.

Dating couples gave each other a wide berth, knowing they could get anything from five demerits for a small offense up to seventy-five for egregious infractions like holding hands. In fact, a couple seen doing something so scandalous would be "socialed," meaning they were forbidden from speaking to anyone of the opposite gender for the rest of the semester. Their only form of communication would be through on-campus mail and the phone.

The dean's office kept a record of every infraction so BJU could monitor offenses and know if they were dealing with a "troubled student." Anyone who got one hundred demerits would be permanently "campused," which meant that you could never go outside the university gates until the end of the semester. And anyone who hit 150 demerits before the end of the semester got "shipped" (expelled).

The Preacher Boys

BJU has long cultivated a special breed of male college students known on campus as "the preacher boys." When they graduate, these ministerial students start IFB churches across the country and around the world. These ambassadors ensure a steady source of revenue for the Joneses from new students. It's a brilliant business scheme, especially since, as naive young undergrads, the preacher boys confide some of their deepest, darkest secrets to college personnel in an effort to keep their consciences clean. The University has actually encouraged these confessions from future IFB leaders for decades. Whether they have porn addictions, secret same-sex attractions, or a weakness for shoplifting, preacher boys know that if they want to "live uprightly," they must confess and ask for mentoring. BJU mandates tattletaling, so no matter who they spill their secrets to, the recipient will almost certainly tell the administration. The sin can then be documented and tucked safely away in BJU's files, ensuring that the future pastor stays loyal for life. In such cases, if anyone hears rumblings about a possible defector, it's easy enough to dredge up old files and subtly remind the pastor in question how unfortunate it would be if word got out about his homosexual or kleptomaniacal proclivities. IFB leaders generally have access to virtually everyone who ever knew the potential defector (high school friends and teachers, college roommates, youth pastors, and so on), so the threat feels very real. Couple that with access to church and camp decision cards, and the cult can build an airtight case to destroy an antagonist's credibility. If there is nothing incriminating, it's easy to manufacture a plausible scandal and, with absolute control over the IFB rumor mill, character assassination is almost a sure thing.

At least that is the common understanding among those whose lives are most intertwined with the IFB. So much like the FBI during the reign of J. Edgar Hoover even the imagined threat of a potentially devastating revelation exerts its power to control whether or not an incriminating file actually exists.

Sex and BJU

There is no better example of the IFB's culture of domination through repression than BJU's attitude toward human sexuality. Things that every rational person outside the cult would be apt to deem as perfectly natural were "dirty" and "that about which we do not speak." Mild expletives like "wuss" and "that sucks" were strictly forbidden when Joseph and I were students because they had vague sexual connotations. Virtually every fall, Tony Miller, dean of men, would stand up in front of BJU's entire male college population to rattle off a list of outlawed words and expressions.

Worse, as my father demonstrated so brutally in Jeremy's case, masturbation is seen as a sin in the IFB. My husband vividly remembers sitting with five hundred other teenage boys at The Wilds camp, quaking in fear as leaders assured them all that they would never have God's blessing on their lives if they didn't conquer this vile temptation. Once, during a long car ride, one of the camp's most respected staff members told Joseph that God had spoken to him in his twenties and told him, "I am never going to bring a godly woman into your life until you get the victory over masturbation." He said he then redoubled his efforts, refraining from masturbating for a long time, and sure enough, God brought him a godly wife.

When Joseph got to BJU, the staff doled out the same dire warnings again at hall meetings. This heaped tremendous guilt on nearly every male student. Many of them assumed that because they had yielded to the temptation to masturbate, they must be sexual deviants, a conclusion that had horrible consequences for their self-esteem and their futures. If they were unable to control themselves, didn't that make them pathetic and weak? With everybody too ashamed and wary to confide in their peers, boys couldn't even take comfort in knowing they weren't alone in their struggle. Almost no one in the IFB concedes that masturbating is normal behavior for teenage boys. With their general antagonism toward sex education, it is all too common for teens to lack understanding about the biological shifts in their bodies as they head into puberty and their sex drives peak. Why? Guilt is crippling, and nobody knows how to exploit it better than the IFB and Bob Jones University.

IFB leaders often cite the fact that public schools taught sex education as proof of their wickedness. The way they told it, those evil secular humanists were dropping condoms from planes to encourage schoolyard orgies. It never occurred to us that a public school teacher might actually be doing something constructive by explaining natural biological changes to students, handling subjects many parents have difficulty discussing with their own children.

Despite being molested, losing my virginity, and enduring years of my father's lustful boasting about his prowess, I had no idea what a clitoris was or where it was located even as a college student. When I was sixteen, a male bus kid in my father's ministry asked me where babies came out during delivery and I told him they were cut out of our stomachs.

As homeschooling guru Mary Pride put it in her book *The Way Home*, "All forms of sex that shy away from marital fruitfulness are perverted. Masturbation, homosexuality, lesbianism, bestiality, prostitution, adultery, and even deliberate marital barrenness—all are perverted." Pride, incidentally, goes on to warn good Christian women never to dress up in lingerie to excite their husbands because "when women exchange their natural function of childbearing and motherliness for that which is 'against nature' [that is, trying to behave sexually like a man], the men tend to abandon the natural sexual use of the women and turn to homosexuality. When men stop seeing women as mothers, sex loses its sacredness. Sex becomes 'recreational,' and therefore the drive begins to find new kicks." In other words, that lacy black negligee just might make your husband gay.

Unfortunately, banning discussion of a subject has a way of fueling curiosity and even fixation on it. Take the "First BJ" buttons given to fresh-men, for instance. We got them as soon as we arrived on campus. When you wore your "First BJ" pin, you were given "grace" if you were late to class or broke a rule during your first semester, which meant you didn't receive demerits. Unbeknownst to me as a naive sophomore transfer, a frequent joke among the upperclassmen, faculty, staff, and administration was that the pins indicated virgins ready for their first blow job. Furtive smirks and suppressed chuckles would ripple through the classroom whenever a fresh-faced girl walked in with her "First BJ" button proudly pinned to her chest. It wasn't until I walked into the library with the button attached to my backpack that two of my classmates, Sam Gage and Brad Baughm, explained what "BJ" meant to those in the know. I turned crimson with humiliation. No wonder Coach DeVries tolerated so much snickering and lascivious speculation about me during those excruciating Bible devotions back in high school. As a male BJU grad, he was literally schooled in it.

8

MARRIAGE AND MOTHERHOD, IFB STYLE (1995)

> If we say that a person over eighteen years of age has the legal right to make his own marriage decisions, regardless of whether those decisions please his parents or not, we are making the Law of God of no effect by our traditions.
>
> —*"Dr." Bill Gothard*

At the end of my first semester at BJU, I was still conflicted about Joseph, so I sought counsel from older, wiser women in the IFB. My choir director's wife, my former piano teacher, and my best friend's mom were all graduates of the school and they all said the same thing.

"Love will come. The most important part of any marriage is a man's integrity. And Joseph is a man of integrity."

What about compatibility? What about chemistry? Those were frequently scorned as worldly ideas. People often ask me if marriages are arranged in the IFB. I tell them it's difficult to explain. They're not quite arranged, but a woman has no real free will in the cult. She might be desperately in love with a man who proposes to her, but unless her father and the other men in her family consent to the union, she normally can't accept him. On the other hand, she might detest a suitor, but if her father blesses the match, there can be no way out. For girls raised by abusive fathers like mine it can spell disaster because the men who control their marital fate care so little for their daughters' happiness that they're apt to pick a husband who will make them miserable. And if they've been primed early enough, the daughters will submit to just about anything.

Joseph was the furthest thing from abusive and I certainly didn't detest him. On paper, he was everything I'd ever thought I wanted in a husband and most any other girl in my shoes would have fallen in love with him. My father gave his final word on my internal struggle when he told me, "It is God's will for you to marry him and this is simply a matter of surrendering yourself to the will of God, something you've never done very well." I felt incredible pressure. Finally, I decided that God must indeed want me to marry this man, and I told Joseph so in early summer 1995 after my sophomore year. Elated, he called my father right away to ask for my hand.

True to form, Bart told him, "I'll gladly let you take her off my hands. She's your problem now! If you ever need help getting her back in line, give me a call." It struck Joseph as a cruel thing to say, but since Bart laughed as he said it, he decided it must have been intended as a joke. Joseph's parents had been loving and supportive his whole life, so at the time he was completely naive to the tactics abusive men use. He had no idea what my father was really like—yet.

Engagement

Joseph had gotten a job as the music director at Northland Camp and Conference Center in Wisconsin, and I was waitressing there for the summer. My parents flew to Wisconsin to help Joseph pick out a ring for me, then they all invited me to dinner followed by a walk along Bay Beach in Green Bay. My parents headed strategically off into the distance while Joseph and I strolled along the pier. When we had settled into a spot between two large rocks, he reached into his pocket and pulled out a diamond ring. In preparation for popping the question, Joseph had gotten permission from camp director "Dr." Jeff Kahl to hug me, and when I accepted we embraced for the first time. However, like most dedicated young IFB couples, we resolved to save our first kiss for the wedding altar.

We set our wedding date for just two months away, and headed to Maryland to meet Joseph's mother, Elizabeth, who had been battling cancer for seven years and was now dying of the disease. Being an only child,

Joseph was everything to her and she had planned to travel to Colorado for our wedding on August 19, 1995, despite her frail health. It was a heart-breaking situation, and perhaps because I knew that Joseph needed comfort, we held each other one night for a long time and ended up kissing—the end of our quest to remain kiss-free until we reached the altar.

Since we were still on staff at Northland Camp, where policy dictated that any man and woman who touched had to confess to the camp director and risked being dismissed, Joseph questioned whether we should turn ourselves in. I persuaded him that, since we were so close to marriage, God would understand and we kept the secret to ourselves.

A week before our wedding, Elizabeth checked herself into the hospital because her pain was unbearable, under the condition that she be released in time for the wedding. Tragically, she took a dramatic turn for the worse almost as soon as she was admitted. Elizabeth died the night before our wedding and Joseph was devastated by her loss. He knew she loved him dearly and that she had been a good person, doing her best to raise him alone after her divorce when Joseph was four. But she wasn't a member of the IFB, the "one true church," so what tormented him most about his mother's death was the fate of her soul.

The Wedding Day

My best friend Christy Roland was my maid of honor. The big day arrived and I was consumed with looking modest as I walked down the aisle. I chose a large, flowing wedding gown that made me look like a princess, but internally I still had nagging doubts. To put myself at ease, I kept repeating under my breath, "I am not marrying this man because I love him, but because God wants me to." I still bought into the IFB mindset wholeheartedly, and I thought being in the will of God trumped love. As long as I was in His will and under a man's protection, absolute joy and peace would surely follow. Joseph knew about some of my struggles, but I had told him I loved him because I thought God wanted me to and he thought at that point that I was dealing with normal pre-wedding jitters.

Three preachers participated in our wedding, all graduates of Bob Jones University and prominent IFB leaders. "Dr." Jim Van Gelderen preached the sermon. "Dr." Steve Pettit performed the unity prayer. And Les Heinze, who had played such a memorable role in my senior year scandal, conducted our vow ceremony. Being a songwriter, Joseph wrote all the music, though, per IFB tradition, there was no dancing and no alcohol. IFB weddings are serious events, with outreach to the "lost" to embrace salvation frequently mentioned in the sermon.

After the wedding came a reception in the church with cake, nuts, mints, and punch. Some brides and grooms include a meal, but my wedding budget was less than $5,000, so we couldn't afford one. My father rented a horse and buggy to take us to our hotel at the end of it all. As I sank back into the seat facing my new husband for our ride through the streets of Denver, my first thought was, "I will never be hit again." A sense of complete and blissful relief swept over me.

First-Night Jitters

The night before my wedding ceremony, my mother sat down on the edge of my bed, put her hand on my leg, and said, "I just want to say that sometimes things don't happen the way we think they will." That was the extent of her parental advice on sex.

It should come as no surprise that I knew very little about the subject despite my scandalous reputation. The vast majority of my sexual experience at age twenty had come from members of my own family. Joseph was a twenty-five-year-old virgin with even less carnal knowledge than I had.

"Dr." Jim Van Gelderen had done pre-marriage counseling for Joseph and advised him to read *The Act of Marriage* by Tim and Beverly LaHaye a week before our wedding night. The book, which was often recommended to IFB grooms, gave a biblical view of sexuality and marriage, and the husband-to-be was expected to learn everything he needed to know from it—with no hands-on experience, so to speak. Men who strove for absolute purity timed their exposure to the book carefully, lest they be overcome with lust and fail to "control their bodily urges" until they could yield to them in a godly way, within the bounds of marriage.

Though women didn't typically talk about sex at all, several of my friends pulled me aside shortly before my wedding to share their horror stories. One said she had burst into tears on her wedding night and asked for an ibuprofen. Then she sat and watched movies with her new husband, too afraid to have sex. Another friend discovered on her honeymoon that she had a rare condition in which her vaginal opening was too small to allow her to have sex. She and her husband were unable to have relations for an entire year after their wedding. None of the women I knew offered any reassurance or encouragement.

When we walked into our suite at the Hilton, we were surprised to find that my father had left a fruit basket and engraved wineglasses for us, for nonalcoholic champagne. It was late in the evening, we were exhausted, and we had to get up early the next morning, but we consummated our marriage. It happened so fast that I have almost no recollection of it. My sharpest memory is of being jolted awake at 3 A.M. by an alarm blaring in my ear. We leapt out of bed and started looking everywhere to find the source of the noise. At last we located about five different alarm clocks strategically placed under the bed and hidden around the room. It was my father's idea of a practical joke. But to me, it was an unsettling reminder that his presence still hung over us like a shadow, even in our new life together. We climbed shakily back into bed but were up again a few hours later, heading to the airport to meet my parents.

When we arrived, I was light-headed and shaking. Joseph went off with my mother to get the standby tickets she had arranged while my father waited with me. "Man, you're pale as a ghost," he joked. "He's capable of doing that much damage? I'm impressed." Suddenly I felt an overwhelming urge to vomit. I put my head between my knees and ignored him, avoiding further conversation.

When I stumbled onto the plane I was still queasy, but arriving in Hawaii rejuvenated me. We stayed in a hotel within walking distance of Waikiki's beaches. The setting was gorgeous and it was wonderful to be able to relax after the stress of wedding planning. But five days into our honeymoon, I was still unable to reach orgasm. Joseph reread and analyzed the *Act of Marriage* book, trying his best to figure out where everything was located, but I was frustrated and in pain. How many times would we try and fail? Finally, out of pure desperation, Joseph pulled the big black Bible he had packed out of his suitcase and started reading passages from the Song of Solomon. Then he held my hand and prayed that God would give guidance during our next attempt.

I don't remember the earth moving, but we made it to the finish line. You would think bringing the Bible into the bedroom would be a sure libido killer, on a par with Mother Teresa lingerie or vibrators with Scripture inscribed on the battery compartment. But it worked. Bible study was the IFB's solution to every problem. And if prayer could move mountains, surely it could help a man bring a woman to climax.

Biblical Sex

It might seem strange to go into such detail about my sex life, but it's impossible to fully grasp the impact of the IFB ideology on women without it. I was still struggling to understand it myself when I broached the topic on one of our IFB cult survivor forums not long ago. To my surprise, dozens of women came forward to talk about their nights as newlyweds. Many remembered the intercourse as rough, aggressive, and painful. Their husbands made no attempt at seduction and showed little sensitivity to the fact that they were virgins. It opened my eyes to the incredible danger the IFB's philosophy poses for brides. Many have no idea they're vowing their lives to abusers. I was thankful that Joseph genuinely wanted to make me happy and to ensure that I enjoyed our sex life.

To understand how little importance is placed on pleasing a woman sexually in the IFB, it helps to take a look at what Christian patriarchalists write and preach. Purity Ball proponent Doug Wilson, a guru of mine before I left the cult, is a great example. "The sexual act cannot be made into an egalitarian pleasuring party," he wrote in his book *Fidelity: What It Means to Be a One-Woman Man*. "A man penetrates, conquers, colonizes, plants. A woman receives, surrenders, accepts. . . . True authority and true submission are therefore an erotic necessity." Wilson calls that kind of sex a biblical mandate. What does that tell a victim of sexual abuse? It suggests that she's got to "receive, surrender, and accept" sex, even if it's forced on her. In 2012 Wilson lambasted E. L. James's bestselling *Fifty Shades of Grey* trilogy as proof that straying away from biblical sex has so twisted women's psyches that we all long for bondage in the bedroom. The possibility that human beings could enjoy role play or acting out sexual fantasies— and be smart enough to separate them from day-to-day reality—seemed to elude him completely. Unfortunately, many IFB members listen to him.

The First Year

When our honeymoon ended, we moved into a small run-down rental house three miles from Northland's campus. Joseph continued as camp music director, and I started working part-time in the camp office. As a staff wife I had to follow the rules in the employee handbook, which meant I couldn't wear pants outside my home and I had to attend a slew of revival meetings and week-long conferences. Naturally, we weren't allowed to listen to music with a rock beat or see movies at theaters in town and we had to attend an IFB church on the approved list.

Working twelve-hour days was normal for us during our first year of marriage, though it soon became taxing for me because I was pregnant with our first child just two months after our wedding day. My old childhood dream of being a wife and mother was finally coming true. I was married to a kind and loving man, carrying my first baby, and we both had jobs and a place to live. It should have been bliss. But dark memories from my childhood loomed up and overshadowed everything.

Joseph and I would talk for several hours every day and at night we would fall asleep in each other's arms. But within a few hours I would awaken suddenly, racked with horrific nightmares. Night after night in my dreams, my father would burst into my room and suffocate me or pounce on me from out of nowhere and strangle me. I would spring up in bed gasping for air, sometimes in tears, other times shaking with repressed fury. Joseph would wrap his arms around me and soothe me, saying, "You're with *me* now. It's okay. Go back to sleep." Comforting words, but they weren't enough. How could I believe I was safe when for twenty years I hadn't been?

I'd spent a lifetime forbidden from expressing rage and anxiety, so I channeled them any way I could. Some nights I slipped out of bed, went into the kitchen to get the cleaning products, and scrubbed the house obsessively. Looking over my shoulder was a normal part of my behavior, and I would check the locks on the windows and doors over and over.

On the drive to work each morning, Joseph would try to talk with me about my nightmares about my father, but I shut him out. We shared everything else, but this place was too dark to explore. I couldn't bear to go there or drag him in. It would be over a decade before I finally opened up to him about what really happened in my home.

As if sleep deprivation and pregnancy weren't bad enough, my lack of sex education heightened my stress level. I had so little understanding of my own body that at my first ob-gyn appointment, my doctor had to explain to me that I had a vagina and a urethra—and that they were actually two separate openings in my body. I had assumed it was all one and the same "down there" and I couldn't wrap my mind around the idea that having two was normal. I honestly thought I would be incapable of giving birth because of it. I asked my husband if he knew the facts my doctor had related about female anatomy and, though he had a master's degree in counseling from BJU and had read *The Act of Marriage* from cover to cover, it was news to him too. Now I was riddled with fear. What else didn't I know about my reproductive system? Would my ignorance prevent me from having a successful delivery?

I was worried and physically sick all nine months, throwing up almost everything I tried to eat. At seven months, I developed a full body rash known as PUPP syndrome. I itched all day and night, scratching my stomach until it bled. I was exhausted, nauseated, and in such emotional shambles that I started having suicidal thoughts. Joseph was at his wits' end.

"What can I do to help?" he'd ask.

"Nothing," I would groan back miserably.

Northland urged newlyweds to seek counsel from older couples in the college's administration whenever they were struggling, so Joseph turned to "Dr." Marty Herron, a graduate of Bob Jones University and his boss. He and his wife, Tami, met with us and gave us the usual advice—to "surrender" and give our cares over to God, which did nothing to stop the maddening hives that made sleep impossible. Tami said God was "breaking me." How much would I need to endure before He finally succeeded? The "spirit of brokenness" had always struck me as elusive. At this stage, it seemed impossible. What did God want from me?

Word soon leaked out on campus that Joseph and I were having "marriage problems" and were in counseling with the Herrons. People we hardly knew started asking us if everything was okay. We never found out who was spreading the gossip, but it was a significant eye-opener. Nothing we confided in anyone was safe—and people were apt to twist what they heard in the most negative way.

My brother Jason decided to propose to his girlfriend, Jenny, shortly before my due date, and we were all invited to a Janz family get-together in the Colorado mountains to celebrate. My parents rented two condos, but when we arrived there weren't enough beds. My father led us from room to room, telling everyone where to sleep.

"Melissa and Meagan will sleep in here on the queen bed," he said, pointing through one doorway. "Jason and his friends will be in here on the bunk beds. Sandy and I will sleep in the back bedroom on the king-sized bed." At last he turned to Joseph and me and said with a shrug, "I guess that means we're out of beds for the two of you. Jocelyn, you can take the floor and Joseph can sleep on the couch."

"Jocelyn, *you* can sleep on the couch," Joseph said quickly, turning to me.

I fought back tears. Seven months pregnant and yet I was the one my father singled out to sleep on the floor. After a year away from the man, he still delighted in tormenting me.

When Bart saw my expression, he asked Joseph to follow him to the back bedroom for a word. But he needn't have bothered because his raised voice echoed through every room. "She is willful and defiant and if you don't get her under control, she'll destroy your family! You have got to get her in a proper state of submission."

As a new IFB husband, Joseph wasn't sure how to handle this difficult extended family dynamic. He was upset at what my father had done, but he didn't betray his emotions. IFB preachers taught that to avoid God's wrath, Christians had to honor their parents until death and Bart was now his father-in-law. Joseph would have gone to any extreme to keep his conscience clear and the cult specialized in creating overdeveloped consciences. It's hard for anyone who hasn't grown up in the IFB to understand my husband's internal conflict, but this would eventually become the Achilles' heel of our relationship for years to come.

While Joseph was gone, Jason heard the commotion and barreled down the hall to me. "Why do you always have to create drama?" he sniped, throwing me a look of deep disdain. "Just submit already. Do what you're told, without complaint!" Knowing it was useless to try and explain, I sat in silence for the rest of the visit and felt glad when we finally headed home.

Becoming Mom and Dad

Eventually the big day came and I delivered a healthy baby boy, Joseph Thomas Zichterman Jr. I was twenty-one years old and happier than I had ever been. As the nurse placed him on my chest, I looked up at Joseph and saw tears streaming down his face.

"Good job, sweetie!" he said, beaming and kissing me. "He's beautiful!"

In that moment, for the first time, I thought, *I really love this man.* It was true. After a year of marriage, love came. It wasn't a passionate love, like the kind you see in movies or on soap operas. But it was love, rooted in friendship. I knew he would be a terrific father, dedicated, loyal, and completely unlike my own. I also knew I could trust him to love our children unconditionally and to have their best interest in mind.

My parents insisted on flying to Wisconsin to meet their first grandchild before he left the hospital, and just as they always did, they brought instantaneous anxiety. I had dreamed of putting our baby's first outfit on him and asked Joseph to have the video camera ready so we could capture the moment to show him one day when he was older. My mother heard me talking with Joseph and immediately snatched up the baby, plunked him on my bed, and started pushing and pulling his little arms and legs into his new outfit. She had no maternal instincts, and my hair stood on end as I watched her flip-flop him roughly. When he started crying I rushed up to take over, but she used her hips to push me away.

Undeterred, I reached for him again. "I've got it, Mom," I said.

"Fine. I was just trying to help!" she huffed.

"Let her do it, Sandy," my father snapped. "She's always got to have things her way."

I kept my gaze focused on Joseph Jr., but I could feel my eyes prickling with tears.

Joseph wrapped his arm around me. "It's okay," he whispered. "Let's just get home and keep things as peaceful as possible."

Fortunately, my parents had rented a car so we didn't have to drive together. On the twenty-five-minute ride home, I gave way to my emotions. "She always steals my most important moments," I sobbed. "She's done that to me my whole life. If she knows I want something, she sabotages it. Then she acts innocent to make me look overly sensitive."

By this point Joseph had spent enough time with my family to understand, but he took the high road. "When there's conflict, someone has to defer," he told me.

I recognized the words of Northland "oracle" "Dr." Ollila in what he said: "All through Scripture, God always blesses the one who yields in a conflict." It sounded like Joseph was telling me my parents could still do whatever they wanted to me, and I felt deeply wounded. "Dr." Jim Van Gelderen, who mentored Joseph in our marriage, reinforced the notion that Joseph should urge me to be more deferential and submissive. He reminded Joseph that he would have to stand before God and answer for my behavior—and he needed to make sure we would both be unashamed on the Day of Judgment. Joseph assured me that the hardest thing God ever demanded of him was to ask me to submit to his decisions when they caused me pain. Still, asking me to avoid conflict with my parents became standard fare in our marriage, no matter how hurt I was by my parents' behavior.

Bart and Sandy came to see us two to three times a year and stayed about a week each time. They loved visiting the college and summer camp because so many of their friends were on staff. But we had conflicts like the hospital incident every time they came and I soon grew to dread their visits.

Babies Are Us

As long as my parents stayed away, I felt happier than I had ever been. We named Joseph Jr. "JoJo" to distinguish between the two Josephs in the house. JoJo was my pride and joy. Joseph adored him too, tweaking his cheeks affectionately and calling him Chubby Cheeks, to which JoJo would let out a huge grin and giggle. He was the most jovial and good-natured of babies, and even today, now that he's almost grown up, he still has the same warm, cheerful, affectionate nature.

From the time JoJo was three months old, Joseph would sit him in his lap every night and read long passages from the Bible, then pray with him. Afterward, he would get down on the floor and tumble around, saying, "I'm going to get you!" I would sit on the couch watching the two of them and feel an overwhelming sense of joy and love for such a beautiful home life. When JoJo tired out, we would carry him to his bedroom and tuck him into his crib for the night. Then Joseph would turn on an audio version of the KJV Bible and JoJo would listen to it as he fell asleep.

The years went by and, like clockwork, as soon as a new baby was four to six months old, I got pregnant with the next one. I was a bona fide baby-making machine, giving birth eight times in nine years. Many homeschooling families were advocating home births, but I wasn't taking any chances, especially with the closest hospital a twenty-five-minute drive away.

When I got pregnant the second time, Joseph prayed fervently that God would spare me the pain of my first. It seemed to work. My pregnancy with Selah Joy was terrific—not one day of morning sickness and an easy delivery. The hard part came after that because she cried incessantly for almost two months. Finally, after taking her to a myriad of doctors, we found out she had a condition called intussusception, in which the colon folds inside itself. My father had had the same condition as a child and eventually had a large portion of his colon removed to correct it. Fortunately, Selah just needed a barium enema to get well. Selah has lived up to her name and has been a constant source of joy and entertainment in our home.

Sandra Elizabeth came along next and gave me an easy nine months, but a nightmare delivery. She got stuck in a bad position on my pelvic bone, so the doctor had me get up on all fours to shift her into the right position. IFB pastors often told us that whenever we endured emotional, spiritual, or physical pain we should focus on the suffering of Jesus. That would put our anguish in perspective, they said, and make us grateful. After all, our hurts were nothing compared to the agony He bore for us on the cross.

Up on all fours, I did as they told me and imagined Jesus being crucified on the cross. *This is what He must have endured*, I thought. Every muscle in my body felt like it was being torn to shreds. Unfortunately, focusing on His death on the cross didn't increase my gratitude for what Jesus had done for me. We were taught to be good soldiers who endured suffering stoically, but in that moment I threw my role as a warrior in God's army out the window and screamed for more Demerol.

Finally Sandra Elizabeth arrived. We named her after our two mothers because, after all these years, I was still trying to win my parents' approval. But when I called to tell her my daughter's name, my mother said coolly, "That's nice. Dad and I are coming to visit in about two weeks. We'll be staying in Green Bay for a day. I'll call you tomorrow to give you our flight schedule." She showed no emotion about our decision. Eventually, our daughter asked if we would call her "Lizzy," and she has become one of our most insightful and analytical children.

Sarah Faith came next, full of life, silly, and independent. Jennifer Lynn followed. She looked like a porcelain doll, with jet-black hair and big brown eyes just like my beloved baby doll, Emily. She has always been a sensitive soul, a homebody who feels best cuddling up in our arms.

Josiah Daniel, our second boy, is mischievous and loves pranks. Tell him a gross joke and he'll laugh for the rest of the day. Jessica Lou got her name from my sister Melissa Lou. Like Melissa, she's strong and her will has never been broken, a point in which my husband and I now take great pride. She might rule the world someday; she seems to be training for it now. Our baby, Serenity Rae Hope, never stops smiling and is one of our sweetest and most congenial children. And though she's only in second grade, she has her pick of boyfriends.

I delivered my first four children without an epidural. Lots of IFB women say the sign of a real woman is that she can deliver a baby without pain relief. At ladies fellowship meetings, they were always swapping stories about how much trauma they had endured unmedicated. IFB pastors encouraged it by reminding us that our bodies were not our own. They were the Lord's. And the more we suffered, the more like Jesus we would be. "Great men and women in the faith have suffered terrible tragedies, yet they endured to the end," they said. It inspired us all to long for the next trial, the next chance to be purified through our suffering. As I had seen in the wake of Jeremy's terrible accident, it was a badge of honor. And boasting about it was an art form. As the chorus of one popular IFB song, "God's Refining Fire," goes:

> *. . . when the answer comes to us in form of trial and*
> > *test,*
> *We fail to see Your loving hand, Refining fire is best. . . .*
>
> *God's refining fire, God's refining fire,*
> *May it purge me now and make of me what You*
> > *require.*

The most popular slogan on the promotional literature from Northland Baptist Bible College was "God never promised an easy path." Cult

members often took it to heart and became like masochistic priests, flogging themselves metaphorically by choosing the most difficult path available and then "surrendering all earthly desires and comforts." In other
words, we would do nothing to make the situation better for ourselves,
trusting that we would receive greater rewards in Heaven for having endured harsher trials on earth.

The Professor's Salary

We had been at Northland for a year when Joseph was offered a
teaching position on the counseling faculty. He accepted gladly and eventually started teaching Bible classes too. At the same time, he was pursuing a Ph.D. in biblical studies from Pensacola Christian College in
Florida, which had a program that allowed him to work full-time and
complete his coursework during Christmas break and in the summer. All
his degrees were unaccredited by the official agencies almost all other
universities and seminaries use, but it didn't matter to us because we never
planned to leave the IFB. Even though I was not on staff or faculty, and an
at-home mom, I was still required to follow the rules in the college handbook. That meant I could not listen to music with a rock beat, wear parts
outside at my home to grocery shop or run errands. If I failed to follow the
strict guidelines of the college. Joseph's job would have been in jeopardy.

We eventually moved into a doublewide trailer, which gave us more
space than our apartment, though it started feeling pretty cramped by
the time I got pregnant with baby number five. Luckily, Joseph's maternal grandparents gave us an early inheritance and sent us a generous gift.
We were overwhelmed with gratitude because the money allowed us to
start building a home for ourselves, with enough room for the many children we envisioned adding to our family.

One of the significant questions that always plagued me about "trusting God" and taking the Quiverfull approach was how we were going to
afford to meet our children's basic needs. Having a baby every year made
me feel on edge, and thinking about our financial state would send me
into dark bouts of depression. After our home was built, though my
physical and emotional pain persisted, my suicidal impulses tapered off
substantially. I saw a light at end of the tunnel and it helped me make it
through each day.

Before we moved in in August of 2000, older faculty, staff, and administration had often treated us with disdain. But the minute we became homeowners, their attitudes changed. They were more polite and they probed us whenever they had the chance. How much had we inherited? Were we likely to get more? How wealthy was Joseph's family? It drove them wild with curiosity and their questions never ended. Joseph's family began cashing CDs annually, and it was their generosity that allowed us to make ends meet despite my husband's paltry monthly salary. He started at $1,200 a month and, even after eleven years made only $1,700 in take-home pay following health insurance costs, though he was one of the school's most beloved teachers and got incredible student and administrative reviews. Young academics sometimes joke about living in genteel poverty, but this would have been extreme even by their standards.

Government Aid

Despite the low wages we were paid, the IFB leaders typically disparaged people who used welfare. They also railed against food stamps, Medicaid, and the government's Women, Infants and Children (WIC) program. After all, our lifestyles had to appear perfect to draw outsiders to God. This left families like ours in a quandary. On one hand, Joseph was paid so little that we qualified for welfare. On the other, we were encouraged to refrain from using the program, lest we appear unable to meet our family's needs to those on the outside. It was the proverbial Catch-22. In many ways, it was the same strategy my father had used with me as a teenager to keep control. People tended to use food stamps in secret at Northland, and representatives from the college went to the community food bank in Green Bay once a month to get food buckets that contained outdated frozen pizzas, name brand cereals, Pop-Tarts, and other treats the faculty and staff couldn't afford.

Bad as our situation was, many we knew who had come to Northland from the faculty at BJU assured Joseph that salaries there were even lower. Plus, they said that, almost without exception, BJU required faculty wives to work thirty hours per week for even lower wages than their husbands earned. The joke on campus was that BJU could get "two [employees] for the price of half." Most faculty members took positions right after graduation, and, with no money and unaccredited degrees, they often had no way to make a new start anywhere else so they became financially dependent and loyal for life.

Cult Leader Tactics

"Dr." Ollila, the one whose sermons had inspired my brother Jeremy's apology years earlier, was still president of the college, and it didn't take us long to realize he had a penchant for stirring up drama. The man fed off negativity. A few years after we arrived at Northland, the school hired a new dean named Pat Griffiths, who found out firsthand how underhanded "Dr." Ollila could be. In his job interview, Pat had explained that he believed humans were automatically forgiven by Jesus at salvation and that daily confession for every minuscule sin was unnecessary. It was hardly radical thinking in many Christian circles, but Pat soon became a controversial figure among students, because he challenged their thinking. Angry parents called, threatening to pull their kids out of Northland.

"Dr." Ollila went for the jugular and commanded all the students, faculty, and staff one day in chapel: "I want every one of you to bow your heads and close your eyes. Now raise your hand if you believe that there is a faculty member who is disloyal to our administration in your midst."

No one raised a hand.

"Come on," he bellowed. "Be honest!"

Two tentative hands appeared on the front row. (My husband defied "Dr." Ollila's orders just long enough to peek from his seat in the back of the church and count them.)

Frustrated at the lack of response, Ollila launched into such a tirade against disloyalty that he scared everyone senseless. Shortly thereafter, "Dr." Ollila's right-hand man, Sam Horn, stood up and, in a hushed and reverent voice, gushed about our president's uncanny ability to "hear from God" on matters like this, echoing the prevailing sentiment at Northland about "Dr." Ollila's decisions being "divinely guided."

Pat Griffiths resigned the day after that chapel service (effective at the end of the semester) and, under pressure, he made a public apology for being disloyal to the school's philosophy. After we left the IFB, Pat told us that he had been getting ready to defend his dissertation at the time of this incident, and BJU had threatened not to let him graduate because of it, though the university did ultimately grant him his degree.

The Pat Griffiths debacle was far from the only time Ollila stirred up trouble. He liked to instigate an "issue," then swoop in to resolve it like a fireman who starts his own blaze and accepts a medal from the town for putting it out. Whenever Ollila started asking accusatory questions at a faculty in-service meeting, you could feel excitement crackling through the air like electricity. People would snap to attention, morbidly curious to find out who was about to get a tongue-lashing. Every media specialist knows that controversy sells and nobody was better than "Dr." Ollila at stirring it up.

The Problem Is Not Us, It's You

Vice President Sam Horn was even worse. In meetings he would rail against things like "women spreading rumors on the phone all day." He seemed to have a particular loathing for me, and glared in my direction after every one of his snarky remarks. One day, my best friend Dee Dee called to tell me she had just come from a meeting with thirteen other secretaries in which camp director "Dr." Jeff Kahl had said "Dr." Ollila was retiring. I started crying at the thought of losing our campus icon. No one told me the news was confidential, so I called to share it with my friend Vivian, who had been on staff at Northland, but was now living in Michigan and had idolized Ollila like the rest of us. Unbeknownst to me, Vivian's husband was picking Sam Horn up from the airport that night in Detroit for a revival meeting at a local IFB church. He asked Sam if the rumor about Ollila was true.

The next morning, my husband got an angry call from Sam.

"Tell your wife to keep her mouth shut!" he yelled. "She's telling everyone that 'Dr.' Ollila is retiring and he's not!"

Joseph tried to explain that the information had come from a college administrator, who had stated it in a public meeting, but Sam would hear none of it. "I don't care who said what, tell your wife to stop talking!"

Soon the school announced that Ollila would become chancellor, which meant he would preach in chapel but not run the day-to-day administration. I should have known, IFB leaders never really retire. They just give them impressive new titles that justify a paycheck.

By that point, Joseph knew Sam was gunning for me. He worried that his job and, by extension, our family's financial future, might be in jeopardy. So he told me to let the answering machine pick up whenever a call came in and to stay off the phone unless he was in the room. This left me even more isolated while Joseph was at work all day and it meant I couldn't even talk to my friends without being censored. That wasn't Joseph's intent. He just figured that if he heard everything I said, he would be able to refute any accusations Horn made about my gossiping in the future.

I should never have expected privacy or respect in the IFB. I got a stark reminder of this when my old pastor Les Heinze came to Northland to give in-service sessions. There was a lot of excitement over the fact that the leader of a huge Colorado church was gracing us with his presence. But he was only a few minutes into one of his first sessions when he brought up my name. To my horror, he told everyone that I had been kicked out of high school. I knew instantly where he was leading. He was dredging up my decade-old scandal under the pretense of illustrating God's benevolence. In essence, he was telling everyone how God had allowed a disgraced and impure girl like me to walk to the altar just like a virgin. I'm not sure if he saw the expression on my face, but he refrained from giving details. Even so, I knew I would be bombarded with probing questions by the other faculty and staff the minute he was done speaking. Horrified, I held my emotions inside, then ran to the restroom to hide the minute he finished speaking. Even as a mother and wife of a respected IFB loyalist, the man was determined to humiliate me.

Joseph came to find me and took me home. Later that night Sam Horn called, ostensibly to offer his sympathy, though I suspected he wanted to pour salt in the wound. Sam had a tendency to pry into our private lives, and his comments about my "emotional reaction to Heinze's words" also suggested to me that he was hoping for some juicy details. I ignored this and shared nothing personal.

Even though almost a decade had passed since I first arrived on campus at Northland as a freshman, I knew I was still on spiritual probation in their eyes. That meant even Joseph was at risk. Our family's stability would depend on me keeping my head down and being the perfect IFB wife from now on.

9

THE HOMESCHOOLING MOM

It's God on the phone for me? How did he get my
number? . . . Yes, Lord? And you want me to deliver a
message? . . . We know you don't take sides at the elec-
tion, but if you did, we kind of think you'd hang in
there with us. . . . A whole army of people out here, we
pledge we'll do our very best.

—*Mike Huckabee,*
Republican Governors Association, 2004

From 1995 through 2004, my days were filled with pregnancy,
nursing, struggling to lose weight, and then rocketing back up the scales
with yet another pregnancy. The clothes in my closet ranged from size 2
to size 14. I always forced myself to drop back down to 115 on the scale
before I became pregnant again, which meant I had to shed all my baby
weight in the twelve weeks following a delivery. Six weeks after each baby
was born, I would start running four to six miles early every morning
before Joseph left for work. I rode the scales just as I had as a teen, going
from a petite size 0 to a pudgy adolescent with my sudden thirty-pound
weight gain, and then whittling myself back down to a 0–2 again.

My drive to slim down came partly from the fact that I knew at the
rate I was going I could have as many as sixteen to eighteen kids and I
knew I needed to keep my body in good shape. But another driving factor
was the incredible pressure IFB leaders put on wives to maintain their
looks so their husbands' eyes wouldn't wander. After my mother gained

extra weight, my father bought her a Nordic Track and treadmill, and demanded she discipline herself enough to lose the extra weight.

Having babies one after the other naturally took a toll on our sex life. The fear of pregnancy made me worry that I would conceive too soon, so if Joseph caught a glimpse of me undressing and got that look in his eye, an overwhelming dread would rush through me. I knew choosing not to use birth control was playing with fire, and I feigned a headache as often as I could get away with it, just to give myself time to regain my strength before another round of morning sickness. But often when I demurred, Joseph would recite Bible passages and warn that he could be "tempted with ungodly thoughts" if his "needs" weren't met. The following passage from Corinthians was a favorite in the IFB: "Do not withhold yourself sexually from your spouse, except when both of you agree for a brief time, so you may give yourselves to fasting and prayer; then have sexual relations again, so Satan does not tempt you with a lack of self-restraint." The verse made life sublime for libidinous husbands in the IFB; it meant they could get sex whenever they wanted it. One pastor's wife, who was a close friend of mine, told me that her husband demanded they make love every night, sometimes more than once, and she had dutifully met his needs for more than twenty years.

Whenever Joseph gave up, rolled over, and fell asleep, I would lie awake, struggling with guilt for hours, eventually waking him with a hug and kiss. Other times, I would cave in and robotically go through the motions, but it was out of duty, not passion. I had no time or energy to even consider sexual fantasy or foreplay—I was just fulfilling another responsibility to my husband.

I was adamant about feeding my kids organic foods, so after waking them all up with hugs, kisses, and songs I made up, I would blend barley juice, carrots, and Granny Smith apples in a juicer and serve it to them for breakfast with oatmeal. I made all our dinners from scratch and filled the pantry with lentils, brown rice, black beans, grains, and other healthful foods bought in bulk from the local food co-op to save money.

After years of being beaten for sloppy chore work as a child, I was fanatical about keeping our house immaculate. I labeled everything from our kitchen shelves to the bins of seasonal clothes in our garage. Anything that smacked of disorder—even mismatched plates—drove me crazy.

"Cleanliness is next to godliness," as our pastors were always reminding us, "and God requires us to be excellent in all we do." Like everyone else in the cult, I thought mental illness was a myth and psychology was the devil's work, so I had no idea I was suffering from obsessive-compulsive disorder. Having grown up in an unpredictable, menacing environment with no way to protect myself and being trapped now in a lifestyle where the church and the college dictated every move I made, I was using organization to give myself a sense of control over my life.

Determined to Create Superkids

If Joseph had taught at Bob Jones University, we would have been required to put our kids in the Bob Jones elementary and high schools, but Northland did not have a Christian school directly associated with it. Almost everyone chose between nearby Pioneer Christian school and homeschooling. A few families put their kids in public school, but it was generally frowned upon. We opted for homeschooling because with less than $1,500 a month to live on, tuition for eight would have been prohibitive. Besides, I was convinced I could give our kids an outstanding education.

In order to homeschool my children, all I had to do was fill out a form for the state of Wisconsin listing how many hours I planned to school them. There were no state inspections, no credentialing requirements, no mandatory curriculum assessments or tests. For all the state knew, I could have been an illiterate parent, running a child brothel in the middle of the woods. Or I could have been a paranoid schizophrenic, hiding my kids in a tunnel under our home because I thought the world was coming to an end. As long as I crawled out of the tunnel long enough to turn the form in, I satisfied Wisconsin's homeschooling requirements.

Fortunately for my kids, education was important to Joseph and me. We loaded up with Christian homeschooling curricula, using materials from BJU Press, A Beka Books, Rod and Staff, and Accelerated Christian Education (ACE). Eventually I added the Bob Jones University satellite program and Saxon for math, which I deemed the best programs available.

Like a number of other moms in the IFB, I was determined to raise super-children whose achievements would put public school kids to shame.

Even that wasn't enough; I planned for them to outpace all their IFB peers academically too. My kids would learn several foreign languages, read classic literature for hours every day, and master at least two musical instruments. I set up what I called "stations," play centers in various parts of the house with dollhouses, puzzles, Legos, and other educational toys from the Learning Center. I allotted each child thirty minutes per station before rotating. In short, I brought the same obsessive-compulsive approach I used in housekeeping to homeschooling. Being a driven person, who also happened to be female, the greatest thing I thought I could do for God was to raise as many children as possible to grow up to be mighty warriors in His kingdom.

Using a Christian homeschooling Web site called Titus2.com, I purchased materials that helped me schedule our days in half-hour segments. A typical day looked like this:

5:00–6:00 A.M.:	Mom jog/spend time in prayer
6:00–6:30 A.M.:	Mom get ready
6:30–7:00 A.M.:	Mom personal prayer/Bible study
7:00–8:00 A.M.:	Kids up, dressed, hygiene, bedroom cleanup
8:00–8:30 A.M.:	Breakfast/kids listen to Bible on CD
8:30–9:00 A.M.:	Bible memory verses
9:00–9:30 A.M.:	JoJo reading lesson with Mom/kids play at stations
9:30–10:00 A.M.:	Selah reading lesson with Mom/kids play at stations
10:00–10:30 A.M.:	Mom reads group story
10:30–11:00 A.M.:	Kids listen to *Children's Story Hour* tapes (character stories)
11:00–11:30 A.M.:	Clean up and prepare for lunch
11:30 A.M.–12:30 P.M.:	Lunch/Bible memory verses
12:30–1:30 P.M.:	Playtime outside or with toys in playroom
1:30–2:00 P.M.:	Listen to Suzuki (violin) tapes while resting— prepping for naps/Mom pray
2:00–4:00 P.M.:	Nap time/Mom spends time in prayer
4:00–5:00 P.M.:	Older kids help Mom set table/make dinner/little kids play in playroom

5:00–5:30 P.M.:	Get devotional items in place/music prepared/do additional cleanup
5:30–7:00 P.M.:	Dad home. Family dinner. Family devotions. Family sing.
7:00–8:00 P.M.:	Dad play with kids/Mom clean up dinner
8:00 P.M.:	Kids in bed
8:00–9:00 P.M.:	Husband-wife time
9:00–11:00 P.M.:	Personal Bible study/prayer

Into that tightly packed schedule I also squeezed breastfeeding the baby, changing diapers for four kids, cleaning up unexpected messes, and doing countless loads of laundry. I was determined to spend hours in prayer every day too. I would be a shining example of what the IFB called "the hidden woman," one who served quietly and passionately in private, making my relationship with God and my family my number one priority.

Corporal Punishment for Beginners

Whenever I could, I attended homeschooling conferences held by Christian curriculum providers like ACE, BJU Press, fundamentalists like "Dr." Bill Gothard, and homeschooling gurus like Michael Pearl, the spanking advocate who has come under fire recently, accused of being a catalyst for parents who have beaten their children to death.

When I took my "Christian Family" class as a freshman at Northland Baptist Bible College, Wynne Kimbrough told his students that he preferred to use a twelve-inch glue stick on his younger children because it was flexible, like a switch. He also emphasized that it was "easy to hide and carry" and didn't leave "marks." I purchased glue sticks as he instructed, but ended up using them for arts-and-crafts projects. I also bought the PVC pipe Michael Pearl recommended and had a friend cut it down because it was too long and awkward, but, despite what Pearl's book said, it wasn't soft *or* flexible. I knew instinctively that it could cause damage. The pieces soon became "swords" used by the children during playtime.

Pearl, incidentally, didn't pioneer the idea of using the rod on children in fundamentalist circles. "Dr." Bill Gothard and Richard Fugate were among the first IFB leaders to espouse "breaking the will" of the child in the 1970s. Fugate is exalted as a child training "expert" in the IFB and his book, *What the Bible Says About Child Training*, is still recommended reading in child psychology classes at BJU. It's also sold in the Bob Jones University bookstore and featured on its Web site. In his book, Fugate advocates using a wooden dowel just like my father did, even going so far as to specify to parents what size dowel they should use at each age:

AGE:	NAME	SIZE OF THE ROD:
1 to 2	Tot Rod	3/16" x 24" dowel
2 to 4	Mob Control	1/4" x 24" dowel
4 to 8	Train or Consequences	5/16" x 27" dowel
8 to 12	The Equalizer	3/8" x 27" dowel
12 and up	Rebel Router	1/2" x 33" dowel

Fugate recommends a:

> ... balloon stick, willow or peach tree branch, blackboard pointer, or 1/8" dowel rod) with a toddler from the time he starts crawling to about 15 months old ...

and notes that:

> Most parents would admit that it is a waste of effort to chastise through either a diaper or heavy pants, like jeans. . . . You can spank them bare-bottomed as long as you are still washing them in the tub or are otherwise seeing them nude anyway. . . . After then the child should be spanked wearing underwear at the least. When a child moves into puberty, a swim suit or similar clothing would be more suitable, if chastisement is still necessary.

He also writes:

> the child who has not yet learned to trust his parent's commitment to his obedience, or who is exceptionally willful, will require more frequent and more intense

whippings. Such a child is likely to require enough strokes to receive stripes or even welts. Some children have very sensitive skin that will welt or even bruise quite easily. Parents should not be overly concerned if such minor injuries do result from their chastisement as it is perfectly normal.

Pearl furthered Fugate's approach in his book *To Train Up a Child*, one of the IFB's favorite discipline manuals when I was a member. In it, Pearl compares training children to training dogs and horses. He encourages parents to place a tempting object where a child can grab it, then to say no and hit them with a spanking instrument when they reach for it. On the Web site for his ministry, No Greater Joy, he writes that, "God commands parents to use the rod in training their children. . . . The rod purges the soul of guilt. . . . The rod assures the child of his parent's love." Pearl says his book has sold more than 670,000 copies and has been translated into a dozen languages. According to published reports, his Tennessee-based ministry, No Greater Joy, brings in annual earnings of more than $1.5 million according to published reports.

Be Fruitful and Multiply

I was also a big fan of Nancy Campbell, an ultraconservative homeschooling advocate and Quiverfull movement leader. Campbell publishes a magazine called *Above Rubies*, which her Web site claims reaches readers in more than a hundred countries and has a pass-along readership of half a million. She's fond of referring to children as "arrows for God's army." In her book *Be Fruitful and Multiply*, she writes, "We are in a war. Our children must be trained for battle. They must be trained to stand and fight against the enemy of their souls. They must be trained to be warriors for God."

The book's publisher was Doug Phillips, founder of a Christian educational organization called Vision Forum that claims to have more than 200,000 customers. Phillips was yet another role model of mine. In the Foreword to Campbell's book, he seconded her opinion: "We must actively seek to bring forth legions of children for the glory of God."

Mary Pride was my other role model and Campbell's counterpart in the Quiverfull movement. Pride runs a magazine called *Practical Homeschooling*, which she says has more than 100,000 readers, and maintains a Web site of the same name that she claims is the world's most visited homeschool site. Her book *The Way Home* was a lifestyle Bible for IFB homeschooling moms like me. It's filled with sentences like, "My body is not my own, to do with as I please; it belongs to God. . . . Why should you and I not 'honor God with your body' by having babies?"

No Government Interference

Like my fellow IFB moms at Northland, I was inundated with heavy-handed messaging from our homeschooling gurus about the pros of corporal punishment, submission in the bedroom, and popping out more children to fight off the evil secular humanists. I believed everything they said. We were all adamant about keeping the government from interfering with our noble efforts to raise godly super-children. The truth was, we had nothing to worry about. In all my years of homeschooling my kids, there was not one iota of interference.

Sadly, the government's hands-off approach to homeschooling has enabled psychopaths and led to tragedies like the cases of Lydia Schatz, Hana Grace Williams, Esther Combs, and little four-year-old Sean Paddock, who was murdered by the hands of his own mother who testified at her trial that she was following Pearl's teachings. More recently, a fifteen-year-old girl in rural Georgia was reportedly forced to wear a shock collar and locked in a chicken coop repeatedly for failing to complete her homeschooling assignments. Fortunately, in her case, someone tipped off the sheriff's office in 2012 and Child Protective Services finally intervened.

Looking back now, I realize many of my fellow IFB moms and I were so antigovernment that we turned a blind eye to abuse in our own backyards. A large homeschooling family lived down the street from me in Wisconsin, scraping by on welfare and spilling out of two rattletrap trailers. Their yard was a shambles of broken toys and their ragged children were perpetually filthy. Worse, the children were illiterate, thanks to their mother's apparently nonexistent homeschooling. Like everyone else I knew, I overlooked the obvious neglect because this family was following Quiverfull ideology, bearing as many children as God dictated, and protecting their offspring from the evils of public school. Northland faculty made a few feeble attempts to support their homeschooling efforts by bringing them books and tutoring the children, but soon lost interest, because the mother was so unresponsive to their efforts.

I should have called CPS. But I thought they were the bad guys and homeschoolers were the good ones, no matter how they treated their kids. I was also steeped in IFB propaganda about the importance of preserving our cult's godly image. If word got out about a negligent homeschooling family at Northland, it would shatter the facade of perfection we thought we were presenting to the outside world. For the sake of the cause, I looked the other way.

The Home School Legal Defense Association

Right now, homeschooling is enjoying an astronomical rise in popularity in the U.S. That means the stage is set for more egregious and widespread abuse. About 1.5 million children were being educated at home as of 2009, according to the Department of Education's National Center for Education Statistics (NCES). That's a 36 percent jump from 1994 and a whopping 75 percent jump from 1999. The most popular reason parents cite for opting out of public schools? To provide religious and moral instruction. An overwhelming majority (83 percent) of homeschoolers mention faith as a driving force in their decision to opt out of more traditional educational settings. In a similar survey five years earlier, only 73 percent listed religion as a key factor in their choice to homeschool.

The National Home Education Research Institute pegs the number of kids being homeschooled even higher, at over two million. That means there are *a lot* of parents out there like my peers and I were in Wisconsin. Many homeschooling families I knew embraced extremist groups like the Patriot Movement, which advocates building a militia poised to battle the U.S. government—no surprise, considering all the messaging we were getting about giving birth to an army of foot soldiers for the Lord.

The homeschooling movement also has a league of powerful lobbyists like Michael Farris, founder of the Home School Legal Defense Association (HSLDA), who speak at homeschooling conferences across the country and oppose laws that make the homeschooling community accountable. The HSLDA appears never to have taken abused women and children into consideration with its fervent commitment to *keeping the government out of our religious beliefs at any price.* Abuse victims pay a hefty price for that separation.

The HSLDA is diametrically opposed to the idea of oversight and the group seems to bend over backward to accommodate abusers. When I went to their conferences, HSLDA senior counsel Chris Klicka coached us on how to avoid accusations of abuse. Nobody distributed handouts telling victims how to dial 911, but we got plenty of tip sheets telling us what to have on hand if we were accused of abuse, including *"A statement from your doctor, after he has examined your children, if the allegations involve some type of physical abuse. References from individuals who can vouch for your being good parents. Evidence of the legality of your homeschool program."*

It's a veritable how-to for covering your crimes, if you consider the fact that many homeschooled kids go to physicians like Silver State's infamous Dr. Roland. Homeschooling parents who believe in "biblical chastisement" surround themselves with adults who support the same brutal approach to discipline. It's easy enough for an IFB family to find doctors and neighbors who will vouch for their parenting style and combat a CPS investigation.

Klicka also compiled a tips list for the HSLDA Web site, advising parents how to handle a potential inquiry from social services personnel:

> *Never let the social worker in your house without a warrant or court order.*

> *Never let the social worker talk to your children alone without a court order.*

> *Inform your church, and put the investigation on your prayer chain. Over and over again, HSLDA has seen God deliver home schoolers from this scary scenario.*

Like the IFB pastors, many of the homeschooling leaders I considered mentors urged us to spank our kids in private. They said "the world" wouldn't understand our godly approach to discipline. So mothers I knew carried short rulers and glue sticks in their purses, ready to whip their spanking instruments out and discreetly nip bad behavior in the bud if their kids acted out. They also told us to pinch disobedient children under the arm or on the inner thigh because we could pass off bruises and hematomas in those spots as normal play. We felt tremendous peace of mind knowing that if any of us homeschoolers were accused of abuse for practicing "godly discipline," we could rest assured that HSLDA lawyers would be on hand to defend us.

In 2012 the group helped to defeat a California bill that would have required all adults to report reasonable suspicions of child sex abuse. They likened the bill to the rise of the Nazi Party in Germany, calling it "Very Dangerous to the Lives and Freedoms of Everyone" and hailing its defeat as "a tremendous victory for all adults and parents!"

Like it or not, the HSLDA is a formidable driving force in America's homeschooling movement. So is the IFB, with its plethora of Christian curricula for moms teaching their kids at home. And virtually anyone who attends homeschooling conferences or reads homeschooling literature gets a generous dose of far-right religious rhetoric, biblical spanking, and the culture of secrecy endemic to the IFB. Even publicly funded charter schools like North Valley Academy in Gooding, Idaho, are making headlines for wearing red, white, and blue uniforms and touting themselves as a "patriotic" choice for parents, where kids shout out "God bless the USA" in the cafeteria. Say what you want, but the uniforms are almost identical to the ones my siblings and I wore at our IFB school in Wisconsin, and so is the God-fearing, patriotic messaging.

Christian Dominionism, Free Will, and the Current Political Landscape

The homeschooling movement's heavy emphasis on religion and the quest by leaders like Phillips, Campbell, and Pride to build an army for God in America dovetail seamlessly with the philosophy of Christian Dominionism that is becoming increasingly prevalent in conservative politics. The phrase comes from a passage in Genesis (1:26) that says man should "have dominion over the fish of the sea, and over the fowl of the air, and over the cattle, and over all the earth, and over every creeping thing that creepeth upon the earth." From that biblical passage, Dominionists have extrapolated the notion that it's time for Christians to take

America back by getting fundamentalists into positions of political power so they can enact laws that support their viewpoints.

Dominionist ideology had a significant surge in the political landscape with the rise of the Moral Majority in the 1970s and 1980s under Jerry Falwell, who told the evangelical right that America was doomed after it took the Bible and prayer out of public schools. He cultivated an us-versus-them attitude toward the government. Since then, religious fanatics have taken the idea to new extremes. Ironically, many Christian Dominionists call themselves Constitutionalists, though they're far from it.

Every homeschooling guru I met encouraged moms like me to believe that America should be a theocracy and, judging from their speeches, Christian Dominionist politicians agree with them. Not surprising, of course, since Christian Dominionism and patriarchy go hand in hand. These fundamentalist ideologies do not promote freedom of religion for people of *all* faiths, but freedom of religion only for people of *one* faith—their particular brand of Christianity. It's a scary proposition that would undercut our Constitutional rights as American citizens. The field for the Republican presidential primary race of 2011–2012 illustrates just how far the tentacles of Christian Dominionism have wound into politics. U.S. representative and homeschooling mother Michele Bachmann, former Arkansas governor Mike Huckabee, Texas governor Rick Perry, and former Pennsylvania senator and homeschooling father Rick Santorum (for whom TLC's Duggars campaigned) all have ties to the movement. So do former Alaska governor Sarah Palin and political commentator and homeschooling father Glenn Beck.

Huckabee wrote in his book *Character Makes a Difference*, "People say, 'We ought to separate politics from religion,' I say to separate the two is absolutely impossible." In 1998, Huckabee and his wife, Janet, took out a full-page ad in *USA Today* thanking the Southern Baptists for supporting the idea that "a wife is to submit herself graciously to the servant leadership of her husband even as the church willingly submits to the leadership of Christ." It could have been lifted wholesale from every IFB sermon I ever heard. No one should be surprised at Huckabee's action, considering the fact that he has attended "Dr." Bill Gothard's seminars and praised them as "some of the best programs available for instilling character into the lives of people." Even scarier, Huckabee has advocated merging

Gothard's institute's teachings with government programs and posed for fundraising photos with the IFB icon and homeschooling leader.

Huckabee reiterated his misogynistic views in 2012 when he defended U.S. representative Todd Akin for making the incendiary public statement that abortion shouldn't be legal, even in rape cases. As Akin explained his views, "It seems to me, from what I understand from doctors, that [conception after rape is] really rare. If it's a legitimate rape, the female body has ways to try to shut that whole thing down. But let's assume that maybe that didn't work or something: I think there should be some punishment, but the punishment ought to be of the rapist, and not attacking the child."

Even after Mitt Romney called for Akin to resign in the wake of public outrage over his statement, distancing himself from this extremism, Huckabee continued to defend him. "This could be a Mount Carmel moment," said the former Arkansas governor, referring to the holy battle between Elijah and the prophets of Baal in the Book of Kings. "You know, you bring your gods. We'll bring ours. We'll see whose God answers the prayers and brings fire from Heaven. That's kind of where I'm praying: that there will be fire from Heaven, and we'll see it clearly, and everyone else will too.' "

Like Huckabee, Palin and Bachmann have talked about being called by God to serve in politics. That's the quintessence of Christian Dominionism. Born-again Christian Bachmann is an ardent follower of the late Francis Schaeffer, a pioneer of Dominionism, calling him "a tremendous philosopher" and "very inspirational" in her life. She's also fond of talking about letting God's will dictate her every political move.

Just to make sure the nation knew the Almighty was backing his presidential campaign too, Santorum told the press, "We believe with all our hearts that this is what God wants." When his political star was on the rise, I couldn't erase the image that sprang into my mind of the Duggars at the White House in their matching long khaki skirts, teaching American women how to do home perms and shop at Goodwill for inaugural ball gowns.

Santorum's impassioned speeches about "the dangers of contraception in this country," likening homosexuality to "man on dog," and warning that legalizing same-sex marriage would lead to pro-gay indoctrination of schoolchildren echoes countless passages in the books I read and the speeches I heard by Mary Pride and Nancy Campbell. What's more, it smacks of Bob Jones–style extremism. Jones III stood up in a public forum in 1980 and stated that "I guarantee it would solve the problem post-haste if homosexuals were stoned, if murderers were immediately killed as the Bible commands."

In the spring of 2012, when President Barack Obama announced his endorsement of gay marriage, blogger Jeremy Hooper at GoodAsYou.org brought to light a series of sermon responses by IFB pastors that exposed how deeply homophobia has permeated the cult. For example, an IFB pastor named Sean Harris delivered a vicious gay-bashing rant, urging his congregation in North Carolina to beat homosexual tendencies out of their children like they would "squash a cockroach." Harris said, "Can I make it any clearer? Dads, the second you see that son dropping the limp wrist, you walk over there and crack that wrist. Man up. Give them a good punch. Okay? . . . And when your daughter starts acting too 'butch,' you rein her in."

Hot on the heels of those disturbing comments, North Carolina IFB pastor Tim Rabon asked his congregation, "What is stopping them from redefining marriage from a person and a beast? We're not far from that."

Next, IFB Pastor Ron Baity—founding pastor of Berean Baptist Church in Winston-Salem, North Carolina, and head of the anti–marriage equality organization Return America—called homosexuality "a perverted lifestyle" in a Sunday sermon and told his congregation that lesbian, gay, bisexual, and transgender (LGBT) people should be prosecuted. "For three hundred years, we had laws that would prosecute that lifestyle," he said. "We've gone down the wrong path. We've become so dumb that we have accepted a lie for the truth, and we've . . . discarded the truth on the shoals of shipwreck!"

Yet another IFB pastor—Charles Worley, also a North Carolinian— suggested that America "Build a great, big, large fence, a hundred . . . fifty or a hundred miles long. Put all the lesbians in there. Fly over and drop some food. Do the same thing with the queers and the homosexuals. And have that fence electrified so they can't get out."

Kansas-based IFB pastor Curtis Knapp took homophobic rants to new extremes by proclaiming that "[gays] should be put to death. That's what happened in Israel. That's why homosexuality wouldn't have grown in Israel. Oh, so you're saying we should go out and start killing them? No, I'm saying the government should. They won't, but they should."

Finally, Maryland IFB pastor Dennis Leatherman added to the controversy when he stated in one of his sermons, "First of all, there is a danger of reacting in the flesh, of responding not in a scriptural, spiritual way, but in a fleshly way. Kill them all. Right? I will be very honest with you. My flesh kind of likes that idea . . . but it grieves the Holy Spirit. It violates Scripture. It is wrong."

The cult's defenders argue that these pastors are the exception—not the rule. But IFB leaders don't get any more prominent than "Dr." Bob Jones III, and if *he* is willing to suggest stoning homosexuals publicly, you have to wonder: *What are IFB leaders saying and doing to LGBT kids in private?* It's scary to consider.

As a cult survivor, knowing all I do about the dangers of the IFB mind-set, it's terrifying to hear elected officials echo IFB pastors' views and to catch them slipping IFB lingo into their speeches. Could any of these extremists actually maneuver their way into the White House? Considering how far Christian Dominionists have gone already, and watching Santorum enjoy a brief surge to the number one position in the Republican race in 2012, I believe anything is possible.

John McCain seems to be all too aware of the extremism creeping into mainstream politics, judging from the fact that he's distanced himself from Sarah Palin just as he distanced himself from BJU years earlier. If the GOP is to have any long-term chance of survival, responsible Republican politicians will need to purge their party of the right-wing extremist fringe that has infiltrated it—the sooner the better.

10

THE "VIRTUOUS WOMAN"

You can't have a career and be what God intended you to be as a wife for your husband. He didn't mean for marriage to be a woman with her goals pursuing them—a man with his goals pursuing his and doing . . . the kid-house thing together.

—Diane Olson, President's Wife's Address,
Northland Baptist Bible College
International University, 2004

My Darker Days

The truth was that things in my own home weren't as wonderful as I tried to make them appear to the outside world. I put on a happy face, but I was having agonizing doubts about the IFB. I kept wondering what it would be like to live my own life instead of being trapped in one my parents, my pastors, and God had chosen for me. Was this all there was?

All the faces around me seemed grim. The faculty, staff members, and at-home moms were dealing with their own stressors, from seasonal affective disorder to tremendous financial strain, compounded by the knowledge that at Northland they would most likely never be able to provide more for their families.

My bouts of depression intensified. In my darker moments, I considered suicide again. I confessed my conflict to God and asked Him to give

me a heart of gratitude, but no matter what I did, I felt a constant underlying boredom. My life ground along tediously, devoid of intellectual
stimulation—and I knew it would always be that way.

Mental stimuli are hard to come by in a culture that predominantly
says a woman's only place is in the home, and even at home there's no room
for a meeting of the minds. IFB women were expected to submit unconditionally to their husbands. They are slave labor—perpetual worker bees.
Those who kept their mouths shut won praise. We were allowed to do the
grunt work of paying bills, but crucial decisions about finances and other
important matters were our husbands' domain. We were bound to them,
as dependent as children. It didn't dawn on me until after I left the cult
how the men in the IFB relegate their wives to toddler status. If a wife
disagrees with a husband's choice, she is told, "you just need to submit to
my decision," just as I would tell my three-year-old to "sit on the couch until we're ready to leave" while I prepped the other kids to go to the park.

My mother was an anomaly in IFB circles, working for United Airlines all those years. My father still ruled with an iron fist, but he "permitted" her to work because he couldn't resist the extra income and the
steady supply of cheap airline tickets. The more common scenario for IFB
wives I knew was that we never got a chance to use our educations. If a
husband died, deserted, or found himself unable to work, cult wives often
ended up in dire straits, unable to support themselves and their quivers full
of children.

Racked with guilt over our own ingratitude (we were supposed to be
elated with our lots in life) and entrenched in a culture of backstabbing,
we seldom turned to each other for true solace. I remember a speech by
Diane Olson, wife of Northland's president and a mentor to us younger
wives, in which she confessed to having been depressed as a young mom
and giving in "to ungodly temptation" by watching soap operas. She said
she repented and determined never to turn on the TV again during the
day. To avoid the risk, Joseph and I didn't own a TV. I heard about 9/11
over the radio and rushed to a friend's home with all my kids in tow to see
the news footage.

Ambitious women were often made to feel "sinful" for wanting a
career. That was not God's intention for us, we learned. Olson said she had

always longed to be a doctor, like her father. But he told her she couldn't be a godly wife and mother if she went into medicine, so she never tried. I kept a recording of one of the talks she gave to women at Northland in which she said: "You can't have a career and be what God intended you to be as a wife for your husband. . . . What are you involved in that you really don't need to be involved in? . . . Is it detracting [sic] for me from meeting his needs? . . . We are his helper. His task is what's important to us. We are oriented to Him. And I really believe only then are we going to find the fulfillment and really accomplish the purpose for which God created us."

Homeschooling guru Debi Pearl, wife of Michael Pearl, echoed the sentiment in her book *Created to Be His Help Meet*, which was sold at BJU and other IFB college bookstores and which we frequently used as a manual. "You were created to make him [your husband] complete, not to seek fulfillment parallel to him," Pearl wrote. "You are not on the board of directors with an equal vote. You have no authority to set the agenda."

Pearl expounds on the culture of submission so familiar to my peers and me, writing, "When you obey your husband, you obey God. The degree to which you reverence your husband is the degree to which you reverence your Creator."

For good measure, she throws in a threat that if you don't knuckle under, you might find yourself alone. "If you want to keep your man and the father of your children, you are going to have to forget your rights as a wife. . . . A man is attracted to vulnerability in a woman—the blush, the need, the dependence. . . . A perfect help meet does not require a list of chores, as would a child. Her readiness to please motivates her to look around and see the things she knows her husband would like to see done."

Another one of my favorite speakers was Beneth Jones, wife of "Dr." Bob Jones III. She preached that a good wife treated her husband as if Jesus himself had walked through the door. She admonished us about keeping up our appearances. No man wanted to come home to a frazzled hausfrau who looked worn out from a day spent minding scads of children.

She and Mary Pride told us even our bodies belonged to our husbands, not to us. That meant we should gladly meet any sexual desire he had whenever he asked. Jones used to talk about being a "Proverbs 7 woman in the bedroom," which meant acting like a street harlot, and a "Proverbs 31 woman in the kitchen," which meant acting like the ideal housewife. She even told a story in her all-female class at BJU about walking across the campus wearing nothing but a trench coat and going to her husband's office, unbuttoning the coat and sending him into a state of shock. Even though sexual conversations were discouraged for the unmarried college students at BJU, the rules never applied to the upper echelons of the IFB—and Jones's point was not to titillate but to stress that we were 100 percent responsible for our husbands' sexual pleasure. Cult survivors joke about how men love IFB wives because, "In the morning they feed you eggs and at night they spread their legs." It was hardly a recipe for female self-fulfillment.

The Need for an Intellectual Pursuit

Joseph knew how unhappy I was, and he agonized over my depression. He talked with me every night at length about how I could find happiness in the IFB. Eventually he came up with a creative idea to help me break out of my slump. Each day he would go to the college library and check out a new teaching tape for me. When the kids were in quiet play, I would pop in a tape and listen to yet another IFB leader's wife discuss baking, sewing, being a handmaiden of the Lord, or a similar topic. He also challenged me to read as many books on the home and family as I could. Over the next five years I became a voracious reader. Every night, after putting the kids to bed, Joseph and I would discuss what he had taught in his classroom that day and what I had listened to or read.

For quite a while, it kept my mind occupied and gave me a renewed sense of purpose. I convinced myself the only work God wanted any woman to do was in the house. Surely, a woman who chose joyful submission to her husband and excellence in her home would hear "Well done, thy good and faithful servant" when she stood before the Lord on the Day of Judgment. I embarked on a quest to be a more godly wife, asking older, wiser IFB wives for their advice. One named Louise Champlain assured me, "A woman's role is to do all the manual labor in the home, to free her husband to do the work of the ministry. Wake up every morning and ask your husband what you can do for him," she urged. "Never question his authority." I determined to be as much like her as I possibly could be. To encourage me in my desire to please God, Joseph put gold plaques engraved with phrases like "Embrace the Work" above the stove and sink in the kitchen.

In fact, he had Bible verses engraved on plaques for every doorway in our home. When JoJo walked into his room, his verse read, "Blessed are the humble, for they will inherit the earth." The plaque above our bedroom door read, "You will seek me and find me when you search for me with all your heart."

I felt so inspired by my new "knowledge" that Joseph and I decided to start a quarterly magazine for IFB women called *Keeping Hearts and Home* and a mock college called Women at Home University (WAHU). We would challenge women to earn a "Ph.D. in homemaking" by educating themselves on how to run an excellent household. Joseph was the publisher and founder and wrote articles on our Web site. I laugh now when I read some of the things we wrote. I sounded like the classic Stepford Wife. To read those issues, you'd think I couldn't flip a light switch without seeking my husband's counsel.

We fronted all the costs and invited fourteen prominent IFB leaders' wives to be submissions editors, reviewing each issue of the magazine before it went to press and nixing any content that failed to meet their standards of purity. My old nemesis Sam Horn, now a vice president at Northland, insisted we get each copy approved by the college too. Horn threw a fit when we quoted a book by a controversial evangelical figure named James Dobson, founder of a group called Focus on the Family. Horn complained to Joseph's boss, Curt Lamansky, head of the Bible department, and Lamansky told Joseph to get me "in line." We were told later that Horn had badmouthed our magazine all across the country, referring to it as a "newsletter," probably because sabotaging sales would prevent us from making money that could have led to financial freedom.

Despite Horn's efforts, the religious publishing house Zondervan heard about our magazine and contacted us to see if we had an interest in writing books. My heart leapt. Here was a chance to reach beyond the borders of the IFB, to spread the information I'd painstakingly accumulated to a larger audience. But after several calls with a Zondervan editor, we realized the IFB's Doctrine of Separation would be a major stumbling block. The restrictions it would impose on marketing would be fatal to potential sales. The opportunity fizzled and I sank into an even deeper depression.

11

THE TURNING POINT

Has your husband reviled you and threatened you? You are exhorted to respond as Jesus did. . . . Your husband will answer to God, and you must answer to God for how you respond to your husband, even when he causes you to suffer.

—*Michael Pearl,*
Created to Be His Help Meet, *Appendix*

Melissa Elopes

Melissa graduated from BJU in 1999 with a degree in nursing. She was a model student who committed so few infractions that she earned the high honor of being named dating parlor monitor and, later, received the Soul Winning Award. We laugh about this now because my sister swears she didn't lead one person to Jesus in all the time she spent at BJU.

Though she planned to become a missionary eventually, she took a job at a hospital in Greenville, South Carolina, to tide her over. In the course of her work, she met several evangelicals who shared their perspective on Christianity with her. She also started dating Vance, a doctor at the hospital. For the first time in her life, Melissa found herself surrounded by people whose viewpoints differed from the IFB's. She began to question all she had been taught. She stopped attending IFB churches in 2001 and, little by little, started backing away from the cult.

Naturally, my father recognized the signs and went ballistic. Bart

Janz wasn't going to lose control of one of his kids. So he did what came naturally: He started stalking her. He made threatening phone calls. He flew to Greenville and tried to strong-arm her into obeying. He met with IFB pastors, friends, and authority figures from Melissa's years at BJU and asked them to confront her. At his urging, they showed up on her doorstep and at the hospital during her shifts, pleading with her to "return to the truth."

Evangelist "Dr." Tom Farrell and Pastor Danny Brooks (another graduate of BJU), called to warn her, "You're out of the will of God." They knew about her boyfriend, so they added, "You must not marry a lost man."

Jason left gruff messages on her answering machine. "Melissa, call me!" he said, then slammed the phone down.

My sister Meagan called too, pleading for assurances that Melissa was still "born again." Like Jason, Meagan stayed loyal to the IFB and is now married to the pastor of a church in South Carolina.

The harassment campaign dragged on for more than three years, and in February of 2004 Bart finally snapped when Melissa turned twenty-seven and got engaged to Vance. I was at home with my kids as usual when she called in such a panic that she was almost unintelligible.

"Dad just called and said he's had it with me! He's flown in from Colorado. He's in town, Jocelyn!" she cried. "His exact words were, 'Pull up your pants, sweetheart, because I'm coming for you, whether you want me to or not!'"

"Did you lock all the doors?" I asked.

"Yes!"

"Did you lock the windows?"

"Yes!"

"Then call the police, Melissa!" It was something no self-respecting IFB pastor's wife would suggest. Their counsel would have been to run to the nearest IFB church, confess, and turn back to the truth. But I knew her life was in danger. I was sure the next call I got would be from the police, telling me that my father had strangled my sister to death.

To keep him from banging down her door, Melissa agreed to meet Bart in a restaurant. We both thought she would be marginally safer in a public place, but I encouraged her to keep her cell phone set to 911 just in case.

Melissa told me later that the minute she sat down at the table, Bart demanded she break up with her boyfriend. "If you don't, God will kill you," he said.

"No," she told him, trying to steady her shaky voice just as she had before the unforgettable flogging that turned her into an introvert at age eleven.

"No?"

"No. And you need to leave. If you come back, I'll call the police."

Bart ranted and raged, ignoring shocked looks from other patrons, and finally stormed off to the parking lot, his face apoplectic and his fists clenched.

Melissa watched him peel furiously out of the lot and called me as soon as his car disappeared. "Thank God I met him in public," she said. "If I hadn't, I'm sure he would have killed me."

My father took Melissa's threat of calling the police seriously enough that he flew home, where he fired off a five-page handwritten letter outlining all the ways in which she was displeasing God. The Lord's wrath seemed less chill-inducing than my father's, though, given some of his other statements.

"Melissa, you have played a dangerous game and you are about to lose," he wrote. "Remember our hike to Promise Rock? You kissed me and promised me you would marry pure. Maybe I should not have put so much trust in your kisses. Marrying a lost man is one of the Bible's descriptions of a filthy act of fornication. . . . Melissa, you have disgraced your testimony and your Savior Jesus Christ, who is God."

The day Melissa decided to flee the IFB cult once and for all and elope with her boyfriend in 2004 was a major turning point for our family. My father had forbidden us from talking to her when she started "going astray" three years earlier, but I had secretly called her at least once a week. I told Joseph I was trying to win her back to the one true church, but really we talked all about her new life. I found it fascinating. I wanted to hear about everything she was discovering.

Melissa never gave up her personal faith. She and her husband attended a small Bible fellowship together for the next six years and she delivered a beautiful baby girl in 2008.

At the time, I had no idea how much her actions would impact my own future—but sometimes the universe masterminds a plan for us that we could never have imagined.

Dying to Myself: The Outhouse Years

The year 2004 was not only a turning point in my sister Melissa's life, but in mine as well. For eight of the eleven years we spent in Wisconsin, Joseph pastored a small church an hour from our home called Long Lake Community Bible Church. Fueled by the countless audio lectures I'd heard, I resolved to set a good example for my fellow "church ladies." Every Saturday, I donned a long skirt or dress and left the kids with a babysitter to plod through the snow with Joseph on church visitations and canvassing efforts, knocking on doors and inviting people to attend our services. Every Sunday I woke the kids up at seven and helped them into their Sunday best dresses, suits, and ties for the hour-long drive to church, often on icy, sleet-covered roads. It was a dangerous drive in the winter and it always kept me on edge.

I supervised the church nursery while Joseph taught Sunday school to the adults and then led the morning worship service. Our musician friends from Northland provided special music each week or sang. I often sang too or played the violin, since I was one of the few church members who knew how to play an instrument. After that, I headed back to the nursery to supervise my own kids and other congregation members' children.

The low point was taking them to the potty. There was no running water in the building, so I had to escort toddlers through foot-deep snow to an old wooden outhouse that smelled foul and seemed to be full of spiders even in the coldest weather. Invariably, one of my children would seize up with cold and fear, let out an ear-piercing scream, and refuse either to get undressed enough to use the potty or dressed again after using it. I would have to muster up my most saintly demeanor, calm the child down, and patiently coax him back to the nursery. Every once in a while another lady in the church would offer help, but I did the bulk of it on my own. With my feet soaked and my frozen fingers fumbling to get endless cold little hands back into endless winter mittens, I would remind myself that a godly, submissive wife would not feel resentful about having to spend so much time in a rank latrine.

That worked reasonably well until several of my children got sick enough for a visit to the pediatrician's office. I happened to mention that every Sunday they were using an outhouse that no one ever seemed to clean, and the doctor was flabbergasted. "Do other people in the community use it?" she asked.

"I guess so," I told her. "It's open."

She ran a battery of tests right away, fearful my children had contracted hepatitis. Thankfully, they hadn't. Still, I came home sobbing at the thought of what might have happened.

"We have to come up with safer facilities," I told Joseph. But he was at a loss. All the board members lived within easy walking distance of the church, so they never used the outhouse. They didn't consider it a problem, and they insisted it was too expensive to put in a new bathroom, especially since we needed a new church building anyway. I knew our small congregation had no way to raise enough money for such extensive renovations, so I was stuck indefinitely. Those with homes near the church refused to let me take our kids there to use the bathroom because, they said, it would clog up their sewer pipes. Once again, IFB wives and children came last.

I started to despise going to church. Every Saturday night as I prepared the kids' clothes, I got a migraine dreading what lay ahead. Joseph kept assuring me that we were suffering for the Lord. But *he* wasn't suffering. I was. And it wasn't because of the Lord. It was because the men in the IFB never had to walk in a woman's shoes. It was impossible not to feel resentful. Joseph says now that I should have separated from him as a wake-up call for the way he had started treating me. He says I shouldn't have agreed to come home until he went to professional counseling and promised to put the children's and my needs first—and he would tell any woman in my situation to do the same. But it took him many years to come around to that way of thinking.

The Most Painful Migraine

As 2004 dragged on, my migraines got worse and more frequent. Sometimes I couldn't lift my head off the pillow on Sunday mornings.

"What are people going to think?" Joseph would insist. "You are the pastor's wife and you've missed two weeks in a row now. Even if you have a headache, you should still come."

"I'm too sick," I would mumble.

As further incentive, Joseph would pull out the Bible and sit on the side of the bed, quoting Scripture. "Do not forsake the assembling of your selves together," he would read. "Where two or more are gathered in my name, there am I in the midst of them." Then he'd preach a mini-sermon about the importance of being in the presence of God's people whenever the church doors were open. Joseph thought I was starting to "backslide" away from the truth and that he owed it to both God and me to insist on my doing what was right.

Usually I would relent and drag myself out of bed despite my splitting headache, huddling mutely in the passenger's seat during the ride to church and cringing as I thought about the marathon nursery duty that lay ahead. The hygiene issues never improved. With no proper restroom and no running water to wash their hands, sickness was rampant among the kids, but I could never convince Joseph that the lack of sanitation at the church was the cause. We didn't know it at the time, but the church had a black mold problem, too, which aggravated the sinus infections and strep throat.

Just as I had at camp, I tried to get my heart "right with God," praying for a submissive, broken spirit. But the more I prayed, the more depressed, hopeless, and trapped I felt.

The clincher came one Sunday when I had a shattering migraine, but Joseph felt that he had to stop and visit a woman from church after the service. When we got to the woman's house, I told her I was ill and asked if I could lie down for a few minutes. She led me to a back bedroom, where I collapsed instantly. She laid a blanket over me and I slept for the next hour.

Finally, she came back to get me. As I stood up, I glanced down at the bed. I was horrified to see that I had been lying on a crosshatch of dark, damp streaks.

"Oh my!" she exclaimed, following my gaze. "The dog just had puppies. She must have wiped her afterbirth all over my bed. I'm sorry."

I fought back an urge to gag and assured her it was okay. On the long ride home, I tried to erase the sickening image from my mind, but the second I got the kids tucked in for their late-afternoon nap, I started crying uncontrollably. I was cracking under the pressure of my crazy schedule, my nauseating headaches, constant nightmares, financial worries, an endless succession of pregnancies and child care duties, and the stranglehold the IFB had over every aspect of my life.

I got no sympathy from Joseph. Instead, he scolded me for being ungrateful, rattling off a laundry list of all the wonderful things God had provided. Then he prayed with me that I would become more submissive to God's will. It's a beautiful belief system for men, isn't it? You get treated like a king and called "God's representative over your family," and if your wife objects to *anything*, it's her "sin problem." This patriarchal philosophy was turning my once kind and gentle husband—a man who genuinely loved me—into a monster.

My Father: The Instigator

My father still insisted on coming to visit us and, whenever he did, he stoked the fire by coaching Joseph to be *more* patriarchal, *more* domineering. At this point in our marriage, the two of them spent hours talking shop in our living room. Bart had been officially ordained as a senior pastor by Les Heinze and taken the helm of a church in Brighton, Colorado. After years of pastoring children and teens, he was reveling in his newfound power over adults. He took great pride in a series of draconian rules he had imposed on his church members, including mandatory nursery duty for women and keeping tithing logs on everyone. He even went so far as to knock on people's doors during the Christmas season to remind them of their financial responsibility to the church. Erupting into boisterous fits of laughter, he'd talk about how surprised his church members were when he reprimanded them for failing to give what they had promised in their faith mission statements. Joseph listened, out of filial respect, but internally, he cringed at Bart's tales.

Invariably, the conversations would turn toward our marriage. By now, he was at a loss as to how to lead me into "proper godly submission," so he started seeking my father's advice and sharing details of our disagreements out of desperation.

"She's trying to control you," Bart would warn. "You need to put your foot down." I would sit at the top of the stairs, listening to the two of them in the living room and cry, knowing Joseph was absorbing every word.

My Brother: The Hero

Bart always held Jason up as the gold standard of IFB leadership and his wife as the ideal of sweetness and submission, and urged us to be more like them. By now, my brother was an outspoken voice for the cult, standing on the capitol steps in Denver and railing against the state of Colorado for allowing shock-rock singer Marilyn Manson to perform. His theatrics earned him a clip in filmmaker Michael Moore's documentary *Bowling for Columbine*. Moore was holding Jason up for ridicule, of course, but in my father's mind my brother was being persecuted for righteousness' sake.

My father also sang Jason's praises for "having the guts" to take on the producers of a Christian movie called *End of the Spear*, which starred an openly gay actor named Chad Allen. Jason launched a campaign to convince IFB pastors to boycott the movie—and to demand that the producers apologize for choosing Allen as an actor. His efforts backfired in the evangelical community, a market he had always wanted to break into, after IFB theologian Kevin Bauder from Central Baptist Theological Seminary posted a blog comment about fire-bombing gay men's homes in connection with the movie, and *The New York Times* picked it up. The evangelical community blamed Jason for sabotaging a movie they saw as a way to spread the "Good News."

Despite what "compromisers" thought, Jason was a hero to my father, and he took full credit for having broken Jason's will sufficiently to mold him into a true warrior for God. In a way, Jason's influence was now so strong in the IFB that his power was eclipsing my father's, and Bart was keen to stay on his good side.

My Husband: The Enabler

Joseph was never physically or sexually abusive, but emotional abuse of women was part and parcel of the IFB lifestyle—and Bart reinforced the message to my husband whenever he had the chance. Men in IFB organizations understood that if they couldn't keep their wives in line they could lose their jobs, so they lived under tremendous pressure. As a result, Joseph grew more autocratic and critical with every year of marriage. He started thinking any problems we had were my fault.

Whenever we disagreed, he would dredge up a convenient anecdote about another IFB leader and his wife. One of the worst was his story of how prominent IFB evangelist "Dr." Jim Van Gelderen, one of our wedding pastors, wanted to make sure he was getting a submissive wife before he tied the knot. So he waited until a storm was forecast, then he took his future bride, Rhonda, on a hike to the top of a mountain. When the downpour started, he told her to stay put while he fetched umbrellas from the car. She did exactly as he said, without question, standing stock-still in the wind and rain until he returned. After that test of Rhonda's obedience, Van Gelderen said, he knew she was the one for him.

When Joseph was in college, he spent six months traveling on Van Gelderen's revivalistic team Minutemen Ministries, a promotional student group sent out by Bob Jones University. On several occasions, Joseph saw him literally command his then thirty-year-old wife to take a nap in the back of the van, in spite of her repeated, humble biblical appeals that she wasn't tired. Van Gelderen would always say that he knew best and that she needed to be fresh for the service that evening. With that, Rhonda would go submissively to the back of the van, wanting to set a good example of a godly wife to the college team.

I knew a lot more inside stories about the marriages of key IFB leaders because of my husband's position. Many women were quite frank with me about how two-faced their husbands were—gentle and charming in public, while treating their families like dirt in private. Some told me they had shut down emotionally in their marriages, but, as long as they still provided sex on demand, their husbands never seemed to mind. "Dr." Bob Jones III's wife, Beneth, famously taught IFB wives for decades that they must learn to submit when their spiritual head made what seemed like bad decisions. "Duck so God can deck your husbands," she would counsel. That statement always baffled me. Would a good wife want her husband to be "decked" by God instead of trying to spare him from making a wrong decision that would hurt his family? Would she want to say, "I told you so" instead of protecting him? It was as twisted and sadistic as the philosophy that parents had to inflict pain on their children as "God's refining fire" to their soul.

My friend Tami Herron often expressed contempt for the way decisions were made at Northland and the fact that her husband, Marty, who was vice president of the school at the time, wouldn't intervene. Once, when Joseph sought counsel from Marty about his struggle to keep me in line, Marty advised, "What my wife, Tami, has had to learn through the years is that she is responsible *to* me before God, not *for* me and the decisions I make in our family and ministry. Jocelyn has just got to learn the same thing."

During some of our own marriage conflicts, Joseph even reminded me about how my father had grounded my mother, taking away her checkbook and banning her from the den, when he discovered she had gone through his things. "At least I don't treat you like that," my husband told me. There was nothing I could do. If it got out that we were having marriage struggles, I would certainly be blamed for my lack of submission and my husband could lose his job.

Suicide was looking more and more appealing. With my usual methodical approach, I spent hours devising a plan. I didn't want to kill myself in a way that my children would find out about and be damaged for life. What if they blamed themselves? So I started running through scenarios that would let me avoid that. If I slit my wrists, it would be obvious. Leaving the car running in the garage was a possibility, but people would probably still figure it was suicide. I finally settled on running my car head-on into a semi. It would be a tragic accident. I never thought about the driver of the truck. I was just looking for an avenue to escape the pain.

Welcome to the Boys' Club

While I sank ever deeper into despair, Joseph's career was ascendant. His influence in the church leadership got stronger every year. The year before Melissa eloped, "Dr." Bob Jones III awarded him with an honorary doctorate at the commencement ceremony. Joseph was just thirty-three. Only one other man had been given this high honor at such a young age and that was Billy Graham, before he fell out with the IFB in the 1950s.

Joseph had been writing music since he was sixteen and more than forty of his songs had been published in the IFB music venue. Technically Jones was awarding the degree to Joseph and three of his fellow composers for "not crossing the line of music by publishing in the Christian contemporary music industry." In reality, though, it meant "Dr." Bob Jones III was officially inducting Joseph into the boys' club. The IFB godfather himself was bestowing one of the cult's greatest laurels on Joseph. In mob terms, he was a made man.

I find it uncanny now when I think about the fact that one of the men who stood on the BJU platform with Joseph receiving the same honorary doctorate was Ron "Patch the Pirate" Hamilton, the man whose songs about cleanliness my siblings and I had listened to growing up, the songs that had convinced us the poor unwashed children who huddled in the corners of our school, friendless and ridiculed, deserved no compassion. He was also the man who wrote "I Want to Marry Daddy When I Grow Up," which still sends chills down my spine. Hamilton played a major role in indoctrinating children with the idea of first-time obedience to all authority figures and, in my view, his songs contributed to building a culture where abused children believe they have to obey adults—even in the extreme, who molest them.

I remember sitting in the auditorium feeling disgusted by the hypocrisy of the presentation and the people all around me. I knew that when a popular Contemporary Christian artist named Steve Green hosted a concert in town in 1994, "Dr." Bob Jones III spent an entire chapel service lambasting him for being worldly and for compromising biblical purity. Jones warned that any student who attended the concert would face severe disciplinary repercussions, but a popular church in the area called Southside Baptist decided to support the concert in spite of Jones's decision to boycott it. From that point on, the church was blackballed and BJU students were forbidden from attending. The irony of this was that Bobby Wood (son of the former university vice president Bob Wood Sr.) told me that his dad listened to country music behind closed doors. He also said he knew "Dr." Bob Jones III listened to select rock and roll music. Bobby himself was friends with Steve Green's manager, and a short time later privately asked Joseph if he wanted to get some of his music to Green's organization for a possible inroad into the CCM industry. Joseph could have published his music under a pseudonym, but he turned down Bobby's offer in order to take the IFB high road. Many members of Northland's administration, including vice president Sam Horn, kept Christian contemporary CDs in their cars and played them with the windows up and the doors locked.

All the young IFB up-and-comers like Joseph bought into the IFB standards even if the leaders didn't. I'll never forget the day when my husband's boss, Curt Lamansky, found a contemporary worship CD in Horn's Jeep and came to Joseph asking if he should resign because he felt like his leader at Northland was willing to compromise on biblical convictions. Joseph assured him that, though things didn't make sense at times, God was still in control. "Perhaps God has strategically placed you to keep people from crossing the line of biblical impurity," Joseph suggested.

The musical double standard was the biggest nonsecret in the IFB. Meanwhile, the students at BJU still could get kicked out for sneaking off to Christian Contemporary concerts in the Greenville area and lose every college credit they had earned that semester.

Now here was "Dr." Bob Jones III assuring a huge roomful of students that the men on the podium were a cut above them, perpetuating a lie. It was just another smokescreen, another way to keep the sheep in the pen: All other evangelical churches used Contemporary Christian Music, so the IFB was your only option if you wanted to remain pure before God in your music standards.

My Migraines

In May of 2004, I was struck with a migraine that lasted four straight days. By Sunday night I was so sick I thought I might have had an aneurysm. Joseph was in bed with the flu, so a friend drove me to the emergency room. The hospital staff that night gave me a shot and sent me home, but the pain intensified. The next day I was headed to see my doctor, but instead I drove to the emergency room. I have no memory of it, but I staggered in rambling incoherently and patting the top of my head. The staff immediately took me back for a CT scan and a spinal tap, but found nothing. They decided to keep me overnight and do an MRI the next morning. The following Thursday I met with a neurologist, who told me the MRI had revealed a mass in my brain.

"What does that mean?" I asked.

"It means you have a brain tumor," she said. The neurosurgeon wanted to do a biopsy to find out more but, because of the tumor's location, she explained that if she decided I needed surgery, she would have to operate within twenty-four hours of the biopsy.

I let out a nervous chuckle, a coping mechanism I had developed when dealing with traumatic circumstances. Then I thanked her and left. Still reeling, I drove to my husband's office to tell him the news. Joseph was devastated.

We met with the neurologists again, but we ended up with more questions than answers. They said the mass might be an astrocytoma, or a benign growth. We returned for a few more visits, and another specialist said it could be a fungal infection. Without a biopsy, it was difficult to tell.

I called my family to break the bad news as soon as I found out about it myself. Being in the medical profession, Melissa and her husband knew what we were talking about and offered to fly out to lend moral support. Meagan, Jason, and his wife, Jenny, came to visit too. But when my father heard Melissa and her husband would be there, he refused to visit with "unsaved" members of our family present. "Call me when they leave," he said. "Then maybe we'll come."

For the first two nights, my siblings and I sat up into the wee hours talking and reconnecting in a rare show of unity and warmth. After four days, Melissa and her husband left so my parents could have a turn to visit.

That's when a series of strange events unfolded. First, my mother went out and bought an absurd amount of food and paper goods, including six mega-packs of paper towels. I was struggling to find a place to put everything and getting frazzled with so many guests, so few answers, and so much chaos in my normally orderly home life. My sister-in-law, Jenny, noticed my black mood and, rather than offer sympathy or help with the groceries, she reprimanded me. "The reason you're frustrated is because you're proud about your home and keeping it in picture-perfect condition," she told me. "This brain tumor is God's lesson to you to release control."

"I'm exhausted!" I snapped back. "I need sleep. This has nothing to do with pride but everything to do with finding a place to put these paper towels."

I shoved the last pack of paper towels into the pantry and hurried upstairs, leaving Jenny standing in the kitchen alone. "You know Jocelyn," I heard my sister Meagan say sarcastically. "Always a drama queen." My mother's derisive laughter carried up the stairs to me, where I stood crying.

My old high school flame Will Galkin, now an IFB evangelist, did something even more insensitive. After our brief relationship, Will had gone on to marry my best friend from childhood, Christy Roland. No sooner did my family leave than Will called to ask Joseph if he could come to our house to meet with us. A few days later, as our respective spouses perched awkwardly on the sectional sofa with us, he told me, "I was bitter at you for the way you broke off our relationship when you were in high school and I was in college. I want to clear my conscience, since I know you've been diagnosed with a brain tumor and you might not live."

People seemed to think about my diagnosis only in terms of how it affected them. For Jason, it provided another "Jeremy incident" to preach about and to hold up as proof of the Janz family's pious suffering. He put posters up all over Iron Mountain announcing to the world that I had a brain tumor and beseeching everyone to pray for our family. Within a week, news had reached IFB communities across the country that I was on my deathbed, despite the fact that Joseph and I had spoken only to our closest friends and had never said anything remotely close to that. The college was also nagging Joseph incessantly to provide written updates on my condition for the Northland Web site, ostensibly so people could include us in their prayers, though it felt like another invasion of privacy. I didn't want to be a source of speculation and gossip. When one of the new doctors who examined my scans told me he thought my tumor was probably benign, Jason urged Joseph *not* to send an update to the IFB community, saying we should "not downplay" the potential severity of the illness. Joseph sent it anyway.

Exasperated by the lack of answers from the hospital staff in Iron Mountain, I met with a neurosurgeon at the Mayo Clinic in Minneapolis. He ran a battery of tests and concurred with the original doctor's assessment: There was no way to know what type of mass was in my brain. He advised against surgery because, given the tumor's location, the side effects might be worse than any problems the tumor would cause. "A biopsy would be just as dangerous as surgery," he warned us. "I would recommend watching this carefully to see if it changes and having MRIs done every three to six months." He also ruled out the idea that this was a fungal infection, and, knowing how severe that would have been, I was relieved.

Taking a wait-and-see approach about what might be brain cancer would be agony, but what else could we do? When I told my family about our decision, Jason couldn't conceal his disappointment and pressured me to go ahead with the surgery in spite of the neurosurgeon's counsel. "Jason, this is my body and my life," I told him. "This is not a story to tell." He seemed shocked that I would defy him, but this was one time I refused to be pressured into making a decision. I knew if I opted for surgery he and my father would have fodder for the pulpit, whether my saga had a happy ending or a tragic one. It would be just like Jeremy's accident. My brain tumor seemed to have a potential upside for everyone but me.

The same week we went to the Mayo Clinic, I found out I was pregnant with baby number eight. My ob-gyn was worried that all the tests I had gone through would affect my pregnancy. "We'll just have to hope for the best," he said, adding to our long list of anxieties.

Not long after that, we got a call from the evangelical radio show called *Focus on the Family*, hosted by James Dobson. One of Dobson's staff members invited me to be a guest on the show to discuss how I was coping with seven children, a pregnancy, and a brain tumor. We were still publishing *Keeping Hearts and Home*, and Dobson's representatives promised to promote our magazine and its mission. I was eager for the opportunity, but Dobson wasn't IFB, so Joseph asked fellow IFB leader John Vaughn for advice. Vaughn was the president of the Fundamental Baptist Fellowship, the second most powerful organization in the IFB next to Bob Jones University itself. Vaughn was vehemently opposed to the idea. He said he had appeared on Dobson's show years earlier and regretted it. "Do not participate with those who compromise the gospel," he warned.

Joseph's announcement that we had to refuse Dobson's offer left me more discouraged than ever. I wanted desperately to get out of the IFB box, but the cult quashed every opportunity. The nail in the coffin came when Vaughn published a letter of apology a short time after speaking to Joseph for having ever appeared on *Focus on the Family* in his IFB magazine *Frontline*. At this point, any hopes I had of convincing Joseph to reconsider evaporated. The great leader John Vaughn had singled Dobson's show out for criticism. To work with *Focus on the Family* now would be seen as an act of deliberate defiance.

Bad to Worse

I delivered Serenity, but the year that followed was the worst yet. Though the MRIs showed no significant change in my brain tumor, two of our other children were diagnosed with illnesses that required extensive treatment. To add to our troubles, my father was getting increasingly overbearing and insisting on visiting more often. I sank into my darkest depression yet, suffering from migraines almost daily, trying to manage eight children, two of whom were ill, and getting few answers from my doctors. Maybe the tumor was God's answer to my suicidal fantasies. If so, I asked Him to get it over with and kill me. "Just let this brain tumor take over," I prayed. "I'm done. Exhausted. I can't take another day. I'm ready to go now." In spite of this, I was scrupulously careful about eating only healthful foods and taking expensive supplements to boost my immune system. I was desperately confused, my will to live and my desire to die vying for dominance.

Given my mental state, perhaps it's not surprising that I lost patience with Joseph's frequent reprimands. "You are not being properly submissive," he would chastise. In the past, I would have redoubled my efforts to please him or walked out of the room to calm down, but now I snapped, "My father's planting ideas in your head. You need to set boundaries!"

Joseph didn't think my father was brainwashing him and his refusal to see what seemed so clear to me sent my temper to the boiling point. I tried to stifle my anger, but it didn't always work. The more "incidents" I caused by standing up to him, the more controlling he became. He had to "command his family" to keep God's law, just like Abraham, no matter what that meant. He was sure I would thank him someday when we got to Heaven.

One of our worst clashes happened when we outgrew our car. For months, I had dreamed of a new minivan, scanning car lots for a model that would suit our family. Meanwhile, Joseph followed the IFB's practice of asking everyone in faculty and staff meetings to pray that God would help us find a vehicle that met our budget. After the meeting, one of Joseph's colleagues pulled him aside. "I've got the perfect solution to your family's situation," he assured him. It turned out he and his wife had a twenty-year-old station wagon with seven seatbelts in the back—and they felt "led of the Lord" to hand it over to us free of charge. Joseph and I went to look at the car that night. It was a clunker, covered in rust and obviously on its last legs.

"There's no way we can drive such a wreck," I told Joseph. "You know how harsh the winters are here. Think about our children's safety. What if it breaks down in the middle of nowhere?"

"This is the way God has chosen to answer our prayers," he said resolutely. "We should be submissive to his decision."

"But we've been saving money for a minivan," I reminded him. "We have enough in the bank to buy a new one debt free."

I begged, cajoled, and tried repeatedly to reason with him for his children's sake. Eventually, he relented, but he held it over my head for the next year, reminding me regularly about my willful behavior about the car.

Joseph had changed. I realized I no longer recognized the kind and loving man I had married. And the higher up the IFB ladder he climbed, the worse things were going to get for me.

It become harder to control my anger. I finally got so fed up with everything that I whipped my jewelry box across the bedroom one day. Joseph heard the crash and ran upstairs.

"What was *that*?" he asked. I didn't trust myself to speak. I was teetering on the edge of a nervous collapse. Joseph must have sensed it because he didn't goad me. Without a word, he bent over and started picking up the pieces of jewelry scattered over the floor. Red-faced and close to hyperventilating, I muttered through clenched teeth, "I'm done!" Then I stalked out. What did it matter now if I offended my husband? I was probably going to die anyway. And even if the brain tumor didn't kill me, I couldn't live like this anymore.

That's when something clicked in Joseph's mind. After nine years of continual internal conflict about how to "lead" me as the head of our home, he finally decided that the IFB's patriarchal model of submission and demand to honor one's parents couldn't possibly be what God taught in the Bible. He decided my father had to be the root of my rage and sorrow, so he called Bart and told him to stop talking about me in such a derogatory way. Naturally, it sent my father into a towering rage.

"Are you telling me what to do?" he screamed at Joseph over the phone. "No one tells me what to do!"

My father kept calling and spewing venom, trying to cow Joseph into an apology. But Joseph held firm. Finally, he said, "You're no longer welcome in our home until you're willing to change your behavior and apologize for the abuse in the past."

For the first time in nine years of marriage, Joseph was about to see my father's darkest side. We both knew that defying a powerful man like Bart Janz could cost us dearly, but it was the right thing to do. Sure enough, my father started making frequent trips to Northland and, though he didn't knock on our door, he met in private with all his friends in the college's administration.

After Joseph started taking my side, I finally began to open up about what had happened during my childhood and we met with Matt and Diane Olson to discuss the physical abuse from my past as well as my father's emotionally abusive behavior in the present. I confided privately to Diane that I was worried about my husband's job, because I sensed that the men were siding with Bart in discrediting my allegations. She assured me, "You have nothing to worry about. Your husband is known as one of the favorite teachers on campus." Unfortunately she misjudged. Northland VP "Dr." Marty Von proved a particularly sympathetic ear to Bart. We found out later that he had a hand in key aspects of the horrendous treatment we were about to endure.

The Beginning of the End

The fatal blow came on January 12, 2006. Sam Horn called Joseph in for a meeting and told him unceremoniously that his contract would not be renewed for the following school year. After eleven years of phenomenal employer and student reviews, he was out. The explanation? "Budget cuts," Horn said.

Joseph loved teaching in the college classroom, so he asked whether he could remain a full-time professor if he raised money to pay his own salary like a missionary, as other professors at Northland had done in the past. Sam said no. We found out later that the college offered Joseph's position to a man named Matt Morrell, who was ten years younger than Joseph and didn't even have an unaccredited IFB doctorate. It doesn't take a rocket scientist to figure out what happened: Joseph wasn't keeping me sufficiently in line, and that is not acceptable in the IFB.

Our world came crashing down. Everything we had known was gone. We lived in a house we couldn't possibly afford without Joseph's meager salary. His degrees were not regionally accredited, so he had no hope of finding a job outside the IFB and he would surely be blacklisted at every college inside it. We now had eight children under the age of nine to support, and we were dealing with three serious medical conditions. The economy was crumbling, and blue-collar jobs were vanishing. We were devastated. And scared out of our wits.

My father took our plunge to rock bottom as a sure sign that he was winning the battle for control over us and redoubled his harassment campaign. He started leaving enraged phone messages, demanding visits with our children. My nightmares got worse. I started having panic attacks, envisioning Bart getting my children alone and then beating them black-and-blue with his horrible wooden rod. I was desperate to protect them from him.

We had to find a way to get out of the IFB.

12

THE ROCKY ROAD TO FREEDOM (2006)

Today [pastors are] looked upon like some mealy-mouthed, little pansy-wansy, little guys that . . . just hold everybody's hands and say, "God bless you. God be with you. Oh, I'll pray for you." Shut up! Man, take the lace off your underwear, will you? Be a man! . . . I believe I'm a man's man!

—*Bart Janz, sermon,*
"Reading Between the Lines," 2005

I was beside myself as the end of Joseph's tenure at the college drew nearer, breaking down and weeping sporadically throughout the day. My past had been bleak and hopeless enough. Now the future looked even darker. And that's when an utterly unexpected life-changing moment occurred, like a ray of morning light in a night sky.

Earlier in 2005 Joseph had finally decided to allow a television into our home, provided I watch only educational news programs. For me, it was a lifeline to the world outside the cult. One night when he was working late and all the kids were tucked in bed, I decided to take a few minutes away from my endless housework. I sat down on the king-sized bed in the master bedroom and turned on the TV. A newscaster was interviewing a woman named Carolyn Jessop about her flight from a polygamist compound in Utah with her eight young children in tow.

As I listened, I got goose bumps. Her story was remarkably similar to mine. She had married young in an intensely patriarchal subculture and had been told practically from infancy that she had to produce as many babies as possible to please God. She had been raised to fear everyone and everything in the "wicked" world outside her own isolated religious community. She believed hers was the only true church on earth. Her church leaders exercised totalitarian control over their members, and women were utterly disenfranchised. When pictures of Carolyn from her cult days flashed on screen, I did a double take. She looked like she had just come from Sunday services at an IFB church, in ankle-length floral dresses and denim jumpers just like the ones I wore.

As Carolyn told the interviewer about her harrowing escape and her struggle to acclimate herself to the real world, I sat there in shock. I felt as if I had just rammed my head into a cement wall. *Was I in a cult?* It was the first time that word had entered my mind. My head started throbbing intensely, a sure sign of an impending migraine. At the bottom of the screen, a crawl read, "If you are in need of help, please contact the HOPE organization." Then a hotline number appeared. I jumped up off my bed, grabbed a pen, and, with trembling hands, wrote it down.

I didn't have the courage to call that night, but the next day, after Joseph left for work, I mustered up the nerve to pick up the phone. Polygamy was just starting to gain national media exposure, and the HOPE organization was small, so the operator passed me on to Carolyn Jessop herself. The moment she said hello, I started crying and shaking.

Lately it seemed that every word I said behind closed doors mysteriously circulated among college personnel, only with a negative spin, so I was extremely paranoid. "I think my church leaders might be recording my phone calls, so I'm really scared," I began. "But I had to call because I think I might be in a cult."

"Do you practice polygamy?" she asked.

"No, no, no," I stammered. "We don't practice polygamy. I'm from a Baptist group that call themselves fundamentalists, but I was watching your program last night and it sounds just like what I'm in aside from the plural marriage part."

Kind, empathetic, and wise, Carolyn Jessop spent the next hour patiently asking me all kinds of questions about the practices and doctrines of the IFB. By the end of the call, she said firmly, "Jocelyn, you are in a cult. You need to leave as quickly and quietly as you can. They will try to take everything from you."

When I got off the phone, I sank down on the floor of my walk-in closet and sobbed. I knew the truth now. But I was no closer to finding a way out for myself and my family. Joseph would think I was crazy if I suggested that the IFB was a cult. I didn't breathe a word about the phone call, but I couldn't get Carolyn Jessop's words out of my mind.

Finally, I resolved to broach the subject of leaving the IFB with Joseph. If we were ever going to get out, now was the time. I began to encourage Joseph to consider the possibility of exploring the world outside our own tight-knit subculture. I suggested we take a trip to Chicago together to look at evangelical ministries as potential options. "You don't need to make a commitment," I assured him. "But maybe we should consider the idea of you going back to school to get an accredited Ph.D. Then you could look into evangelical churches in the area." Joseph was hesitant about even considering a degree from a non-IFB school. A few years earlier, Sam Horn had enrolled in a doctoral program at Master's Seminary in California, where ultraconservative evangelical leader John MacArthur was president. After the news broke, Horn stated publicly that he would counsel no one to follow his example unless they had served in the ministry for at least twenty years because the danger of being corrupted at a place like the Master's Seminary was too great.

It was a huge step for me to suggest leaving and an even bigger one for Joseph to consider it. I knew that in his mind, I could be Eve in the Garden, tempting him to make the biggest mistake of his life. After all, women were temptresses. In our natural "flesh bent," we were manipulators, beguilers who led men into a life of sin.

Time to Explore

Fortunately, Joseph agreed to explore non-IFB alternatives. He confessed that he had always wanted to know what it was like "on the other side." Eventually I even persuaded him to send his résumé to Moody Bible Institute in Chicago, though the IFB had always condemned it as "liberal" and "compromising."

Even though we had lost everything, Joseph and I were working together as a team for the first time in our marriage. We didn't tell anyone where we were going, but one weekend we left the children with a sitter and took a day trip to Moody to meet with the vice president and dean of the faculty, Larry Davidhizar. I'll never forget the drive to his office.

Traveling down the highway on our way to Chicago, we were both exhausted and overwrought, holding hands to reassure each other. Joseph prayed aloud, "Dear God, be merciful toward us and if we are making the wrong decision in this, please stop us now. You know that all we want to do is follow your will."

We walked into Larry's office like deer in the headlights of an on-coming semi. We spent a lot of time crying in those days, and we both welled up as soon as we sat down. Within fifteen minutes, Larry called his wife, Donna, explained that there was a couple that needed help, and asked if she would meet us for dinner. That evening marked the beginning of a deep friendship. Larry and Donna listened with endless patience and compassion as we cried and talked. During the twelve months after our final departure, they came to our home for countless visits and continued to listen, letting us pour out all our fear and doubt and guilt and anguish. They came along like angels and showered us with love, acceptance, encouragement, and understanding.

The Davidhizars set something in motion that first night over dinner that would forever change our lives. We started taking trips to Chicago nearly every weekend. We visited Trinity Evangelical Divinity School (TEDS) and Willow Creek Community Church in Illinois and we got to know sincere, strong Christians who shocked us with their warmth and their nonjudgmental attitude toward us. We also met with Dr. John Woodbridge at Trinity, whose father had been a faculty member at Bob Jones University in the 1960s and had written one of the most influential IFB books on the Doctrine of Separation. John had left the Doctrine behind as a young man and eventually became a well-known evangelical author and professor, but the IFB spread the word that he had gone into demonism. When we told him about the current theological positions and isolation within the group, John said it had become worse than he could have imagined. After we finalized our decision to leave the IFB, he pulled me aside. "Are you sure you're ready for what is to come?" he asked. "You know that they are going to demonize you. You're the one they are focusing on."

I had wanted to leave the IFB my entire adult life, so I answered confidently, "Of course, I'm ready!"

I had never been so wrong in all my life.

Demons of the Past

Sleep was harder than ever to come by in the midst of all this chaos, and after one fitful night, I woke up lying on my back. It was an unusual position to find myself in because I always slept on my side or my stomach. I closed my eyes and a strange, unsettling, yet somehow familiar image flashed through my mind. My body seized up instinctively and a feeling of panic rumbled through my mind. *What was that?* I froze as a horrible memory re-formed itself against my will like a monster rising out of the mist.

My father was rolling my nightgown up to my armpits. He tucked the excess material under my back. He then lay down on top of me, naked, and started pushing his hips hard against my stomach. Unable to breathe under the weight of his body, I turned my head to the left. I tried to stop myself from hyperventilating as I gasped for air through a space under his armpit, nearly gagged by the smell of his sweat. I was going to suffocate to death. Pinned down and too terrified to try to wrestle free, I turned all my attention to my drawing a thin stream of oxygen into my lungs. The second I lost concentration I started hyperventilating. "I can't breathe! I'm dying," I thought, in silent panic. Talking to myself, I tried again to focus my mind. "Slow and steady ... breathe in and out ... slowly ..." At last, I felt his body unclench. Without looking at me, he stood up, grabbed a cloth, and rubbed my stomach roughly. Then he pulled my nightgown back down over my knees. I rolled onto my side, facing away from him. My stomach hurt and I felt like I needed to throw up. I pressed my hand against my belly to quell the nausea, and my nightgown stuck against it. I reached underneath the fabric to free it and my hand touched something wet all over my stomach. I thought it was Vicks VapoRub, the gel my mother put on our chests when we had colds.

As the memory came rushing back with the force of a freight train, I felt the sticky flannel against my body again. I saw the ruffle across the bottom of the gown. My mind cast around frantically for answers. *How old was I?* Realizing I couldn't have been more than six given my memories of my bed, the room, and the nightgown, I started heaving and the room tilted at a crazy angle. With my pajamas still on, I staggered to the shower, turned on the cold water, and rolled into a fetal position under the spray. "I hate you! I hate you!" I screamed, years of striving for godly forgiveness washing down the drain and uncovering a raw, visceral emotion I had never experienced before. Suddenly flashes of my mother's face over the years came back to me, her eyes boring through me with a look of pure loathing that left me both devastated and puzzled. "No wonder! No wonder you hated me!" I cried. It all made sense now.

Finally, I called Joseph and begged him to come home from work right away. I poured out everything about the long repressed memory that had suddenly and inexplicably returned, leaving him ashen.

"What do we do now?" I sobbed.

He shook his head. "I don't know," he said.

We decided to call a crisis center in Michigan and set up a meeting with a counselor. The next day I spent several hours talking through my childhood with her. She explained that what I had experienced was a repressed memory. Introduced by Sigmund Freud in the late 1800s and still the source of debate among psychologists, repressed memories are a phenomenon that can occur when an event is so traumatizing that the mind buries it in some remote corner of the unconscious as a coping mechanism. Sometimes, decades later and for no apparent reason, it resurfaces in the conscious mind.

I told the counselor that I had always been able to remember my father rubbing his erect penis against my back while watching TV and in the swimming pool. He would even grope me in front of the family so obviously that they would shout out in disgust, "Gross, Dad! Stop that!" Then I told her about the way I'd been beaten until I turned eighteen, and how my father removed my clothing before each session.

"Even without the memory that returned this week, the things you're describing are sexual abuse," she assured me. "None of that was appropriate behavior for a father."

I had always understood that my brothers had molested me, but it had never occurred to me that my father's actions might be sexual abuse and I had never mentioned any of these incidents to Joseph. I also hadn't remembered any naked touching until now. Besides, my siblings were well aware of what went on in our home. They were all beaten, just like I was. I thought it was normal because so many of my friends had experienced the same thing.

I confided in my sister Melissa, who, to my astonishment, had similar memories. She still hadn't come to terms with the label "sexual abuse," but she knew what she had experienced was wrong—and she could clearly articulate the fear she had lived in as a result. Foolishly, I told Jason too, and he wasted no time in telling Bart.

Jason Intervenes

In cases of interpersonal conflict, IFB protocol was for both parties to meet to "clear offenses," as Will Galkin had done after my brain tumor diagnosis. Apparently, Jason was taking it upon himself to orchestrate an offense-clearing session because he called back a short time later to say that Bart would meet with me.

"How did he react to what you told him?" I asked. "Did he show any emotion?"

"No," said Jason. I wondered if Bart had half expected a call like this to come one day. My psychologist explained later that abusers prepare for this moment their entire lives. Now Bart was poised and ready to spring into action to discredit me.

Joseph's contract was set to end shortly after graduation on May 13, so we were braced for a full-fledged attack. I knew my father and the cult leaders would maneuver against us and attempt to push us into checkmate before my husband's official ties to Northland were severed. A few months earlier, after one of Bart's particularly vicious phone calls, we contacted the police and they told us to record any future calls he made for our protection. So when Bart called on April 30, Joseph had his voice recorder next to the phone and put the call on speaker so I could listen silently in the background. For the first twenty minutes, Joseph tried to talk Bart out of coming to his workplace to force a public confrontation. My father ignored his pleas and insisted that he was going to "disclose our family secrets" to the "entire faculty and staff" whether we liked it or not. Finally, Joseph told Bart he was going to call the police and start the process of issuing a restraining order. My father exploded. During the next thirty minutes my husband barely got a word in edgewise.

"You are being so deplorable, it gnaws at my craw. . . . You are a dog, Joe! A dog! This is war! This is going to trail you, buddy, for the rest of your life! . . . If Northland doesn't deal with you, I'm coming to the next place you go! . . . You picked the wrong guy to dis! . . . I can tell you something young man, God is watching you, Joe! . . . I'm in total control and that's what you don't like. . . . Go ahead and call the police on me, Joe. And I'll tell you what, Joe, you'll wish you never did!"

As soon as Bart slammed the phone down, we called the police.

Northland Administration Backs My Father

The next morning, my father faxed a letter to one of Northland's vice presidents, "Dr." Marty Von, telling him about the restraining order. Then they all pounced at once.

When Joseph arrived at work, "Dr." Les Ollila confronted him. "It was a faithless and fear-filled decision for you to threaten to take out a restraining order against a man of God," he admonished, refusing to hear Joseph's side of the story.

A short time later, Northland president Matt Olson also reprimanded him sternly, "It is *not* God's will for you to handle conflict in this way, Joe."

Next, the following long, rambling e-mail dropped into Joseph's inbox from "Dr." Marty Von:

> *I received an unusual fax from Bart Janz outlining a phone conversation with you about his desire for clearing offenses from the past. I believe I know what you would teach in your classes on this: that offense clearing is so critical to leave your gift at the altar and clear up the offenses if they have not been resolved. This is a clear, Biblical command from Matthew 5. Then, the fax included a court restraining order. Wow! Something is being severely hidden here. I realize there are two sides to every story, but you are in a place of higher accountability, as is he, as pastors, and you as a faculty/staff member. Where is the Christ-like model? This tells me there are things under the table that are being hidden. The most likely agenda from my almost 40 years of counseling tells me: there*

may be deceit that is being covered, protecting the family which usually means severe problems in the home, a manipulation to carry out a game plan that nobody knows, using people to accomplish desired ends, outside control that you have bought into, fear of exposure that could hurt reputation and acceptance. When a person goes out on a limb, they have to come up with other legitimate reasons to keep from doing right. Any believer would welcome an offense-clearing opportunity, particularly if you could have another believer as a witness. I know I have had many good conversations with Jocelyn, and some regarding her past relationship with her father; so any way I can help her or you now I'm open to consider. But, please, for the sake of Jesus Christ, and your personal walk with God which trumps all other issues—otherwise Satan will blind the mind, and you both could become something you would never want to be. I know there is a time to pray, but God told Joshua to obey. What is the first step in God-ward obedience that needs to be taken now? My suggestion is that since Bart is on campus now (today); it is time to make things right. I can't imagine you teaching your classes or your children that Godly obedience is delayed obedience versus obeying right away. We are either broken and Davidic or Saulish and covering and excusing. Obedience is not geared to our convenience or schedule. Joe, you may have to make a choice between God and all others. As a Campus Pastor, I would ask you to move on this today.

The irony wasn't lost on Joseph. Before the return of my repressed memory, he had tried for more than a year to get my father to meet with us to clear offenses related to his past physical and emotional abuse of me. However Bart insisted, "The only thing I will ever apologize for in respect to Jocelyn is that I never taught her how to respond properly to authority!" Since Bart was denying every accusation I made, Joseph suggested a private family meeting with all the siblings present to verify what really happened in our home when we were children. That's when Bart lost it. "I will never get my pants pulled down in front of my family!" he roared.

My father was bent on "resolving the conflict," surrounded by men of his choosing. It was like rigging a jury. I was convinced that these men would back Bart no matter what he did because they needed to destroy our credibility when we left the IFB. And Von, the man Jeremy had poured his heart out to about molesting me so many years earlier, was, in my view, the worst of the lot. Suggesting to my husband that I had confided anything about my father in him was a bold-faced lie. Though Von taught a large portion of the counseling classes at Northland and insisted his students call him "Dr." (just as honorary "Dr." Les Ollila did), he held nothing more than an honorary doctorate and he had no credentials to counsel someone about sexual abuse. Besides, he was the last man I wanted privy to anything about my private life. He had harassed me shamelessly, insinuating himself into my conversations at college events, standing too close, and slipping his arm around me. He had even leaned over and kissed me at an IFB wedding in front of my friend Dee Dee, to our mutual shock because touching was never permissible under the IFB's rigid social code. Of course the IFB never ran seminars on sexual harassment in the workplace, so we had no words to codify his inappropriate behavior. The thought of "Dr." Marty Von hearing the sordid details of my childhood was more than I could bear.

"Dr." Marty Von: Mission Almost Accomplished

Though my husband and I had been working as a team for more than four months by this point, "Dr." Marty Von's plan worked precisely as the IFB leaders had hoped. Joseph finally snapped and became completely irrational, insisting that we meet with Von first thing in the morning. I went into hysterics and begged Joseph to change his mind. But he just lay on the couch, arms folded, eyes closed, not making a sound. He seemed to be refusing to cave in to what he viewed as a six-year-old temper tantrum thrown by an unsubmissive grown woman. I ran to our walk-in closet and lay on the floor crying for hours. How could a man who had promised to love and honor me until death, a man with a master's degree in counseling, expect me to walk into a room full of male-chauvinist

IFB hard-liners and describe the most degrading abuse I had ever suffered? In hindsight, I realize Joseph had been enduring profound psychic trauma for months and wasn't cognizant of what he was doing. But I was still at my wits' end and devastated by the whole ordeal.

To an outsider, the whole scenario probably sounds absurd and cruel. There would be no rape crisis counselor present, no other woman in the room to balance the numbers. In the cult, offense-clearing sessions like this are deliberately designed to intimidate and shame the victim, especially when she's female. Pressuring abuse victims into "talking to" their abusers to offer the abusers forgiveness is standard operating procedure in the IFB. The leaders tout it as the biblical way to handle being wronged.

Rand Hummel: Speaks in Chapel at BJU

The prominent IFB preacher and youth counselor "Dr." Rand Hummel, program director at the popular IFB camp The Wilds, and adjunct professor at BJU, shared one such incident in a sermon he gave for university students at a chapel service:

> *I was preaching at another camp and a girl responded and I went to the counseling room. She was weeping… the longest time. And finally she looked up at me—she said, "God hates me.… I don't even know who my real parents are. They dumped me off at an orphanage.… From the time I was 13 to 15, my stepdad took physical liberties with me. Mom found out and divorced him. God hates me." I said, "Young lady, you've lived a very difficult life— very hard life. But, let's look at your sin in this situation." When I said that, she lost it! She said, "My sin?! It wasn't me. My mom, my dad, my stepdad." I said, "Yeah, you've allowed the sin of these folks to create such anger and hatred and bitterness in your heart."… If you're bitter, if you're angry, it's not God's fault, okay? He offered the grace to get you through this.… Finally, God broke her heart and she got on her knees and asked God to forgive her. When she got off her knees, I said, that's the first part in handling this bitterness and anger. Now you need to*

go home and ask your mom, your dad, and your stepdad
for forgiveness for your hatred toward them.

After I left the cult, I told my psychologist about the IFB's standard protocol for handling abuses this way, and he was appalled. He explained that statements like Hummel's give abusers an incredible amount of power and control over their victims. Not only are victims made to feel shame for anger and "bitterness" that are natural by-products of abuse, but by forcing victims to talk to their abusers before meeting with law enforcement, the abusers get a heads-up whenever a victim starts to break their silence. Perpetrators are master manipulators, so this enables them to mastermind a preemptive attack to discredit the victim, as well as to take measures to silence any *other* victims. It puts the victim at a tremendous disadvantage and heightens the danger they face in coming forward.

It's also less risky for a pastor, especially one untrained in sexual abuse, to come down on the side of an alleged abuser because the perpetrator tends to have a lot more social power in the church than a child does. That's one of the many reasons most states deem pastors and teachers "mandatory reporters" when it comes to sex abuse allegations. Most members of law enforcement are trained professionals and many police departments have sex crimes units, which enables them to conduct unbiased investigations when accusations arise. My psychologist's explanation was a profound revelation to me, one I wish I had known before leaving the IFB.

Joseph Comes to His Senses

I'm not sure what clicked during those long hours of pleading, but Joseph finally came to his senses, took pity on me, and relented. We would decline to meet with my father and "Dr." Marty Von. Instead, the day before college graduation, we agreed to meet with Northland president Matt Olson and "Dr." Les Ollila (now the chancellor of Northland). Joseph always referred to Ollila as a "spiritual father in the faith." He had taken Joseph to breakfast regularly for years and candidly shared his "secrets of effective ministry" with my husband. Joseph felt certain he could get his mentor to understand our side of the story.

In spite of Joseph's confidence, the night before the meeting, I was scared to death, so I decided to share everything with Tami Herron. By this time she and Marty had taken a new job in Guam, but they had flown back in for graduation. Tami told me that after working as the dean of women at the college for many years during her husband's tenure as a vice president, she estimated that seven out of ten female students came to Northland already having been sexually abused. This was a shocking revelation for me, since the girls who attended our college were from what we considered some of the "godliest" homes in the IFB. Tami also confided that she had tried to deal with several sensitive issues involving "Dr." Marty Von being too "touchy-feely," only to be quietly removed from her position as a result. "These men will probably not respond well to what you have to tell them," she cautioned me gently. "Just brace yourself."

"We *Are* in a Cult!"

As we entered Matt Olson's office the next afternoon, the hostility in the room was palpable. Within five minutes Les Ollila laced into me, hurling insults. "You're a liar and a deceiver!" he yelled.

My whole body seemed to be boiling, as if I had a raging fever, but I hung my head and waited until Ollila calmed slightly. Taking a deep breath, I finally decided to tell them. "I have memories of him sexually abusing me," I muttered.

This sent Ollila over the edge. He leapt out of his seat and pointed his finger at me as I sank lower in my chair, cowering like a whipped puppy. "If what you are saying about your father is true, we will fly him here from Denver! The two of you can stand before the entire faculty and staff while you tell your side of the story," he raged. "We'll let *them* decide if *you* are telling the truth!"

Joseph was flabbergasted. He had always been a member of the boys' club and had never seen these men act this venomous. "I don't think my wife should have to talk about this with *anyone* she doesn't feel comfortable with," he said, trying to bring a note of rationality to the proceedings.

Ignoring Joseph, Ollila shouted at me, "Do you want *me* to mediate this conflict?"

"I don't know. I . . . I . . ." I stammered.

Now hovering directly over me, Ollila screamed at the top of his lungs, "Do you or do you not want me to mediate this conflict between you and your father? Yes or no?"

For the first time in my life, I stood up to a man of power in the IFB. "No," I said quietly but firmly. I didn't dare look up to see his reaction. Staring at my shoes, I braced for another verbal onslaught.

Ollila threw up his hands. "Then I'm done with you! This meeting is over!"

We sat in stunned silence for a few seconds, but once it was clear that we were not going to cave in to his manipulative tactics, instead of storming out, Ollila tried a new tack. "You need to be willing to meet with your father," he said in a calm voice. "What about Les Heinze in Denver and your brother Jason? Would you meet with them?" At least he was talking instead of yelling.

It wasn't the most palatable solution, but it would get us out of this room and remove the Northland administration from the equation, so I agreed. We would meet with them in Denver to discuss my allegations of physical and sexual abuse. Ollila rose from his chair and strode to the office door. Before he left, he turned to Joseph.

"You know we love you," he said, reaching out to embrace my husband. It was the classic IFB hug-slug—punching you one moment, praising you the next—to keep you reeling emotionally. I'm convinced Ollila knew that if he lost Joseph's confidence, he could lose control of me. I could see the disillusionment in Joseph's eyes as we left the office. I believe Ollila had orchestrated this entire event to shake Joseph up, but instead his cruelty and dishonesty finally opened Joseph's eyes to the hypocrisy I had seen in this IFB icon for more than a decade.

We found out later that numerous former employees of Northland had gone through similar ordeals. Ollila had summoned them in for final meetings, during which he hurled accusations at them about previous "wrongdoings." Now I understand that it was a tactical maneuver meant to terrify them into remaining loyal or to rattle them enough that they would stumble into a useful confession he could file away to discredit them in the future if it proved necessary.

Bobby Wood had told us that when he first left BJU and became an administrator at Northland, he questioned whether he should go into the president's office and confront Les about this kind of behavior. He asked Vice President Sam Horn what he thought and Sam stopped him dead in his tracks. "Don't you dare go in his office, Bobby," Sam said. "You don't confront Les Ollila—*nobody* confronts Les Ollila." Even Bobby, with all his family's political influence in the IFB, decided to back down and "let God deal with it." Les truly was untouchable in our world—a man with absolute power.

As we hurried down the steps of the administration building a few minutes later, I whispered, "We *are* in a cult!"

"Shhh!" Joseph whispered back. "Wait until we get in the car."

I had hinted at my fears several times in the past few weeks, but he had dismissed them as an exaggeration. Now he slammed the van door shut and turned to me wide-eyed. "You were right," he said. "This *is* a cult!"

I felt a rush of relief. Somehow I knew that if we worked together, we would be able to find a way to get out and get our children to a safe place.

Our Trip to Colorado: The Statement of Silence

The day after the confrontation with Olson and Ollila, Joseph and I flew to Denver to meet with Bart, Jason, and Les Heinze. Looking back, we were in no mental or emotional condition to have the meeting and should never have agreed to it. However, we felt obligated to try to make peace and we naively hoped that we could get Bart out of our lives once and for all. Without realizing it, we had fallen prey to the IFB leaders' backup plan to regain control over us.

Jason asked us to have lunch with him beforehand because, as he explained it, "I don't want you pulling out anything new. I want everything to be known to both parties, no hidden agendas. And, Jocelyn, you need to admit to doing something wrong in this meeting."

"I haven't done anything wrong in this," I said, starting to cry. "He molested me and beat me. He showed up at our house without warning, in spite of Joseph's repeated insistence that he stay away. He made threatening phone calls over and over again. He came to my husband's workplace, even after Joseph threatened a restraining order, forcing us to make this conflict public. I'm just trying to get away from him and he won't let me go."

"You should admit some part in all of it," Jason insisted. "Do whatever you can to make peace and move on. You are responsible for that much." Before I had time to respond he concluded with, "And you should be kind enough to give Dad a hug at the end of the meeting."

A burst of anger surged through me. "I will NEVER hug that man ever again!" The fact that Jason would ask such a thing showed how little sensitivity he had for me. Ironically, after I refused, Jason broke down and admitted that he had wanted to confront Bart for a long time about hugging his own wife in a way that made them both profoundly uncomfortable.

That afternoon, as soon as we sat down at a table in the church Les Heinze pastored, Heinze said, "Jocelyn and Joseph, we have this meeting all set up for recording. Jason has the computer ready. Are you okay with that? Of course, we will give you a copy too."

My mind started racing. *I thought there weren't supposed to be any surprises. Now they tell me they want to record this?* I felt coerced, but in order to keep the peace, I agreed.

"We are here to talk about the abuse from Jocelyn's childhood and to hear about these new memories that have returned," Heinze stated. I had written out a number of things for Joseph to say on my behalf in the meeting because I wasn't sure I could handle talking through it myself. He started with the physical abuse, but when he got to my new memories of sexual abuse, I told him I would elaborate. No sooner had I opened my mouth than my father turned to Heinze and blurted out, "I'm not going to sit here and listen to that!"

"But, Bart, isn't that why we're here?" Heinze asked. "To sort this out?"

"That's disgusting!" Bart said. "I won't even hear it!"

He grabbed a stack of papers from my mother and rifled through them, quoting passages the two of them had evidently collected online and printed out about false repressed memories. He didn't realize all the research he had collected was about victims whose "memories" had been coaxed out or coerced by others, through hypnosis or therapy. Mine had returned spontaneously. He insisted that my memories couldn't possibly be true. Then he produced a paper he had typed up for me to sign and the others to witness, which said:

> *My claim of sexual molestation is erroneous and ground-less. I withdraw all my allegations toward you, my fa-*

ther. I am confident that you have never touched me
sexually or inappropriately at any time.

"I will not sign that," I protested. "I'm not lying! These memories
are there. I don't understand them yet, but I'm telling the truth." It was
obvious to me that they had planned a number of surprises to spring on
me. I felt horribly betrayed.

"You withdraw this allegation tonight because this is the only chance
you're going to have!" Bart shouted.

Heinze was shocked. "Bart, that sounds a little bit like a threat." I
looked at Heinze dumbfounded. *A little bit like a threat?* Just like every
other IFB leader, he was downplaying my father's behavior.

Bart's black eyes were fixated on my every move, and I knew him
well enough to grasp the underlying message: This was my last chance to
agree to stay quiet—or else.

In an attempt to diffuse the rising tide of animosity in the room, Jason took the paper from my father and looked over it. "What if I rewrote
this in a different way?" he asked. "Would you sign it then?"

Nothing mattered more to me in that moment than getting out of that
room. So, when Jason revised my father's letter, turning it into a "statement
of silence," I agreed to sign it, just so we could leave. (Only later, understanding that it had been procured from me under duress, did I disavow
the statement.) His revision read:

> *After careful evaluation of the unproven results of re-*
> *pressed memory studies, I have come to a solid conclusion.*
> *Due to the fact that my claims are tenuous, I withdraw*
> *my former allegation toward you, my father, regarding*
> *sexual molestation. I will never revisit this issue again.*

Bart also agreed never to contact us again under any circumstances,
unless we initiated it. Shortly thereafter, we closed the meeting. We felt
as if we had run a marathon, drained emotionally and physically. I later
learned from our lawyer that this agreement had no legal binding, since
I signed it under emotional duress. Still, I thought I had finally been set
free—all I had wanted from day one.

Preparing to Slip Away Quietly

The next day we flew home from Denver and discovered that Bart had left another threatening message on Joseph's voice mail. In this one, he accused me of sharing details from our meeting with Jason's wife—an accusation that Jenny herself said was false. Joseph called Jason to insist that Bart honor his agreement to leave us alone.

A few minutes later, Jason called back and said Bart had made the story up to scare us, but he wanted to tell me in no uncertain terms that he would not tolerate me violating my statement of silence. A few weeks later, Bart left another angry voice message, demanding that Joseph return his call "away from [our] house," presumably so I couldn't be a part of the conversation. Bart also said he had another list of demands, which included, among other things, that I sign a written statement that I had violated the biblical teaching of Psalm 1 by seeking counsel from a secular professional. At that point, Joseph called Les Heinze and demanded that the pastor call my father and convince him to back down. Heinze returned Joseph's call later that day and told him that Bart had screamed at him on the phone for more than twenty minutes. Heinze pleaded with Joseph to keep in contact with Bart by mail, sending him updates on our family and pictures of our kids.

"Absolutely not," Joseph responded. "Tell that man never to contact me or my family again! I'm done!"

By this time Joseph's contract had ended, so he packed up his office and we decided to lie low for the rest of the summer. It felt like a flashback to my disgraced summer after high school, keeping our heads down and avoiding attention. In the midst of all that drama, almost every weekend, we drove to Chicago to firm up more details for our move. Joseph and I spent countless hours meticulously charting our exit strategy, writing down the steps, scribbling them out, and revising them. We came up with endless *what ifs* and hypothetical ways to field problems that might occur. What if my father heard about our plans and showed up on our doorstep in a violent rage? What if the moving company didn't show up? What if the van broke down as we were trying to leave? What if the college administration discovered our plans and sabotaged them? Contemplating everything that could go wrong was a recipe for panic, but it was better to be prepared for the worst.

Confrontations

We didn't discuss what was going on with our children for fear that they might make an innocent remark to a friend that would reach the wrong ears. So far, no one knew if we were leaving our home, the cult, or taking new jobs in the area. Most people speculated that we had our sights set on Chicago and the rumor began to circulate that my husband was joining the faculty at Moody Bible Institute. We couldn't understand how the rumor started, since we had told no one about my husband submitting his application online or his subsequent contact with the organization through e-mail. Soon after that, Curt Lamansky called to ask if it was true that we were moving to Nashville to get involved in the Contemporary Christian Music industry. My husband had recently placed a secret phone call to a childhood friend who was the manager for a popular Christian performer. Years earlier, the friend had told Joseph to give him a call if he ever left the IFB and wanted to break into the industry. But again, Joseph had told no one about his e-mails or phone calls. How were the IFB leaders finding out what we were doing?

Christy Galkin showed up at my house one day to admonish me. "You're causing IFB members to sin, because you're not sharing your plans," she scolded. "You're fostering a climate of gossip. You should repent." So much for girlhood friendship. Gone were the days of wearing "best friends" necklaces and the deep bond we had felt when she served as the maid of honor at my wedding. It was clear to me that Christy's loyalty lay with the IFB, not with me. But her entreaties made no impact. I was sure our lives were in danger, and I was eager to put a safe distance between ourselves and the IFB as fast as I could. It struck me as absurdly ironic that after being accused of talking too much and forced to sign a statement of silence, I was now being criticized for not talking enough. It was obviously the cult's way of trying to maintain control over our family.

Watching Our Every Move

Our neighbors were keeping an obvious watch on our comings and goings and I was growing more afraid than ever that our phones were being tapped. We soon became convinced the administration at Northland was reading our private e-mails, since my husband's account was on the college network, which granted them full access. To test my hunch, I sent a stream of e-mails to his Northland account regarding real estate worth millions of dollars and said we could set up appointments to see the houses the following weekend. We both laughed about it. But then, sure enough, a friend came over within the week and said she had heard a rumor that we had inherited millions of dollars and were moving to Chicago. She wondered if it was true. It was proof positive that the cult was monitoring everything we did.

Actually, we *had* found a home, but it was a modest rental that we planned to live in until Joseph completed his accredited Ph.D. at Trinity. The university had taken pity on him and agreed to admit him to its doctoral program as long as he completed a long list of extra prerequisites, including taking remedial courses throughout the summer to make up for the deficiencies in his IFB program. After fourteen years in IFB colleges, he was now facing another five to seven years of school. And although his unaccredited degrees made it virtually impossible for him to get a job in his field outside the IFB, we were still going to have to somehow come up with hundreds of thousands of dollars for tuition and living expenses. At a time when many men with legitimate credentialing are hitting the height of success in their careers, my husband was starting over at the bottom. It would be a long, arduous academic road for a thirty-six-year-old father of eight, but it was the only road that led to freedom, the only hope he had of a *real* career at a *real* university.

Final Preparation

I spent the week before our departure driving to Walmart late at night to collect boxes and quietly filling them with our essentials during the days. It would be wrenching to leave so many cherished belongings behind, but I steeled myself and pushed on. *You care too much about things of this world.* My mother's criticism from years ago floated back into my mind. Now I was proving her wrong. China and tablecloths and sweaters and even the house itself meant nothing compared to protecting my children's lives. Maybe it would be better not to take too many reminders anyway, considering how desperate I was to leave the life I had known in the IFB behind me.

As I packed, I reviewed our escape plan again and again in my mind, searching for holes, weak points, and overlooked details that might trip us up. Sometimes I would run compulsively to the desk to make another note or change a step in the sequence Joseph and I had written down.

In late July, Jeff Miller, one of my husband's former colleagues at Northland, stopped by to visit with him. Jeff said he was disturbed because he had brought up our names in a recent administrative meeting. "We won't be discussing Joe and Jocelyn Zichterman. Things came out about them," "Dr." Marty Von had replied. Now we finally knew how Joseph's employers had decided to spin our situation. "Things came out about the Zichtermans" could imply anything from sexual impropriety to embezzlement to something worse. The IFB faithful would assume some grave sin had caused Joseph to lose his job and leave the community. The strategy was flawless: It allowed the administrators to look magnanimous, as if they were refusing to discuss the details in order to protect our reputation.

A short time later we heard that another board member, "Dr." Harold Patz, claimed I was losing my mind and making insane allegations against my father.

What were Joseph and I going to do now? Should we defend ourselves? Should we walk away? Most people in our position would have filed a lawsuit as well as complaints with the appropriate government agencies. However, IFB leaders taught that in almost every situation, the Bible forbade Christians from filing civil suits and involving the government in ministry matters, citing the following New Testament passage: "Do any of you who are in conflict with one another, dare to go to law before unbelievers? . . . Why do you not rather allow yourselves to be cheated?" In the end, Joseph and I decided to take what we considered the high road and trust God to protect our reputation. All we wanted to do was get away.

Off to Chicago: August 1, 2006

Perhaps it was a lapse of judgment, but we couldn't bear to leave our closest friends without saying farewell. So on the Saturday night before our Monday morning departure, Joseph and I had dinner with them and confided that we were planning to move in a few days. We asked them not to share the news.

For eight years Joseph had been the pastor at a little IFB church, one of many in northern Wisconsin, in a town about an hour away. He cared deeply about his forty-member congregation, so on Sunday morning he told them this would be our last worship service. He explained that we were moving away within the week so that he could go back to school. We kept the details vague and recited the line we had rehearsed: "As soon as we can tell you more, we will."

They were thoughtful enough to throw an impromptu going-away party that afternoon, though we knew that as soon as we drove home the phones around town would be jangling with the news. Would the leaders show up at our door and try to intimidate or browbeat us into staying? Would they take more extreme measures? We didn't know very many people who had left, so we weren't sure what was in store for us. Our biggest worry was getting away before my father could find out and book a flight from Colorado.

Joseph had gotten home early Sunday evening and gone to sleep in the basement bedroom so he could be alert for our escape the next morning. We turned off all the lights in the house. It was too early for the kids to go to bed and we wanted to avoid having to talk to any of our neighbors, so I piled the eight of them into the van. First, I took them to a McDonald's an hour away from our house, where there was a huge playground with a jungle gym and where, I hoped, we wouldn't run into anyone we knew. So far, so good. Then I treated them all to dessert at an ice cream parlor, biding my time until our departure. I kept them out until I knew all our IFB neighbors would be settled in for the night. By 9 P.M. I thought it would be safe to head home, but to my dismay, as I turned down our street, I passed my husband's boss, Curt Lamansky. I could tell from his expression that he was intent on stopping in to see us. *He must have gotten word from someone at church*, I thought. And he was going to do his utmost to dissuade Joseph from leaving the cult. Abruptly, I turned the van around in our driveway, gave him a wave, and sped away. He swung his car around and started following me. Panicking, I took a sharp left around a curve and kept driving. A few minutes later, I ventured a glance in the rearview mirror. "Whew! I lost him," I muttered under my breath.

I drove around for hours and finally got the kids into their beds a little after midnight. I felt dazed. Sleep was out of the question. The whole week had been surreal. My body was tight and tense from fear. I knew my husband's boss hadn't given up that easily. He was probably assembling the church leaders right now, hatching a plan to force a confrontation, an intervention at which forceful IFB leaders would do their utmost to break Joseph's resolve and to shame, bully, or intimidate us into staying. Worse yet, I was terrified that my father would show up in a rage, wielding a gun, and at least one of us would end up dead. We had to get out before that happened.

Preparing Into the Night
4:00 A.M.

I went down to the basement and woke Joseph, who quickly moved some of our possessions into a small vehicle he had rented. A few minutes later, the moving company pulled its truck into the driveway, right on schedule. The neighbors' lights flew on, and I saw them peering out their windows. Adrenaline surged through my body as I started loading the kids into the van.

"Hey, fellas, can I talk to you for a minute?" Joseph asked the movers, as I buckled the last child into his car seat. The men gathered around him in the dim light of the garage. I stopped too. "We need to leave before you load the moving van," Joseph told them, keeping his voice low. "After we've gone, if anyone comes by and asks you where we're going, please don't give them any information. Our family is in danger."

They agreed.

At 4:30 A.M. Joseph and I climbed into the driver's seats of our vehicles, pulled out of the driveway for the last time, and headed toward the highway.

As I drove away, I could see our beautiful home receding in the rearview mirror. I had designed it myself, believing that we would be bringing many more babies into it, even envisioning our grandchildren running through its spacious rooms. Tears welled up in my eyes as the kids' playhouse faded into the distance. We had it built three years earlier in the backyard as a miniature copy of our home. It had the same light yellow siding, green shutters, and Cape Cod–style dormers in the roof. My children loved their playhouse as much as Joseph and I loved the bigger one. And now it was all gone.

I was filled with a combination of deep sadness and overwhelming relief. I would miss my friends, but I was finally through with the charade. About a mile down the road I called Joseph on his cell phone.

"How are you holding up?" I asked.

"I don't know," he said. His voice sounded low and melancholy. "I can't believe we're leaving like this, but we have to stay safe. That's our number one priority right now." He sounded like he was trying to convince himself.

Somehow his uncertainty made me feel stronger. We were on our way. The impossible was happening.

"You know what we should do? We're not under the IFB rules anymore, so let's try to calm ourselves by listening to our new music," I told him. All my life, Christian contemporary worship songs with a rock beat had been strictly forbidden. Recently, though, I had bought a few CDs and hidden them in the glove compartment in preparation for our escape. At last I was free to listen to whatever music I wanted. The thought triggered a sudden surge of happiness in me.

I heard Joseph fumbling for a CD just like I was. I found a song by a group called Avalon. "*I don't want to go somewhere if I know that You're not there. Cuz I know to be without You is a lie*," the female vocalist sang. "*I don't want to walk that road, be a million miles from home, cuz my heart needs to be where You are.*"

The lyrics were talking about God, but I thought about Joseph and our kids. I didn't want to go anywhere without them. I listened to that song a dozen times during the trip.

About ten minutes later, Joseph called again. "I can't believe the fear I'm feeling," he confessed. For almost twenty-five years, he had believed ardently that the IFB was the only true church on earth. But the harsh reality about my upbringing, the battle with my father, and ugly conflict with the church leaders it sparked had shaken his faith in the sect. Still, he was hesitating. I could hear it in his voice.

"Remember how hard we tried, honey?" I said. "No matter what we did, my father wouldn't stop. He tried to ruin our lives."

"But we're abandoning what we believe," he blurted out.

"Your bosses screamed at me when I told them about my abuse," I reminded him. "They called me a liar. And you and I both know that I was telling them the truth!"

"I know, but I'm still so afraid," he said. "I keep praying that a semi doesn't hit me head-on."

After we hung up, we were both rattled. My husband was afraid that God would punish us for forsaking the IFB. I was afraid my father would hunt us down like prey. I was running from something that terrified me, while my husband was running headlong into his worst fears.

13

BREAKING FREE

*Northland Baptist Bible College does not have to con-
tinue to exist, but we do have to do what is right.*
—"Dr." Les Ollila, Chancellor's Address,
Northland Baptist Bible College/
International University, 2006

Feeling Safer in Chicago

For weeks after our move, we waited for the ax to fall. I flinched
every time the phone rang, and I half expected to hear the furious pounding of my father's fists on the door at night. Sometimes if a car cruised by
too slowly, I would glance at the driver in fear, suspecting that he must be
an IFB spy watching our every move. But nothing terrible happened.

Word reached us eventually that the college switchboard operator
was telling everyone who called for Joseph that the IFB leaders had no
idea where we had gone. We even heard that some cult members were saying I had lost my mind and was dragging my family down to Hell with me.

I no longer cared what they said about us. I was fed up with God.
After all I had endured in the name of religion, I wanted no part of it.
Joseph, on the other hand, felt our children needed a church to attend, so
we became members of Willow Creek Community Church in Barrington,
Illinois. He and the kids dragged me to Sunday services like a conscien-
tious objector to the front. My only solace was that the church had more
than twenty thousand in weekly attendance, so I could blend in with the
crowd.

During the week, Joseph would come home from his classes at Trinity and find me lying in bed. For those first few months I was so grief-stricken I could hardly get out of my pajamas to participate in any normal activities. A torrent of sexual-abuse memories returned as well—spiraling me into turbulent sobs. Joseph would climb into bed with me and try to console me, but it had little effect.

All IFB Rules Go Out the Window

I had to acknowledge the fact that I couldn't be a perfect mother and homemaker now; my grief was too all-consuming. I stopped resisting and accepted my shortcomings, but the house went to hell. All the rigidity of the past ten years dissolved. The kids reveled in their newfound freedom and embraced the opportunity to act like children for the first time, watching cartoons, eating pizza and hot dogs, and running around the house with snacks, sometimes leaving a trail of dry cereal in their wake.

Since it was fall, school was about to start and we were still planning on homeschooling the children because we were so heavily indoctrinated to believe the public school was full of secular humanists who would destroy the souls of our kids. I didn't know what I believed, but Joseph was holding tight to his faith. Fortunately, a new friend from Willow Creek recognized how depressed I was. She worried that our home life was becoming chaotic for the children—and she knew I was in no shape to teach them—so she staged an intervention. She encouraged us to enroll our kids in the local public school, assuring us that lots of children from the church attended the school and were thriving. Our new friends arranged for us to meet with the principal, who gave us a thorough explanation of the curriculum and assured us that a number of teachers in the school were fellow members of Willow Creek Community Church. Joseph and I were astonished at how rational he was and how nonthreatening the place seemed. I couldn't shake the images the IFB pastors had painted in my mind about public school—of orgies on elementary playgrounds and condoms being handed out by teachers around every corner. But the principal assured us that no such thing was taking place. Four weeks into our arrival, the children started their first day of school and soon they were happily ensconced in their new classrooms, able for the first time to interact with peers in an educational setting.

I stayed in bed for long stretches the next year, grieving. Joseph couldn't sleep well either. Night after night, he woke up overcome with anxiety and reliving the traumatic events of the past. We rushed him to the emergency room several times, convinced he was having a heart attack, but the doctors explained that he was suffering panic attacks from severe stress.

True Friends

One remarkable couple, Matt and Melanie Harper, stayed loyal to us when we fled the cult. Though they were still members of the IFB themselves and received subtle threats from the cult's leaders, who suspected they were staying in contact, they spent countless hours on the phone with us during our long and agonizing transition to the world outside the IFB. At one point I told them it felt like everyone I ever knew had perished in some terrible bus accident. "But in their eyes," the Harpers reminded me, "you're the ones who are dead now."

Joseph tried diligently to find a job as a Christian counselor to bring in some income for our family, but no place—not even evangelical organizations—considered his master's degree in counseling from Bob Jones University a legitimate credential. BJU's staff had duped us into thinking that accreditation was a meaningless term, but we were learning the hard way that it mattered a great deal. In fact, accreditation serves a vetting process—validation that the education a college or university provides is reputable and high-quality based on standards set by a peer review board. It would be impossible for my husband to get licensed as a counselor in any U.S. state with his counseling degree from BJU, a fact the folks back in Greenville conveniently forget to tell their students.

My sister Melissa and friend Melanie were my lifelines, and when I called to tell them the bad news, they weren't surprised. "In our nursing classes, they always said that mental health issues were a sin," Melissa explained. Her psychology "professors" had lectured that bipolar disorder, depression, anxiety, ADD, and ADHD were spiritual problems, not worthy of medication or therapy. Greg Mazak, the head of BJU's psychology department, told Melissa and her fellow nursing students that the teachers and parents in our country were lazy and that they wanted to keep kids on drugs to create zombies so they could keep order in public school classrooms. That statement naturally segued into a rant on the necessity of Christian school education.

Mazak, incidentally, holds a master's degree in counseling and guidance from BJU and a Ph.D. from BJU in New Testament interpretation. With those degrees, as of 2012, he was teaching nine master's-level courses in counseling and two bachelor's-level psychology courses, including abnormal psychology and clinical psychology. Steven Cruice, his colleague in the psychology department, held no degrees in counseling or psychology listed in the university catalogue as of 2012, yet he taught eight master's-level courses in counseling at BJU that year.

"But the school gets federal grants," I told Melissa. "How can the government give money to them if their professors' degrees are bogus and the professors aren't even teaching legitimate psychology?"

BJU having national accreditation is an anomaly in our country, since it's a liberal arts university. It has been suggested TRACS was allowed in as a campaign favor and exception for religious schools, under Ronald Reagan. However, national accreditation is usually reserved for tech schools with specialized degrees, such as ITT tech, or aviation, etc. This means, BJU is not required to follow standard procedure—and the students are the ones who lose out.

I finally called the Transnational Association of Christian Colleges and Schools (TRACS), which is BJU's and Northland's Christian national accreditation agency. I told the president that a number of men with bogus degrees had tried to "counsel" me about the sexual abuse I had suffered and that they were now covering for my abuser. I also explained that Joseph couldn't get a job anywhere with his degrees and that BJU had lied to us in saying that regional accreditation didn't matter.

"I'm sorry, but there's nothing I can do to help you," he said.

"That's not good enough," I insisted. "There is no accountability. BJU needs to get regionally accredited."

"Well, don't hold your breath," he responded. "I can tell you *that* will never happen."

He chuckled, but I was fuming. We had escaped one nightmare situation only to plunge into another. I felt betrayed, not just by the cult leaders, but by the government. Why couldn't it regulate these organizations? It was a question I would ask countless times in the years to come.

The next night I went to Willow Creek Church and shared my frustration over the accreditation issue with our friends. "People at BJU always used Harvard as an example," I said. "They pointed out that since Harvard isn't accredited, no school needs that type of oversight."

"What do you mean Harvard isn't accredited?" one of my friends said. "Of course Harvard's accredited."

I was flabbergasted. How many other lies had we believed? Why hadn't any of us ever bothered to vet the so-called "facts" we were fed by the IFB?

Trying to Find Jobs: Harder than It Seems

Joseph applied for every part-time opening he could find, but with no luck. He even got turned down for a job as a bus driver. Finally, he found part-time work pastoring a small church near our new home. I took a job as a waitress at TGI Friday's to help out, but it brought in very little income. We were forced to use a private loan to make ends meet, watching helplessly as Joseph's school loans racked up. By the time he graduated, we would be several hundred thousand dollars in debt.

Just when things seemed to be settling down, Jason called me. The IFB, it seemed, had tracked us down. To my horror, my brother informed me that my father had flown to Northland and that he and all the college administrators were planning to show up at Willow Creek to confront me. "They heard you've been talking and violating the statement of silence you signed," he said accusingly.

I knew he was baiting me. Aside from the fact that the famous statement of silence was not legally binding, we had agreed that I could seek counseling for the abuse I had suffered. The only person I had confided in about the gory details of my past was my counselor. There was no way these men could know who I was talking to or what I was saying. They were trumping up charges, looking for any excuse to attack me.

Our home address was unlisted and we had left only a PO box for forwarding mail, so I didn't think they had found out where we lived. Although we gave Jason and Melissa our cell phone numbers in case of emergency, we specifically asked for numbers outside our area code. Still I was terrified. I envisioned them frog-marching me out the front doors of

Willow Creek and spiriting me away to be imprisoned under my father's tyrannical Umbrella of Protection forever, unable to reach my precious children or my husband for the rest of our lives.

There is no privacy in the cult. None. Right after we left, Jason called my cell phone and insisted that we tell him our whereabouts so he could get in touch with us in an emergency. We told him about Trinity and Willow Creek, though we refused to reveal where we were living. I'm afraid we still didn't understand the consequences of talking to him at all. He acted as if he were trying to help us, but word about us spread like wildfire all over the cult. Fortunately, Willow Creek was a big church with parking lot ushers and lots of services every weekend, so we knew it wouldn't be easy for them to find us there.

Still, Jason sounded supremely confident that Willow Creek's pastoral staff would be sympathetic to the IFB godfathers' cause and would force us to meet to "clear offenses." After all, that's how the IFB works. Surely, every other church would be the same. When I got off the phone with him, I was shaking and my head was starting to throb as if one of my old migraines was returning to debilitate me.

Feeling Some Protection

Panicked, Joseph and I immediately called Willow Creek. We explained the situation to one of the pastors.

"Don't worry," he assured us. "We would never allow anything like that to happen in the church. I'll put the security staff on alert. And if those men show up for a confrontation, they'll be ushered out the door."

It was all I could do not to cry as I thanked him and hung up, overwhelmed with gratitude. For the first time, I felt protected by people who claimed to be Christians. Joseph and I called Jason and told him what the pastor at Willow Creek had told me. He was shocked.

"They wouldn't be willing to sit down for a confrontation on this?" Jason was exasperated.

"No. They won't," I told him. "And the men will be escorted off the property. That's not how they do things here."

I could declare their position now with certainty. Relief swept over me, and the men from Northland never tried to show up after that.

Firing "God"

Despite all the care and support showered on us by our friends and pastors from our new church, I spent my first months in Illinois raging against God in private. I blamed Him for everything that had happened and I hated Him with a passion. I would go to my room and scream to the sky, "I fucking hate you! Fuck off!" Then I'd thrust two middle fingers toward Heaven. Every day, I would rage in my bedroom. All the negative emotion I had dammed up inside myself for years, never allowed to show "sinful" feelings in the IFB, came pouring out in a torrent—along with enough four-letter words to make a sailor blush. Thirty years' worth of pent-up profanity came spewing out of my mouth.

"I fuckin' hate your goddamn church! I fuckin' hate you and everything about you! Fuck off and leave me alone!" I would shout. "You are nothing but a bastard and I want nothing to do with you or your sick sock-puppet followers!"

It felt good. I tried to string together the worst sentence I could think up and aimed it right at God. "You cocksuckin' piece of shit! Fuckin' lunatic monster, motherfucker, bitch, cunt!" Out of all my new words, "fuck" was my new favorite. I screamed it all-out, glaring at my ceiling.

I had been taught my entire life that God was waiting to strike me dead if I ever turned my back on Him, so I waited for the lightning bolt. But instead, the more I vented, the better I felt.

"What are you doing, motherfucker? Trying to woo me back! Well, I ain't going back to you or your stupid groupies! You can brainwash them all you want, but you ain't gonna brainwash me again! No way, sucker! We're done!"

I waited for the floor to crack open and drop me screaming into the lake of fire from my childhood nightmares, but instead, I felt a sense of peace and comfort. I could almost hear a still, small voice assuring me, "It's okay. Let it all out. I'm with you. You're not alone. I'm here whenever you want to talk." I thought that was another figment of my imagination, another delusion. And I didn't want to listen. I wanted to hate God for the rest of my life.

One night, I ranted to my friend Rory after a service at Willow Creek. "I hate everything about God!" I told him. Before joining Willow

Creek, Rory had been a pastor in a strict religious denomination, and its rules took such a toll on his relationship with his wife that they ended up divorcing. He had lost everything and was rebuilding his life piece by piece.

"Jocelyn, please don't give up on God," he pleaded, tears in his eyes. "Don't lose your faith. The light will shine again one day, I promise."

But the truth was, I didn't *want* the light to shine again. My life had been one long horror story and I had no energy left to rebuild it. I just wanted to die.

Joseph knew what deep turmoil I was in and he apologized profusely for the role he had played in my suffering. After a year of sleepless nights and intensive counseling to come to terms with his own anguish, at last Joseph understood the pain I had endured at the hands of the IFB. Finally, he convinced me to meet with some of the pastoral staff at Willow Creek to see if they could help me. When Ron Erkley, a licensed psychologist who worked with the church, met with us and asked what I was feeling, I let it all out.

"I hate God! I hate this church!" I shouted at him. "I tell God to fuck off every day! And I want to say that you can fuck off too!"

I braced myself, expecting IFB-style wrath, but Ron seemed unmoved. "Can I try to help you?" he asked calmly. "Jocelyn, what those men did to you, none of that was God. That was abuse. That god, the one they believe in, that's a fictitious and false god. He doesn't exist. God is a God of love and compassion and humility. And you should FIRE that god from your childhood! Just fire him! That is not the true God. Fire that false god and hire the God who does nothing but love and care for you and want the best for you."

Throughout his previous sessions, Ron had listened patiently to Joseph drone on and on about all he had given up for me, leaving all he knew behind so I could be happy. But now he turned to Joseph and said, "You simply did what you should have done years before. Your family was deeply hurt by you. You should have been a partner to your wife the day you married her. She needs you to step up and do the right thing now."

Joseph sat in stunned silence. This was my husband's epiphany, his wake-up call. Throughout our transition he had thought he deserved a medal for his "incredible sacrifice." Suddenly, he understood fully his role in all of it. He realized he was just as culpable for his *inaction* as others were for their actions.

"I honestly never thought of it that way before," he said at last.

Ron continued to reason with him. "You have a hyper-sensitive conscience," he told him. "What they drilled into you has warped your view of God and robbed you of any peace. Now you think this god that they created is unreasonable and ready to exact punishment on you the minute you do the slightest thing wrong. The IFB's mantra of 'if you doubt, don't' has debilitated you, crippling your clarity in decision making. So, my suggestion for you is for the next six months, if you doubt, DO IT! Have fun! Test the boundaries of your conscience and see what it can handle. At the end of the day, you'll know what you feel comfortable with and then you can draw a healthy boundary."

Ron hit the nail on the head. For as long as I had known him, Joseph had been tormented by doubts about whether he was really "born again," even though he was one of the most committed Christians I knew. He was also continually stressed about whether he was following God's will in every detail. The IFB ideology drove nonemotional members like Joseph toward perfectionism by instilling an irrational fear of an unreasonable God in them. Meanwhile, it drove emotional people like me to an irrational fear of people by filling our heads with guilt, shame, and fear. But we were both so consumed by the tortured, guilt-laden belief system our pastors had ingrained in us that we were like addicts, insecure and frightened without it.

My wheels started turning. Could I really *fire* the "God" I had always known, the "God" of hellfire, brimstone, and eternal damnation? Could I erase the images burned so deeply into my mind of Him as a wrathful old white man, an omnipotent version of my father and every other IFB pastor that had ever made me cower? Could I replace him with a loving, forgiving, magnanimous God?

I finally decided to start reading the Bible again—but only The Message version, a modern language edition that summarized the spirit of each passage. I couldn't handle reading much of it, but what little I did read made me realize the IFB had lied to me and severely skewed my childhood belief system. I also began to grasp the power of language. Subtle rephrasing could shift the implications of a sentence dramatically. Take the ubiquitous IFB phrase "You just need to forgive." Worded that way, it's a chilling bit of cult lingo meant to silence victims. But if someone tells me, "Forgiveness is for you, not them," I can embrace the notion as a victim, knowing that bottling up anger and thirsting for revenge can hamper my own path to healing. I realized that sometimes we fail to get through to people because we don't understand their background and culture and, by extension, their language triggers. You might be telling the truth, but if you say it the wrong way, your audience won't hear you. It was a lesson that would serve me well in the years to come, when I began working to help fellow cult survivors.

Living in the Moment: Exploration into the Unknown

In 2007 I discovered Eckhart Tolle's books *A New Earth* and *The Power of Now*. Later, I started watching Oprah Winfrey's new *Lifeclass*es on TV. Tolle gave me an inspiring fresh perspective on spirituality, something I desperately needed as I reevaluated everything I had ever been taught. I was still reeling from my grief, but this spiritual exploration gave me hope for brighter days in my future. I became even more adventurous and started reading books like *Spiritual Solutions* by Deepak Chopra, *Living Buddha, Living Christ* by Thich Nhat Hanh, and *Be Here Now* by Baba Ram Dass. Even though these books would have been banned from IFB bookshelves, I found them packed full of new thoughts and insights I'd never considered. It was wonderful to be able to question the "truths" posited by other spiritual teachers—instead of categorically denying their veracity. With such an exciting new world to explore, I was convinced I would never feel bored again.

IFB members sometimes called Oprah the Antichrist. They've even made YouTube videos to that effect. But I admired her a great deal. I was forbidden from watching her talk show as a kid, but during my year of unmonitored homeschooling I would sometimes sneak off to watch. Even at that age, I knew she had answers to problems I was unable to solve. So at the age of fifteen, I did what came natural to me and I got on my knees and prayed that I would meet her someday. I wonder now if I unconsciously was drawn to her because she stood up for victims of abuse. But now I was meeting her in a different way, thrilled to be able to watch her *Lifeclass* every day and to absorb her advice.

Between Ron Erkley's counsel about firing the vindictive "God" of the IFB and the fresh views on spirituality I was discovering, I started to see God in a whole new light. After years of apocalyptic IFB thinking and belief that our time on earth was just a dress rehearsal for the afterlife, the idea of living in the moment seemed wonderful to me. I read Tolle's *The Power of Now* so many times it grew dog-eared and torn. I created a gratitude journal and started writing down all my joys and blessings. At first it was a short list: my children, my husband, and my sister Melissa. But gradually it expanded to include our home, our friends at Willow Creek Church, our friends at Moody Bible Institute, our friends at Life on the Vine Church, and many more wonderful people whose love and encouragement guided us through the eighteen months we spent slowly detoxing from the cult. I also gained new insight on the mind control techniques cult leaders use by reading books about the Amish by Beverly Lewis.

I got another big shock when Joseph told me that the men in his classes at Trinity treated the female students and faculty as intellectual equals, taking their opinions and beliefs into serious consideration. Unlike those in the IFB, women in our new community didn't preface their insight with self-deprecating statements like "I could be wrong but . . ." or "My husband believes . . ." or "I'd like to confirm this with my pastor, but I think it might be true that . . ." We had truly entered a different world.

Studying church history slowly began to free Joseph's conscience too. In the IFB, almost every acceptable opinion on any issue had come down from Bob Jones and his university. But now Joseph began to believe that sincere Christians could hold many different beliefs about what the Bible taught.

People who have no experience with cults often find it hard to understand how an intelligent person could be brainwashed so profoundly. But a child's conscience is easily trained and if you spend your entire life in a cloistered community, isolated from dissenting viewpoints, there are almost no limits to how much your mind can be manipulated. This is

among the most humiliating realizations you have to face once you leave
a cult. It was especially hard for Joseph, who had devoted his life to gain-
ing and sharing knowledge.

Another one of the hardest aspects of leaving a cult is relinquishing
the concept of yourself as spiritually elite, the focus of heaven's attention.
Like other religious cult leaders, IFB pastors indoctrinate you from childhood into believing that what your tiny group is doing is the most important thing happening on earth from God's perspective. The sense of higher
purpose and mission gives you a high almost like a drug. When you leave
the cult, you realize how utterly unimportant you are in the larger scheme
of things and it's a profound letdown, a staggering blow to the ego. It's
hard to come to terms with the fact that you are just an ordinary person,
a very small fish in a very big ocean when you've been told your whole
life that you are superior to the rest of the human race because of your
"special enlightenment."

The more acclimated to my new life I grew, the more my spirits lifted.
Even my migraines receded slightly. I'm positive now that the stress of
my situation in the IFB was a strong contributing factor to my years of
pain. And even though I needed to continue my MRIs and have medical
professionals monitor my brain tumor closely, I resolved not to continue
obsessing over what might happen if it started growing "fingers"—an
indication of malignancy. I wanted to live fully in the present, enjoy every
moment with my family, and continue to hope for the best.

The Surprise Letter

I was in such a positive frame of mind that even the letter that
arrived in the mail from Bob Jones University in May of 2007 couldn't
dampen my spirits. It informed Joseph that he had been kicked out of the
BJU Alumni Association.

Dear Joseph,
I am writing this letter with a heavy heart. One of the
criteria for continued membership in the BJU Alumni
Association is that the individual be in good standing
with the University. We understand that is not so in your
case at this time. In light of that, we regret that we will

> *not be able to continue your membership in the associa-*
> *tion until such time as the problem has been resolved.*
> *Enclosed is a refund check. I trust that whatever has*
> *brought this breach will be dealt with and corrected soon.*

Director of Alumni Relations

Given the fact that Northland had allegedly terminated my husband's contract due to "budget cuts" and Joseph had had no dealings with
Bob Jones University, positive or negative, since then, this was yet another
message from the cult leadership that the IFB would not tolerate defiance, rebellion, or defection. I wouldn't have been surprised if they had
tried to revoke Joseph's actual degrees, but it no longer mattered to me.
We were out for good, and I was thrilled.

Every person who leaves a cult has to overcome three primary hur-
dles. First, he must reprogram his conscience not to fear God's imminent
wrath for leaving the "truth" and instead learn to how think reasonably
for himself. After a year out of the IFB, we were making strides in that
direction. Second, a defector has to rebuild his entire network of personal
and professional relationships. This can be a long and lonely process, but
Joseph and I were progressing. The third and often the most difficult step
is to find new employment and sever old financial ties to the cult. That
was the most arduous task for us, partly because, no matter how hard we
tried, we couldn't sell our house in the small IFB community surrounding Northland International University. And regardless of how strapped
we were, the mortgage payments still had to be made.

Sabotaged House Auction

In the spring of 2007, we borrowed $10,000 from Joseph's grand-
parents to hire the region's best auction company to advertise our house
and host a series of open houses. More than a hundred people toured our
beautiful onetime dream home, traveling from a five-hour driving radius
in all directions, and about thirty showed up for the auction. At the time,
our house was priced at $450,000.

On the day of the auction, our auctioneer told us that a man who
identified himself as a member of the faculty at Northland offered $40,000

and argued with him in front of everyone for the better part of half an
hour that we had to accept his bid. After that, no one else made an offer
and our $10,000 was wasted. Joseph and I have no doubt that the alterca-
tion disconcerted potential buyers and suggested to them that there was
something extremely strange about the situation. We had long suspected
that the college leaders were discouraging people from buying our house,
telling them it was overpriced, and this incident made us wonder once
again if they would ever let us sell our home.

We Are Not Alone

During our first year detoxing from the IFB, Joseph and I met
many fellow "defectors." At first we thought our experiences were unique,
but we soon began to realize that the leaders used the same basic tactics
to discredit, intimidate, and threaten everyone who left the cult. Finally,
Joseph decided to post a ninety-minute audio on the Internet explaining
why we had left the IFB, sharing many of the insights we had gained
over the previous year. He knew that appealing to IFB leaders, whose control and income would be threatened by his comments, was a waste of
time. However, he hoped that rank-and-file members of the cult might
start to open their eyes to the brainwashing we had all experienced.

Within three days of posting his lecture, the audio file had been
downloaded close to thirty thousand times and the IFB blogosphere lit up
like a Christmas tree. "Joseph Zichterman should be officially turned
over to Satan in church discipline for his rebellion against God and the
Bible," one listener wrote. Another remarked, "Zichterman is a heretic
and an apostate, seeking to make those he influences 'children of Hell.' "
And still another wrote, "Joseph is part of the 'great falling away' from
the Christian faith, which was prophesied in the New Testament to come
immediately before the appearance of the Antichrist." Prominent IFB
evangelist "Dr." Steve Pettit, BJU graduate and board member at Northland, quickly responded on my brother's immensely popular blog ("Sharper
Iron"), stating that Joseph needed to apologize for his "inconsistency in
practise [sic] and dishonesty in message." Little did we know at the time
the lengths they were willing to go to in order to discredit us.

My husband received hundreds of e-mails from the IFB faithful. One
came from a woman named Gloria Everson, a graduate of BJU and a

former co-worker at Northland. She wrote, "I pray that you will come back to the truth. You have been deceived and Satan is using you to destroy the work that you have done." Dave Doran, BJU graduate and president of Detroit Baptist Theological Seminary, wrote accusing Joseph of "shameless self-promotion" and demanding that he "quarantine" himself for a long time. Matt Herbster, BJU graduate and assistant program director at The Wilds camp, wrote, "I'm . . . praying for you to extend God's love and forgiveness to those you feel have hurt you in the past." A short time later, Bobby Wood also wrote Joseph, criticizing him for "attacking" his close friends at Northland, saying, "Don't let bitterness destroy your life."

Joseph had obviously touched a nerve. In the midst of all the attacks, he was also inundated with supportive e-mails. Many were from former IFB members who had left the cult and others from mid-tier up-and-comers still trapped inside—almost all of them scared to death for anyone to find out they were starting to question the leaders.

The Move to Hawaii

By August 2007 Joseph was a few months from finishing his classes at Trinity and contemplating what we would all do during the time he was writing his dissertation. That's when my sister Melissa came up with an interesting proposition. "Why don't you move to Hawaii and live with us?" she suggested. We would have to sell everything we owned to pay for the move and pack only the bare minimum, but we decided to take the gamble. For the plan to work, Joseph would need to stay in Chicago to finish his final course work, while I took the kids to my sister's and waited for his arrival.

Melissa and Vance's home was large by Hawaiian standards, but not nearly spacious enough to accommodate ten extra people. They built two large triple bunk beds for the kids and put them in a closed lanai, and we stuffed all the clothes and toys we had brought into storage bins under the bottom bunks. The mattresses came from a Navy ship and were spacious enough that our two small children could share the bottom bunk. Meanwhile, Joseph and I slept in the guest bedroom next to the lanai, where our children could reach us easily if they needed us. The kids' quarters were laughably tight, but they were delighted to embark on yet another new adventure. Every day we headed to the beach with surfboards, body boards, Frisbees, buckets, and shovels. It felt like we were on one long, delightful extended vacation. Melissa also introduced us to hundreds of popular movies that almost everyone in America had seen in the past twenty years—except those of us in the cult. There was a mind-boggling amount to catch up on in terms of American culture.

Every night when my brother-in-law came home from the office, the kids would clamber over each other to regale him with the day's escapades and exhibit their latest boo-boos to the family doctor. "Uncle Vance! Uncle Vance! Look at this cut on my toe! Wanna know how I got it?" They were all convinced he had magical powers of healing.

Melissa's house was right on the beach and we sat around a bonfire in the evenings with Clark and Jan, her wonderful neighbors. We were in a terrific new world of freedom, sitting outside watching the beautiful sunsets and the ocean waves hitting the rocks while Beatles and Rolling Stones music played in the background. We sipped wine (our favorite indulgence after a lifetime of fear that a glass of alcohol was a one-way ticket to Hell) and talked about how distorted our perceptions had been, as well as how far we'd come. Melissa was pregnant with her first child and had decided to cut back on her hours at work as her due date drew near, so, while the kids played nearby, we spent several hours every day discussing our childhood, helping us both to come to terms with the terrors of the past. I was there for the birth of her adorable baby girl and was able to help out during the first few months of her life. Those were halcyon times. It felt as if we were starting life all over again together, full of hope and free of fear, something we had never thought possible.

The Bad Girls' Club

During our time in Hawaii, I attended a conference on sexual abuse, where I met actress Alison Arngrim, who played Nellie on *Little House on the Prairie*. The show, based on the series of bestselling books about Laura Ingalls Wilder's life in nineteenth-century rural America, was one of the few my parents allowed us to watch growing up, and I had been an enormous fan. I'd passed my love of all things *Little House* on to my own daughters, building their playhouse in Wisconsin to the floor plan of the Ingalls family's log cabin and even re-creating scenes from the series for Christmas one year. I had white nightgowns and nightcaps hand-sewn for them and gave them cinnamon sticks, red knitted mittens, tin dishes, and *Little House* dresses, aprons, and bonnets. All the outfits were made to match the show costumes, with meticulous attention to detail.

I introduced myself to Alison after her speech and told her about my obsession with the show. She wasn't surprised. In fact, she surprised *me* by knowing all about the IFB. No matter where she goes, Alison seems to get cornered by adoring homeschooling moms and their daughters, all wearing long matching gingham and calico *Little House* dresses.

Next, I told her a bit about my personal history. I said I found it ironic to know that she had been sexually abused by one of her relatives while she was a child star in *Little House,* when I had so often longed to escape similar abuse in my own life by plunging into the Ingalls family's perfect world. There, fathers were as kind and loving as its protagonist, Pa. Alison explained that Michael Landon, who played Pa, had created the series with kids like me in mind, to offer them a sunnier, gentler world.

We hit it off immediately and ended up spending the weekend together, bumming around the island. I loved hearing her memories of the actors I had adored as a kid and finding out what had become of them all after the last episode. We even went to a party together, where she showed me how to smoke my first cigar.

It was a full-circle moment for me. Whenever we had played *Little House* as kids, I insisted on being good girl Laura Ingalls. My sister Meagan was blond, so she played Laura's golden-haired sister Mary. I always cast Melissa as Nellie, Laura's nemesis and the stereotypical bad girl. In the IFB's eyes, Melissa was still playing that role. Now I had joined her. And both Nellies, Alison and Melissa, had stepped in to guide me on my journey from IFB enslavement to freedom in Hawaii. I had come a long way and I was proud of who I was becoming.

Devastating Revelations

The kids were starting school partway through the first quarter, and the air crackled with anticipation as they prepared for the first day of class. Joseph and I gave them the standard parental advice every child hears. "Don't chew with your mouth open." "Don't talk in class." "Make sure all your papers come home in your backpacks." But Melissa felt it was also important to discuss inappropriate hugging and touching to make sure they would know how to protect themselves.

To her horror, a puzzled frown crossed several of my daughters' little faces. They explained to her that Bart had often touched them in the ways she was describing. Making a monumental effort not to betray her outrage for fear of upsetting the girls, Melissa hurried out of the room and told me.

My knees buckled as a crushing flood of grief, fear, shock, and guilt engulfed me. Hadn't I always been terrified of him harming my children the way he had harmed me?

My first instinct was to rush to them, wrap them in my arms, and promise never to let anything bad happen to them ever again. But I didn't dare participate in any conversations with my daughters about sexual abuse. I knew that if I wanted to press charges against him, my father would produce his reams of Internet "research" and tell everyone I had provoked false memories in my daughters just as he claimed I had fabricated memories myself. So instead I called 911 and was connected to the Honolulu Police Department's special sex crimes unit. My daughters were ready to talk, so we brought them in to meet with detectives for video-taped forensic interviews. Afterward, the detectives met with us and said they were convinced that both of our children were telling the truth. They offered to send the videotapes to the police detectives in Dunbar, Wisconsin, where the crimes had been committed. I was touched by the sensitivity and genuine concern they showed for our family. The detective who broke the news had tears in his eyes when he spoke.

Our next move was to get our daughters started in therapy with qualified counselors. One of our girls had been particularly distant and cold with us, but after she came forward about the abuse and sobbed out her pain, vomiting for three straight days, she became a different child. She was lighthearted, funny, and quick to show affection. The transformation was miraculous to watch, but I couldn't help grieving over all the years we had lost with her. I knew all too well what deep pain she had suffered and kept locked inside herself for so long.

"How could I be so stupid as to let him around my children?" I kept asking.

"Jocelyn, you were beaten bloody," Melissa assured me. "He had you locked in fear of death. They didn't even tell us what sexual abuse was. How could you have known? You didn't even understand it yourself!"

Melissa had gone through a lot to gain this perspective. She had been making this slow, arduous journey along with me and had decided to go to therapy herself. She had done extensive eye movement desensitization and reprocessing (EMDR) therapy, a treatment most often used to rehabilitate soldiers who were prisoners of war, to put the terrible ghosts from our past to rest. Melissa and I were both diagnosed with PTSD—a common side effect of extreme abuse. She understood me like no other person could. I couldn't have asked for a wiser, more empathetic confidante, but her words gave me little consolation. Knowing I had failed to protect my children was a heartbreak greater than anything we had yet gone through. I cried myself to sleep every night while my sister consoled me. I wouldn't have made it through that time without her by my side.

Marinette County detective Tony O'Neill's voice sounded gruff over the phone. "Why do you want to press charges against your father?" he demanded.

"Because he molested my daughters," I explained.

That didn't seem to be enough for O'Neill, though. He kept pressing, firing questions at me. O'Neill was the senior detective in a town of fewer than 2,000 residents, and I knew he had investigated other criminal cases at Northland. I was beginning to wonder if Northland had prejudiced him against me because he seemed disinclined to believe everything I said.

I couldn't handle his unexpected bullying, so Joseph took over. O'Neill was just as rude and dismissive with him. He seemed incredulous about our desire to press charges against Bart and skeptical that a case would be prosecutable without DNA evidence.

"We want this man arrested!" Joseph said emphatically. "Why hasn't anyone moved on this? Didn't you get the videotaped interviews of our daughters that the police in Hawaii sent?"

"Nope," O'Neill said.

We were exasperated. Bart Janz had threatened to kill us. His molestation of our daughters had been confirmed by the Honolulu sex crimes unit. But with the police in Wisconsin unwilling to take action against him, the man would remain a senior pastor with access to vulnerable children every week. "How can the justice system be so unfair?" I fumed to Joseph. "Vulnerable children get wronged at every turn!" Joseph even sent a letter to the district attorney in Marinette County, insisting that something be done, but we received no reply. We couldn't believe it.

Not long after this, we got word from a relative that my father was planning a vacation to the island of Oahu where we lived. The news threw us all into a panic and we went to the police to get a more extensive restraining order. My sister documented her side of the abuse and submitted it to the court while I documented mine.

Bart attended the hearing by phone and was brusque even with the judge, who granted a twenty-year restraining order for my children and me, effective in all fifty states. My father asked for the right to retain his firearms, and when the judge asked, "Why?" Bart responded that he "went to the gun range to practice hitting targets." The judge glanced toward my direction and I shook my head no emphatically, using eye contact to plead with him because I was sure it was yet another veiled threat on my life. To my immense relief, the judge denied his request.

The Marriage Contract

Joseph had been looking for work every day for several months on the island, but again, no one would hire him because of his unaccredited degrees. Finally, even though he hadn't completed his dissertation yet, he decided it was time to start sending his CV to colleges across the country for a teaching position in theology. Unfortunately, the economy was still sluggish, and job openings were scarce. He got a few job offers from smaller schools, but nothing seemed to fit our family's needs. Then one day he opened his e-mail account to find a message from an evangelical university in Portland, Oregon, inviting him to interview for a position. Excited at the prospect, he Googled the school's Web site.

"I don't know," I told him warily. "It looks extremely conservative."

"Let's at least check it out," he said. Our roles seemed to have reversed. He sounded like me back in our last days with the IFB, when I was gingerly coaxing him to send out feelers and keep an open mind about new possibilities. "It'll be fun to do the interview and get away for a few days," he said. But what if he saw the campus, fell in love, and let his old passion for teaching guide his decision, regardless of what it meant for me? To put my mind at ease, I asked him to sign a contract before we left. It said that if the school didn't take an egalitarian position regarding men and women, he would walk away and wait until the right opportunity came along. I guess I had learned this "tactic" from the IFB rather well, but this time I was putting it to good use. He signed—and we both laughed about it—but I was determined never to sink into a patriarchal subculture again.

We flew to the school and met the co-chairman of the Bible and Theology Department. He was friendly, humble, and unequivocally egalitarian, which took me completely off guard. He said he understood our history and was glad we were free. I was delighted to discover that he and I were passionate about many of the same issues. Even more unexpected, the employment committee invited me to join Joseph during his first interview, explaining that having a wife onboard when a husband accepted a new job was crucial. Oregon's rain could drastically affect anyone with seasonal affective disorder, and they had lost more than one new faculty member because a spouse couldn't take the dreary climate.

I had to make a conscious effort to keep my jaw from dropping. I had come out of a culture where women were supposed to be meek, submissive "help meets" who didn't even *have* opinions of their own, let alone voice them. I had lived in a place where the sky was dark and gloomy most the year, in minus-20-degree weather, where men required women to wear skirts while trekking through drifts of snow. Now an entire group of men at an evangelical university were concerned about *my* mental health?

Our interview devolved into fits of laughter when the committee mentioned reading the glowing employer reviews my husband had saved from his IFB days. In one written long before anyone knew we were leaving the IFB, Joseph's old boss Curt Lamansky had said, "I'd like to assure you that Jocelyn is a submissive and faithful woman who serves as a wonderful helpmeet for her husband." The very idea that an employer would write that in a letter of recommendation for a job seemed crazy to the entire committee. It seemed like a different lifetime to us now too.

We bonded quickly, and the committee felt comfortable enough with us to reveal that one member had seen Bob Jones University and Pensacola Christian College on Joseph's CV and thrown it in the trash, saying "he wouldn't be a good fit here." However, this man's curiosity eventually got the better of him and he Googled Joseph. He didn't have to read much to realize that Joseph had been banished from the IFB boys' club—and that convinced the committee to give his résumé a second look.

Joseph couldn't conceal his delight. All this time he had been afraid that the vicious comments circulating in IFB chat rooms and on IFB message boards would keep him from getting a job. But the cult's penchant for backstabbing and denigration had turned out to be better than a letter of recommendation to sensible academicians in the real world. The committee made it clear that they would be happy to have another "apostate" join them, all laughing at the thought.

A few days later, Joseph was offered the job—and accepted. Soon we were packing our bags, showering Melissa and Vance with thanks and well wishes, and moving to Oregon to embark on the next stage of our journey.

14

FROM IFB TO LIBERAL

We are addicted to counseling in America today and we've got to get over it. Do you know why we're addicted to counseling, because you're not reading your Bibles, that's why.

> —*Bart Janz, sermon, Holly Ridge Baptist Church, "When Men Don't, Women Do," 2007*

Hopes for the Future, Ghosts of the Past

We found a suitable house, enrolled the kids in the local public schools, and settled in to Portland in July of 2008. In addition to teaching full-time at a conservative evangelical university, Joseph soon took a weekend job pastoring a local Baptist church, which is *not* part of the IFB. (He is a pastor there even now, which means I am still a Baptist pastor's wife—humorous, given my work exposing abuse in the IFB.) However, by this time, our family conversations were getting quite lively, as our kids starting calling me "the liberal" and Joseph "the conservative."

Soon after arriving in Portland, we attended a student body function at Joseph's university, where the student body president gave a talk about growing up in a hyper-perfectionistic homeschooling family and having a complete mental breakdown at age seventeen from the pressure. He ended up in a psychiatric hospital and took a year to recover any semblance of a normal life. Chagrined and horrified, I remembered my own drive to raise "super-children" who would master foreign languages, play musical instruments, and surpass their peers academically. Now my children reveled in their freedom—singing and dancing to pop songs, living in the moment, and brimming with happiness. I hugged them all a little tighter that night, profoundly grateful that they had been spared from the life he described—the life we had left behind in the IFB.

Barack Obama was running for president when we moved to Portland and I contemplated joining his campaign, but there were two major stumbling blocks: homosexuality and abortion. In the minds of the IFB and many other right-wing evangelical organizations in the U.S., no "good Christian" could ever vote for a Democrat because the party's stance on these two issues opposes "God's biblical guidelines." The pastors thundering from their pulpits made it perfectly clear that voting Republican was the *only* option. It had been drilled into my head even as a little girl. Now I find it dismaying that IFB churches, schools, and universities claim tax-exempt status and yet shamelessly promote a specific political position. Don't they understand what "separation of church and state" means? Why can't the church develop a mutually respectful relationship with the government and vice versa? What about a "middle ground" of pro-choice (the state), yet anti-abortion (their church)—in other words, you can oppose the concept of terminating a pregnancy but respect other women's right to have opinions and make decisions that differ from yours? Or pro–gay marriage (the state), yet anti-homosexuality (their church)? Once again, it seemed clear to me that the IFB's stand on these issues was about power and control over other people. It's one thing to have a personal moral belief based on a literal interpretation of the Bible. It's something entirely different to demand that the rest of society adopt your beliefs. By this time in my journey, I was glad the government allowed me to make my own choices about my body and my personal life. I had become an advocate of free will and would never ask another person to give up his rights. With that, I took a pro-choice and pro-gay marriage position and have never faltered in my political positions on either.

I went to work for the Democratic National Committee. Campaigning for Obama made me feel marvelously liberated. A few years earlier, I would have thought "I will burn in Hell" was part of the job description. But now I was on the side of freedom, progress, and forward-thinking.

Every morning after my children left for school, I would slap magnetic "Yes We Can" magnets to the side of our twelve-passenger van and haul DNC staffers all over Portland, dropping teams off at strategic locations. I drove the only "Obama van" in town, and we called it the Dancemobile. Every day, we popped Obama's playlist into the CD player and the college students working with me rocked out in the van at all the stoplights. We got either a thumbs-up or the middle finger, depending on whether the driver in the next lane was a Democrat or a Republican. I loved my work and I met some of my closest friends through it. They had all been raised by hippies, businesspeople, and progressive professors, so they were fascinated by my life story. I read books they recommended, such as *The End of Faith* by Sam Harris, *The God Delusion* by Richard Dawkins, *Letting Go of God* by Julia Sweeney, and *The Lucifer Principle* by Howard Bloom. While I didn't agree with the authors' conclusions, it was another fascinating step in my spiritual journey. Our diametrically opposed backgrounds set the stage for lots of great conversations.

In the fall of 2008 I also enrolled in a community college, later transferring to George Fox University and graduating in 2011 with my bachelor's degree in social and behavioral sciences. It was quite the job, having eight kids at home and being in school full-time, but I was proud to be a real student in real schools. I literally cried my way through my psychology and women's studies classes, realizing how miseducated all my years at IFB schools had left me. There had been yawning gaps in some subjects and outright lies taught in others. My only brush with "feminist history" had been the many diatribes I heard on how those evil working women were destroying the American home. It had never dawned on me that I was sitting in a classroom at Bob Jones University because feminists had risked everything and devoted their lives to fighting for a woman's right to higher education. I knew even less about African American history and music. I made some close friends at college, and one brought me a towering stack of CDs from her collection so I could catch up on all the music trends I had missed. The kindness and warmth of the people I met continually amazed me. How many sermons had I heard in the IFB warning me about the evil and dangerous sinners outside the cult? The truth was, the cruelest, most spiteful people I had met in my life were those *inside* the cult.

I also took my first domestic violence course and read *Why Does He*

Do That? Inside the Minds of Angry and Controlling Men by Lundy Bancroft. It convinced me that every seminary, rabbinical school, and teachers
college should make the subject mandatory and put Bancroft's eye-
opening book on its required reading list.

The criminal justice class I took had an equally profound impact on
me. I became a passionate advocate for the restorative justice model,
which stresses repairing the damage criminal behavior leaves in its wake
and enabling offenders to repair it. Having been raised under a punitive
justice model, I knew firsthand how debilitating that approach is to
the soul. Studying restorative justice convinced me that change is possible but that abusers don't often get proper treatment or face stiff enough
consequences. It also prompted me to start asking tough questions about
the roots of my father's violence and whether the model might be helpful
for a man like him.

When I wasn't crying over all the years I had wasted misinformed
and ignorant, I felt angry—angry at the U.S. Department of Education
for allowing schools like First Bible Baptist Elementary School in Wisconsin, Silver State's K–12, Northland Baptist Bible College (now Northland International University), and BJU to exist without appropriate
accountability. Because I'd had the misfortune to be born into the right-
wing extremist fringe, the government had turned a blind eye to my basic
human rights and catered instead to the extremists who controlled me. I
was a casualty of the shipwreck the religious right had caused, sailing
under the religious persecution banner. Realizing this ignited a passion
in me to push for changes in the laws.

Another Shattering Revelation

I was out with my college friends one night when Joseph called
me. From the tone of his voice, I knew instantly that something was
wrong. "What's the matter?" I asked urgently, worried that one of our children was sick.

His answer left me winded and weak, as if I'd been blindsided by an
invisible punch. Another one of our daughters had just come to him, crying hysterically, and told him that my father had molested her too. I made
a hurried excuse to my friends and rushed home, where Joseph and I
called 911 and filed yet another police report.

The next day we contacted an organization called CARES Northwest that specializes in conducting abuse assessments for victimized children. The group knew about our two daughters who had already come forward and now, hearing about a third little girl, the staff asked us to bring our five oldest children in for forensic interviews. Knowing that we had escaped from a cult, they devoted an entire team of specialists to our family. Our children were interviewed by a mental health specialist, examined by a pediatrician, and forensically interviewed while the police observed from behind a one-way mirror. CARES even brought in the FBI to gather as much information about the cult as possible.

After their in-depth assessment, the staff met with us and assured us that they didn't suspect Joseph or me of child abuse. They knew I had spanked my children in my cult days because I had been convinced it was the only way to save their souls from Hell, though I was always very careful to administer minimal "swats" because I didn't want to be like my father. Joseph, since he was working two jobs to make ends meet and spent long hours away from home, was rarely the one who doled out corporal punishment.

I found a wooden spoon preferable to any other spanking instrument. Somehow it sounded more *Little House on the Prairie* and less sadistic than pipes, rods, or glue sticks. I had heard lots of women I knew—even those who hadn't been raised in the IFB—mention that their mothers had used a spoon to spank them, and that normalized it for me. I always wanted to be as "normal" as possible—though that term seems strange now, realizing there was *nothing* normal about my parenting style in my cult days.

Understanding the warped mind-set that had guided my actions did nothing to console me. Having spanked my children was one of my deepest regrets and I lay awake at night sobbing about my past actions. My remorse intensified now, because I realized that my children had probably been acting out as a cry for help. I had been so heavily indoctrinated to believe they were "in sin" when they showed negative emotions that I had completely missed the warning signs suggesting that they were being molested—signs any mother, especially one who is an abuse victim herself, should have seen. I couldn't think of anything worse.

More horrifying to me was finding out that one of my daughters recalled being spanked by a Northland faculty member and close friend of our family. My daughter cried as she explained how much she had feared him from that day forward. How could he do that to her and not tell us? Neither my husband nor I had ever spanked a child from another family. We couldn't imagine having done so. Then we found out that several baby-sitters from the college had spanked our children too, even using the IFB method of pinching the kids under their arms and between their thighs. Our children remembered every incident as if it had happened yesterday.

How could it be legal to spank children in the state of Wisconsin? Why didn't the government protect me from myself? As the popular saying goes, "When you know better, you do better." Having grown up the way I did, I didn't know better, but I was proud to be a law-abiding citizen. If the government said I wasn't allowed to spank my kids, I wouldn't have done it. You can't hit an *adult* in our country without the potential of being charged with assault and battery. How could our laws allow a two-hundred-pound man to hit a thirty-pound child? I got incensed whenever I read comments online espousing the "terrific results" of corporal punishment and calls to use the rod to rid our country of "spoiled brats." One post read, "I was beat with a belt and there isn't anything wrong with me." It was more than I could handle. How could the writer know? Had he had psychological tests conducted to make sure he hadn't been harmed? Didn't he know about all the scientific evidence proving that hitting children can cause brain damage?

Then I realized that fundamentalists were the ones dominating the debates I was reading and that they were refusing to look at the data. They had been unhappy when women got the right to vote, to work outside the home, and to use birth control. They were never champions of disenfranchised individuals, like women and children in a patriarchal subculture. It made sense that they wouldn't want the government to label brutal forms of "spanking" abuse. When would the government stop catering to them and protect the children?

The specialists at CARES Northwest told us that all three of our daughters had given exceptionally detailed descriptions of their molestation by my father. This led them to believe the girls were telling the truth. The staff assured us they would write detailed reports and send them to Detective Tony O'Neill in Wisconsin.

I felt like we were heading into the ring for Round Four. First, I had discovered that the statute of limitations would make it impossible for me to criminally prosecute my father for abusing me. Second, Melissa had heard the same news about her abuse. Third, our two remarkably courageous daughters had spoken out about their own ordeals, only to be ignored by small-town police.

Once again, Detective O'Neill seemed evasive. After some time passed, He insisted that the reports from CARES Northwest still had never reached him. Then he said he had interviewed my father in July 2008 and Bart was denying everything. "There's not enough evidence to prosecute," he insisted.

A Family Death

Right after Bart was interviewed by the police, my brother Jeremy passed away. During the years I spent at BJU and through many after that, Jeremy endured seven brain surgeries and seven brain shunts. He lingered in a vegetative state for fourteen years because my father seized on a Bible verse that told him to choose life at all costs. He refused to let my brother go even though he was long past hope. None of us could legally intervene. He finally died in 2008.

Jason called Melissa to tell her that neither she nor I was welcome to attend his funeral. He said Bart had reserved several locations, just in case we showed up and they needed to move the service at the last minute. We found out later from friends that my father had an armed guard at the church door, ready to prevent our entering. It was a very sad time for Melissa and me because we still loved Jeremy deeply despite the abuse we had suffered at his hands.

The Lawsuit

Two months after Tony O'Neill interviewed my father in 2008, we received official notification that my father was suing us for libel and slander. We couldn't find anyone in law enforcement willing to help us build a case to protect our children. But the man who had molested my daughters, my sister, and me had no trouble finding a lawyer ready to do battle to protect his "good name." It was too much. I understood right then how unjust our justice system could be for those who have lived through sexual abuse and domestic violence. And it was now obvious the countless warnings we had heard in sermons about avoiding "worldly" actions like lawsuits didn't apply to the church leaders when their empire was threatened.

We soon pinpointed the root of the lawsuit. When our third daughter spoke up, Joseph sent an e-mail to my brother Jason, telling him that another victim had come forward and warning him to keep a close eye on his own children around Bart. It had been well intended but, we now realized, supremely naive. Jason wasted no time forwarding Joseph's e-mail to my father, and he was now using it to claim defamation in court. Colorado happened to have a so-called "long arm statute," which dictated that, if a lawsuit was accepted, the defendant had to travel to Colorado for all legal proceedings.

We were stretched thin already—working three jobs between us, making two monthly house payments, paying off massive loans, trying hard to put food on the table for eight children, and helping them settle into their new surroundings despite obvious emotional trauma for at least three of them. Now my father was coming after us with the full weight of the cult behind him and, no doubt, unlimited funding. I knew he would be as ruthless in maneuvering against us as he had been at Northland. Bart's actions had cost my husband his job that time. What would we lose now? It left us with two options: let him silence us forever, while the cult leaders spread whatever lies they wanted about us and Bart enjoyed free rein to continue his abuse, or fight back to protect our family and all the children who might fall victim to him in the future.

I knew most lawyers would caution a defendant like me to "keep quiet" until the trial, especially when the suit involved defamation, but doing something out of the ordinary was the only way to protect ourselves from a cult. And I had to fight for my freedom of speech. I had been guarded about sharing my history of abuse, always keeping it within a small circle. But now I knew I needed to get the truth out. Over the next two weeks I created a Web site and an audio file describing in detail for the first time what had happened to me at Northland and what the cult had tried to do to our family over the past three years. The night before I put it up on the Internet, Joseph and I lay in bed, petrified of what might happen next.

"Once that goes public, we could all be killed within a very short time," Joseph warned me. "He said this is 'war' and I know he meant it."

"But what other choice do we have?" I asked. "They're going to try to take everything from us. And if the cult members don't hear our side, they'll do and say anything to back him. If Bart has other victims, it is very possible they may come forward as well, knowing they are not alone." We knew the best way to protect our family was to bring as much public awareness and accountability to the situation as possible, so I uploaded the audio to the Internet and braced myself for the fallout. (Later I took the audio file down in the course of the litigation with my father.)

E-mails came flooding to my inbox from victims across the country. Later, it was reported to the court that the audio file had been viewed 32,000 times. I started to understand that I was far from alone; abuse was epidemic in the IFB subculture. That realization prompted me to call the FBI. Agents came to my home to meet with me, and I gave them as much information about the cult as I could, even drawing a large map of IFB connections and perpetrators throughout the country. Over the next few years I stayed in close contact with the FBI and wrote reports to the Department of Homeland Security. My number one goal was—and is— securing government intervention and accountability before the cult is able to do more harm.

After going public, Joseph and I hired one of the best lawyers we could find and tried for five months to get my father's lawsuit dropped. When the judge ruled it would go through, I countersued for sexual assault and battery.

I found out later that the IFB leaders had successfully circulated the story that I had initiated the lawsuit against my father unprovoked so their followers couldn't blame them for involving the legal system. The way they spun it, Bart was simply acting in self-defense.

Meeting the Media

My Web site hadn't been active long when Gary Tuchman, a national correspondent from CNN's *Anderson Cooper 360*, contacted me. He wanted to know everything about the cult, the abuse I had suffered, and my reasons for creating the site. I told him everything I had discovered about the "religious loophole" in the country that enabled untold abuses in private schools, colleges, group homes, and homeschooling families.

His next question surprised me. "Could CNN help expose the abuse you're warning about in your audio file?" he asked.

Gary had done some preliminary research, but the IFB had lots of different names for itself at the time, and he was confused. He'd found information on the Fighting Fundamentalists, Separatists, Militant Fundamentalists, Independent Baptists, Fundamental Baptists, and numerous other groups. Growing up, we all knew these names were synonyms for various branches of the cult, all united under the Doctrine of Separation created by Bob Jones. But Gary explained that it would be impossible to expose them on a national level without a unifying moniker. He suggested I pick one default name to use for clarity and see if it caught on. That's when I started using the term Independent Fundamental Baptists or IFB because it encompassed all of the various factions loyal to Hyles, Gothard, Jones, and other prominent pastors in independent Baptist churches.

That wasn't the only sage advice Gary offered. He also encouraged me to develop a game plan and to set specific goals. So I enlisted help from several IFB cult survivors I knew and we developed five main objectives, which are now posted on my Web site:

1. **COLLEGES/UNIVERSITIES:**
   Mandated accreditation (mandated regional accreditation if not a trade/tech school) of all colleges/universities who want to make the claim that they are giving out professional degrees in liberal arts fields (in order to call the institution a "college" or "university").

2. **PRIVATE SCHOOLS:**
   Mandated school counselors (unbiased and state licensed) for private schools (a person victims could turn to for help). Each private school being required to follow basic curriculum plans that ensure children are getting a thorough education.

3. **STATUTE OF LIMITATIONS:**
Longer statute of limitations for childhood physical/sexual abuse.

4. **GROUP HOMES:**
Mandated licensure of group homes in every state and more government oversight of reform schools.

5. **HOMESCHOOLING:**
More oversight of homeschooling families (at the minimum, required testing in public schools to ensure documentation in the system and to ensure each child is being legitimately educated).

Gary spent many hours with me, finding out everything he could about the cult's beliefs and practices. Over the next few years, whenever news surfaced about the IFB, he would look for a way to weave it into a story for CNN. Meanwhile, I worked around the clock to keep the dialogue going through the cult survivors' forum on my Web site because I knew there were children, women, and even men who needed rescuing from the clutches of the IFB just as my family and I had.

The IFB's Fake "Doctor" Brigade

As the trial date approached for Bart's lawsuit, my father lined up an IFB "dream team" of well-dressed white men who looked more like Fortune 500 CEOs than religious extremists. He put a slew of "doctors" on the witness list against me: "Dr." Matt Olson, "Dr." Steve Pettit, "Dr." Wynne Kimbrough, "Dr." Marty Von, and "Dr." Les Ollila. Having no knowledge of IFB colleges and their unaccredited degrees, the judge would almost certainly fail to realize that not one of those men was a legitimate doctor with valid credentials. In fact, most of them had honorary doctorates just like Joseph's from BJU, handed to them by high-ranking administrators as fast passes into the IFB's old boys' club. IFB college presidents are notorious for giving honorary doctorates to each other, sometimes even to leaders at their own colleges. They're also famous in IFB circles for insisting their students and underlings call them "Dr."

The cult has trotted out ersatz dream teams like Bart's for decades to successfully discredit anyone who threatens it. On the rare occasions when a victim has attempted to confront her abuser in court, a posse of IFB big guns usually shows up in $1,000 suits and ties calling themselves "doctors"—and the judges generally buy into the lie. Women have escaped from the IFB only to lose their homes, their children (during horrific custody battles), their friends, and all their financial resources because the IFB "doctors" disparaged them as attention seekers and pathological liars—all the while protecting their abusers. If a disenfranchised victim of domestic violence is squaring off alone against a crew of powerful IFB godfathers with deep pockets, she has little hope of coming out on the winning end.

What's more, the IFB leaders almost always have access to every person the defector from the cult has ever known—parents, siblings, high school teachers, college roommates, former colleagues, and employers—all of whom are eager to help protect the "cause of Christ" by providing whatever information is needed to discredit the "apostate." It doesn't matter if it's true. It just needs to sound believable.

When I came forward, they planned to attack and discredit me in the same way. They decided that the most plausible story to explain the drastic measures they were taking against our family was to claim that I had faked having a brain tumor. I found out later that they had used the false-medical-claim tactic successfully in the past, giving their "expert opinions" that the victims were mentally or emotionally unstable. If a victim turned over medical records that didn't note the illness she claimed, she could be discredited as a liar. If her claims were proven true, the victim could be painted as mentally or emotionally unstable. It had proven in the past to be a win-win strategy. Nearly every legal motion my father made was about medical fraud—not libel, slander, or false allegations. Not surprisingly, when the judge saw the names of a dozen or so IFB leaders on Bart's witness list—each preceded by the title "doctor"—she assumed these were credentialed professionals ready to invalidate my medical claims, so she ruled that I had to produce all my medical records. I would also be forced to reveal my new address, my place of employment, and my telephone number to the man who had beaten me and threatened my life. It felt like the judge was giving him carte blanche to abuse me again and to endanger my family. It was appalling to see how adept the cult was at foisting its deception onto the public in a court of law. Joseph and I were brand-new to this, but they knew exactly what they were doing.

Bart's years of brutal parenting worked to my advantage in one respect now: He had so drilled the importance of meticulous neatness, organization, and attention to detail into my head that I had kept scrupulous records of all my medical visits. I had no trouble producing documents from doctors at the Mayo Clinic and other respected authorities to support my diagnosis.

Depositions: Evading the Truth

During our deposition, Joseph and I had to answer all sorts of questions unrelated to defamation. How much did we owe on our house? What were our house payments? What other loans and income did we have? On and on it went. Finding out precisely how much money we had would enable the IFB leaders to know how effectively we could fight them and where we were weak.

A short time after releasing the medical records that validated my brain tumor to the court, we received a letter from the state of Wisconsin informing us that our daughters qualified for victims' compensation and were entitled to counseling services. In essence, the state was admitting that it recognized my children as legitimate sexual abuse victims but telling us it was unwilling to take action to prevent other little girls from being victimized.

Around that same time, almost a year after my husband's inquiry, we *finally* received a letter from Marinette County DA Allen Brey stating that there was not enough evidence to prosecute my father for abusing our daughters. The letter went on to say that if more evidence surfaced the DA's office would consider moving forward. How could two separate police departments' assessments and a group as meticulous in its investigation as CARES Northwest not be "enough" evidence to prosecute these crimes? There were *five* alleged victims. How many more did they need? We were livid not only about the news but about how long the DA had taken to inform us, in spite of our repeated inquiries.

In his deposition, Bart denied every claim against him. He said the wooden dowel was only one-eighth-inch thick. He swore he had never removed our clothes and that I was exaggerating the beatings; they were no more than mild spanking sessions.

My brother Jason followed suit, downplaying the childhood abuse we had suffered. He didn't deny the murders of the cats, but he said there were just a few "drops of blood" after only one beating that he could re-member. It was insane! Jason had also hired the top criminal lawyer in Denver, and when our lawyer pressed him about sexually abusing me, he pled the Fifth Amendment. Six months before Bart filed his lawsuit, Jo-seph had written Jason to confront him about kissing and groping me and ejaculating against me in high school. Jason had e-mailed me a let-ter of "apology," which I now believe was an attempt to appease me and keep me quiet. But I wasn't appeased—not when he wrote an affidavit against me a year later, and served as the star witness in my father's lawsuit.

In his letter, Jason said, "Regarding my personal indiscretions, I was inappropriate on several occasions and would not refute the instances you recall. . . . I remember feeling extremely guilty about these. I remember that when these incidents would occur that I would often apologize soon after because the guilt was great. To my knowledge, I have apologized for these actions. I have not endeavored to remember those days, but rather to forget them. If, after looking back twenty years, you feel these apologies were insufficient or you do not recall them, I once again admit to my wrongdoing and ask for your forgiveness."

No, Jason had never apologized before now. He was always the fa-vored child and did exactly what I would expect a man of little character to do. He tried to weasel out of any responsibility. Even though his abuse wasn't as extreme as Jeremy's, his lack of remorse makes it much harder for me to accept what he did.

Witnesses: The Truth Surfaces

Melissa wrote an extensive affidavit that she prepared for the court on my behalf, validating being molested and being severely abused physically in our home, not only by my father but by our brothers. A num-ber of other witnesses came forward to testify against Bart too, validating other forms of emotional and spiritual abuse. We were told that in the previous five years, my father had excommunicated close to forty people from his tiny church in Denver and many were ready to stand up on our behalf. Several childhood friends had e-mailed me to tell me that they too had been beaten by my father with his one-inch-thick wooden dowel when they were kids. A single mom who had been a member of the church he pastored came forward to confirm (and was prepared to testify) that as of 2010 he was still promoting beating children with one-inch-thick wooden dowels in his church. The night before our depositions, this woman received a call from Social Services saying that an anonymous report had just been filed against her for abusing her own children, which was a preposterous claim. We were sure it was an attempt by the IFB leaders to discredit and intimidate us and our witness although we could never prove it. I called Social Services and told them what we were all up against with this cult and, thankfully, no action was ever taken against her.

Bart, incidentally, had filed for a restraining order against this woman and was suing her too for defending me to his church members. Ours was actually one of three lawsuits Bart had initiated almost simultaneously. The third was on behalf of his church against a woman who had sold property to his congregation. My father had found a new power toy called the legal system, which he could use to punish people who wouldn't submit to his wishes.

As we prepared for trial, we desperately wanted the CARES Northwest report about our daughters' claims of sexual abuse to be submitted as evidence to the court. In it, the CARES evaluators asserted that, in their professional opinion, our daughters' claims were credible even though there was no DNA evidence. Unfortunately, CARES prohibited us from releasing a copy unless the judge ordered it—and then, only per request from Bart's attorney. Of course Bart declined to do so and the report could not be used.

My Father Gives Himself Away

In preparing for trial, we obtained a stack of CDs of Bart's sermons from the previous few years, several of which we submitted as evidence against him. Bart made a motion for the judge to rule them inadmissible, but his motion was denied. Among his quotations from 2005 and 2006, we found the following:

"Do you understand what sickness [sexual molestation] is out there today? And it— Listen folks, it's walking right around you. You think it's over there in Florida. I'm going to tell you something. It's right outside the door of this church. Let me tell you something scarier, it's in the church. It's in here. You say, who you talking about, pastor? I ain't telling."

"You spank your child and you put a bruise on them and I'll show you just how much power you have. I'm going to tell you something, the state is taking away your power a long time ago [sic] and I'm going to tell you, in the church we better get back on track! I told you before, you spank your child and I'll go stand alongside of you in prison. . . . Our kids don't need to be registered as sex offenders, they need to be whupped!"

"Finally I told my son in-law [in April of 2006], well, I don't care if you want me to come up there [to North-land] or not, I'm coming anyway. . . . Now you know me, when I'm coming, I'm coming [laughter from con-gregation]. And I got a phone call from a Deputy Lin-coln the next day saying, 'Don't come up here. There's a restraining order against you.' And I said, 'When is it in effect?' And he said, 'Well, it gets served out of Mari-nette County and it will be served in Denver. And when you sign for it, at that instant it becomes effec-tive.' Well, I hadn't signed anything yet [laughter from congregation]. You know, I don't like trouble—I like to avoid trouble [louder laughter from congregation], so I went. And uh, when I got up there, uh, they were very dismayed that I was there. But I had tried to get them to go to the faculty and talk to them. They refused and refused and refused. So finally, I just said, 'I'm going to the faculty' and there was the rub. . . . And I have the power to destroy them. I really do."

In these public sermons, not only was Bart admitting that he had intentionally tried to dodge the restraining order and forced my husband to defend himself in a public confrontation, but he was also publicly advocating beating children. What's more, he was acknowledging the existence of sexual abusers in his own church, whose identity he was unwilling to disclose. Our attorney was elated.

The week of the trial in April 2010, my husband and I flew to Denver, booked a hotel room and rental car, and met for an entire day with our attorney to prepare. Bart had listed "Dr." Matt Olson and "Dr." Les Ollila on his "will call" list, which our attorney said meant that he was asserting to the judge that they had agreed to testify at the trial. "Dr." Marty Von was also on Bart's "may call" list, so Northland's top three administrators appeared to be lined up against me. Our attorney called all three men repeatedly to confirm whether or not they would be testifying, but they refused to answer. Either way, Bart would be able to use them as leverage to pressure us to sign a statement of silence. If the case ended in a settlement, this strategy would enable the IFB leaders to tell their own people that Bart had written their names down without their knowledge, so they had not actually participated in any "unbiblical lawsuit." It was the perfect plan.

The Abuse of the Legal System

The day before we were set to go to trial, my father dropped his claims against my husband and me. We had to make a spur-of-the-moment decision whether to move forward with my counterclaims. Ultimately, we decided the costs and the risks were too great, after our attorney explained that the judge would likely rule much of the evidence we hoped to bring out inadmissible because my father's claims of slander and libel against me had been withdrawn. We could end up having to pay another $20,000 in legal fees without achieving our goal of fully exposing and prosecuting Bart. Ultimately, I refused my father's request that I sign a statement saying I would never speak about the allegations again and my counterclaims (of sexual assault and battery) were dismissed pursuant to a confidential settlement agreement. All told, the process had stretched out over twenty months and many sleepless nights, and our legal fees cost us more than $50,000. In that time, I gained fifty pounds from all the stress and felt as if I had lost a part of myself. Joseph and I had both experienced extended and profound mental trauma all over again. The end result? Bart was free to keep pastoring. I had to hope the truth would come out eventually.

Had my father and his IFB cronies succeeded in proving that I was exhibiting attention-seeking behavior and had faked a brain tumor, they would have argued that it made me an unfit mother, and I believe they would have filed motions to take our children from us. Even though the IFB didn't believe in most mental illnesses, its members had no moral problem using the concept as a legal argument to get what they wanted. If the judge had believed their side of the story, my children might have been ripped out of my arms and thrown into those of their abuser. On his initial list of witnesses to the court, Bart had even included the names of Northland administrator Wynne Kimbrough, the man who taught us to use glue sticks on our young children in the classroom at Northland, and his wife, Vicky, and claimed that they could provide testimony that there were criminal records on file in Wisconsin showing that we had neglected our children. The claim about criminal records was patently false. The hypocrisy was astounding, not to mention the fact that the claims were patently untrue. It was simply another veiled threat from Bart that he would try to wrest our children from us. The Northland faculty member who had spanked one of our daughters without our knowledge was also listed as a witness against us. And "Dr." Marty Von, who had heard firsthand from my brother that he had molested me, was also on the list. We never learned what these witnesses would actually have testified, but it was evident that their role would be to in some fashion support my father's efforts to deny his history of abuse and to attempt to place the blame for our family's problems on me.

One of the most heartbreaking examples of the cult's collective attacks against abuse victims is the case of Zach Scadden, which coincided with my own legal battle against the IFB power brokers. Scadden was a young teenager who had grown up in my father's church in Brighton, but attended Silver State Baptist High School, my alma mater. When he and another minor came forward to accuse principal Daniel Brock, a graduate of BJU, of sexual abuse, the IFB members in Colorado closed ranks against the boys. Prosecutor Dave Lynn knew my sister Melissa had fled the IFB and called her to Colorado for a forensic interview to get a better handle on the school Scadden had attended as well as the man who had pastored him, my father. Lynn was astonished at the size and intricacy of the IFB network Melissa and other IFB members described during their interviews, which connected Christian colleges all across the country. In the center of it all was Bob Jones University.

During the trial, the courtroom was packed with Brock's defenders, almost all of whom were in suits and ties and Sunday best dresses. Scadden, on the other hand, left after testifying with only his fiancée's family to offer moral support. Even his own relatives turned against him. Perhaps not surprisingly, Brock was acquitted. A few weeks later, Scadden woke up to find the word "Bitch" scrawled on the side of his car. Later that night he committed suicide.

Unsatisfied, the media obtained court documents after the trial, and the local CBS station reported revealing that prosecutors had seized Brock's school-issued laptop. According to those reports a forensic search uncovered viewed images, movies, videos, and Internet searches of homosexual male pornographic Web sites, all conducted from Brock's user accounts during the time he had the IFB schools computer. The judge had squashed this information at trial, so the jury never heard it.

After Scadden's death, thousands of survivors had contacted me privately to talk about my audio file and to confess that they had endured similar abuse. But they were all petrified to go public because they didn't want to end up like Zach Scadden. I had to find a way to get our stories out to the world. It was the only way to shatter the culture of fear and set the stage for positive change in a system that allowed every one of us to be victimized.

Our entire family: Sandy, Melissa, and Jocelyn, (front row, left to right); Bart and Meagan (second row); and Jason and Jeremy (third row, left to right).

(All photos courtesy of the author)

Since I wasn't allowed to graduate, my parents took me to dinner the night of graduation. I wore this white dress the following Sunday when I stood to apologize for my "immorality."

Jeremy gave me a teddy
bear as a gift in an attempt
to make me feel better
for not being allowed to
graduate.

Joseph getting his master's
at Bob Jones University.

All my kids dressed up for church, right after I was diagnosed with a brain tumor in 2004.

Me as a college student at Northland Baptist Bible College (far left).

Me and Selah—on my twenty-second birthday.

Me in my cheerleading uniform.

Joseph Sr. and I, with all the men on the deacon board and church staff, at his ordination.

Baby Dedication at church—Josiah is being dedicated, along with David Harper (Matt and Melanie Harper are at the far right).

Melissa, me, and Meagan — taken before Melissa officially fled the cult.

All the kids visiting me at the hospital after Jessica's birth.

Our new home, what I deem the "Duggar House."

Faculty and staff wives from Northland Baptist Bible College at our home for a "thirtysomething dinner."

The new plaque for my kitchen sink and stove, "Embrace the work!"

Joseph at the Bob Jones University snack shop—while on staff and getting his master's.

15

THE SURVIVORS' NETWORK

*So you want to know where a man stands with God?
You have only to ask him one question: What do you
think of this university [BJU]?*

—*"Dr." Bob Jones Sr.*

I knew abuse was epidemic in the IFB. But members had been brainwashed to believe that the Bible compelled them to be "forgiving." How could I get through to people that speaking out was the right thing to do? IFB leaders are only afraid of two things: publicity and the police exposing their misdeeds with respect to sex and money. Otherwise, they are more than able to control their followers through political spin. I knew pedophilia and its cover-up was rampant in the IFB, so I started inviting my fellow survivors to share their stories through Facebook, hoping that an online dialogue would be a relatively nonthreatening forum for discussion.

A mentor of mine who was experienced in working with cults advised me that to get IFB survivors and members talking, I would have to speak the language of the cult. She said that social workers assisting in polygamist compounds were trained to use the more formal speech and expressions children of plural marriage were accustomed to hearing to help build trust and convince the children to open up to them.

"What is the IFB language like?" she asked me.

"They pride themselves on being like warriors," I told her. "They call themselves 'militant fundamentalists' and, boy, do they love to fight.

They are trained to 'do battle royal for the truth.' We were told we were soldiers in God's army and we needed to be willing to take up arms to protect our religious practices. The preachers always screamed and were know-it-alls."

"Then get out there on those blogs and start fighting," she advised. "Use capital letters. Your voice has to be louder than the cult leaders' voices or they won't listen to you."

So every day, Melissa and I, along with a few other survivors, would talk among ourselves on Facebook, about the abuses in the IFB. Neva Anasovich started a group called Independent Fundamental Baptist Survivors, but since she wanted to stay out of the center of things, she asked me to take it and run with it. I asked her if we could add the word "cult" to the title to make it more accurate and she liked the idea. That day it became Independent Fundamental Baptist *Cult* Survivors, and when the name hit Facebook the IFB threw a fit. We whittled the group *down* from eighty survivors to thirty-five. Not a stellar beginning. I started receiving outraged e-mails. "How dare you call us a cult? Mormons are a cult. Jehovah's Witnesses are a cult. We believe the word of God. You are an apostate, leading people to Hell!" A few survivors had left the IFB in the 1960s and 1970s and they didn't understand how the group had evolved over time to become increasingly abusive, so they struggled with the term. They contested the use of the word "cult" and downplayed the IFB by referring to it as "cult-like" instead. Somehow that made them feel better. Finally, we posted a Cult Quiz we found on the Internet and that put it all in perspective. If those who took the quiz said "yes" to three or more questions, the answer key warned that they could be in a dangerous group (i.e., a cult). Our survivors were saying "yes" to almost all forty questions on the quiz.

We also continued our education about the sociological definition of a cult. I started to share everything I was learning in my college courses about mental illness, brainwashing, hierarchical organizations, and more through the group. The advice of my mentor was working like a charm and we became more persistent, peppering our dialogue with capital letters— the online equivalent of shouting. We also continually used the words "evil" and "good" to define behavior, since that was IFB members' only paradigm.

We talked about two movies that fit our "cult" world: *The Village* and *Population 436*. Bobby Wood Jr., son of the former vice president of BJU, had told us in whispered tones about *The Village* in 2005 when Joseph was on the faculty with him at Northland. He said it accurately depicted what life was like growing up at BJU in so many ways, and we found this to be true for thousands of survivors who had grown up in other IFB ministries.

Traffic was slow for the first few months, but my theory was, "If we keep talking, they will come." Eventually, our numbers grew. We had our share of saboteurs, posing as cult survivors but claiming they still felt speaking out on accreditation fraud and sexual abuse cover-ups was "un-Christlike." It threw our legitimate members off balance because they read the posts and started to doubt themselves. "It is unbiblical to appeal to a lost and godless world and secular authorities to rectify conflicts among believers in Jesus," the faux survivors said. They argued, "We should bring the details of these grievances to the IFB leaders so they can investigate and determine the validity of our claims. And even if a genuine victim did not get justice in this life, he or she should leave it in the hands of God. After all, airing these complaints on the Internet is hurting the reputation of the church and the alleged abusers' innocent family members. It is much better to keep everything in-house." Fortunately, I could sniff out the phonies fast and block them. They always slipped in bits of cult lingo, calling us "bitter" and chastising us for not going about our healing in "the right way."

When a victim finally started opening up, dissenters would condemn any foul language they used as a "sin" and that would often shut them up. But, because I had gone through counseling, I understood the importance of the Seven Stages of Grief codified by pioneering psychiatrist Elisabeth Kübler-Ross. I knew that anger was a fundamental part of the grieving process and that there was no timeline for grief—we all go through trauma differently. So I encouraged the survivors to "rant away." After all, if anyone deserves a "Fuck you!" it's a bunch of child abusers. I didn't care what their titles were: pastor, college president, or Bible professor. If they abused children, they deserved no respect from us. Besides, I wanted our group to be a safe haven for survivors, a place where they never had to stifle their negative emotions. I was determined not to put them in a refurbished IFB box, as the others were trying to do. Our group was going to be a safe place for all victims, at any stage in their journey, to heal—they were our priority. Anybody who didn't like it didn't have to participate in the discussion.

When we stanched that flow of negativity, our detractors took a new tack. They launched attacks against us by creating their own blogs and YouTube videos casting doubt on our credibility. They called me everything from "mentally ill" to "Jezebel." The hardest accusation to hear was that I was being "too harsh" and "not loving enough" when dealing with abusers. I spent a lot of time grappling with this before I finally realized that a person's maturity level is often unrelated to his chronological age and that we need to treat people in a manner appropriate to their maturity level. For instance, we can't sit back and allow a playground bully to kick little girls in the stomach. Recess monitors need to say, "No! That is not acceptable behavior!" The monitors can't walk over to the little guy and gently, slowly, and kindly remove him from the situation. They need to rush in and grab him before he kicks the next little girl so hard that she falls and ends up with a concussion. The same is true when dealing with the IFB. They are schoolyard bullies, running wild and metaphorically kicking the littlest and most vulnerable kids on the playground. They are not spiritually evolved enough to understand gentle, loving language. They need to be told, "No! You cannot act that way!" When we don't do so, they end up running roughshod over everyone. Emotionally battered wives, gay and lesbian teenagers tormented by cruel rhetoric, even young children beaten with wooden rods end up losing their lives or killing themselves as a result.

The IFB leaders might be fifty-five-year-old men in their chronological age, but their spiritual maturity—what I deem their "grace age"—is much younger. Once I explained this, those accusations stopped. It was another lesson to me in the language barrier between our progressive culture and a cult.

Despite the relentless assault, we held our ground. We kept talking and we kept telling the truth. Eventually hundreds, then thousands of victims started speaking up about the abuse they had suffered at the hands of IFB leaders and ministries. One of the greatest accusations against us by the cult was that we were "broad brushing" all the IFB churches, but with an estimated eight to ten thousand survivors speaking out on the Internet, telling the same stories from their experiences within IFB churches from all over the country, we finally put that accusation to rest. Dozens of public and private Facebook groups and blogs are now highlighting their abuses. That was precisely what the mob bosses feared: We could prove the entire cult was rife with sexual abuse cover-ups and we had a mountain of evidence to back up our assertions. To my knowledge there is no religious cult anywhere with more people speaking out through social media about their physical, emotional, sexual, and spiritual abuse than the former members of the IFB.

16

TAKING THE CAUSE NATIONWIDE

Fully forgiving offenders brings genuine joy.
—"Dr." Bill Gothard

Two months before the aborted trial with my father, a former member of Trinity Baptist Church in Concord, New Hampshire, shared a story on our Facebook cult survivor site about a fifteen-year-old girl who had been raped and then ushered out of the state in an effort to protect the rapist from prosecution. Whenever a new case surfaced on our groups, I contacted the cult survivor who posted the story and asked if he or she would be willing to get in touch with the police along with me. In this case, the person's name was Matt Barnhart, and he agreed.

The next day, we both called Detective Chris DeAngelis of the Concord Police Department and the investigation began. As the situation unfolded, it revealed one of the most horrendous clergy sex abuse cover-ups I had ever seen. Tina Anderson would later write police statements claiming that in 1997 she had been raped repeatedly by Ernie Willis, a thirty-eight-year-old married father in her IFB church. At the time, she was a babysitter for the Willises, whose oldest children were close to her age.

Tina sought help from her IFB pastor, Chuck Phelps, but instead of offering it, he forced her to stand up in front of the entire IFB congregation and apologize for her immorality, just as I had done my senior year at Silver State. Tina said that she was forbidden from mentioning the word "rape" in her public apology; Phelps even told her that a woman in her situation would have been stoned to death in Old Testament times because she hadn't immediately told anyone what had happened; according to Tina's testimony, Phelps's wife had gone so far as to ask her if she "enjoyed it," a common IFB technique meant to inspire guilt in the victim. Naturally, Tina answered, "No!" but the mere suggestion of pleasure when discussing a rape can sometimes plant seeds of doubt and confusion in a victim's mind. Normally, it works like a charm when an abuser wants to intimidate a victim.

By the time she "confessed" publicly, Tina knew she was pregnant, and Phelps orchestrated her transfer to Westminster, Colorado, where Pastor Matt Olson of Tri-City Baptist Church arranged for her to live in the home of his head deacon. While rapist Ernie Willis went untouched, protected by the IFB community, Tina was forced to give her baby up for adoption within the cult and was homeschooled by IFB members in Colorado for the next few years. Matt Olson, you may remember, was the same man who, almost a decade later, would scream at me and Joseph in my last meeting at Northland—and accuse me of lying about my history of sexual abuse. Small world. No wonder Olson didn't believe me, I thought.

Six weeks after our initial call to the police to report the crime, Tina Anderson contacted me through Facebook to ask if I could help her. Because my role was to be an advocate for victims' rights, I never tried to contact victims. I knew how deeply wounded they were, and the last thing I wanted was to cause additional harm by making them think their story was being circulated throughout the country. I always waited for them to seek me out.

When I saw Tina's message, I was so consumed with emotion that I collapsed on my bedroom floor, crying just as I had done in the dark days before leaving the cult. But these were tears of hope, not grief. The crimes against Tina had happened recently enough that, unlike me, she couldn't be thwarted by a statue of limitations. And unlike my poor daughters, who lacked DNA evidence to corroborate their stories, Tina had living, breathing proof of her rape in the form of a child, who was now twelve years old. If Tina was willing to tell her story, we might be able to prosecute the man responsible.

When Tina and I talked on the phone for the first time we felt an instant bond, having endured such similar journeys of sexual abuse, trauma, shame, and victimization. She still thought the rape was her fault, so she was carrying a heavy burden of false guilt. I had done some baby-sitting during our years at Northland and, in a strange twist, I realized that her baby was one of the children I had cared for, because the adoptive parents were on staff at the college. The adoptive mother and I had become friendly, and I was able to reassure Tina that her child was well taken care of. I was able to give her details that even she didn't know about her baby, because the child had been a playmate of my own children when we were at the college.

When Trent Spiner at the *Concord Monitor* broke the Tina Anderson story in New Hampshire, it hit the networks fast and furious. Tina had no desire to be in the media spotlight, so she asked me to be her family spokesperson. Dozens of programs contacted me asking for interviews with her. She finally said yes to *The Early Show* at CBS. There, she spoke for the first time about the systematic brainwashing she had gotten from her IFB pastors, both graduates of Bob Jones University.

We flew to New York together, where my sister Melissa met us. CBS had me check in under the fictitious name Millie Dillmount as a safeguard against competing networks finding us and scooping them. My sister and Tina had a ball chiding me about my alias. It seemed trite in light of what we were all going through, but it relieved the tension. Though Tina was shaking and deathly afraid to speak, she mustered her courage and described her abuse in detail, knowing her story might help other women and children still trapped in the cult. The second the cameras stopped rolling, she sprinted back to me, threw her arms around my neck, and broke into sobs. It was a moment I'll never forget. I felt like I was comforting my own sister. Everyone on the set stopped and stared. A few welled up themselves and praised Tina for her bravery.

We had just gotten back to our hotel when a representative from *20/20* called and asked to meet us. Tina had seen a few episodes of the program and knew it had integrity, so the next morning we met with senior producer Lisa Soloway and her assistant. Lisa was convinced there was a bigger story to tell and she wanted to get other stories of IFB abuse into the spotlight. She and her colleagues were willing to spend nearly a year investigating the cult with the goal of airing an in-depth report that would expose the abuses it was perpetrating. Lisa said they were planning to put one of their best producers on the story. Soon after, we met *20/20* producer Alan B. Goldberg and his assistant Sean Dooley. Tina and I treated them all to a rendition of Patch the Pirate's "I Want to Marry Daddy When I Grow Up" to give them a window into the mind-set of the cult. It was fascinating to watch their repulsed expressions when they heard those lyrics. Clearly, I wasn't the only one who found the song creepy.

Alan called after we returned home and asked if I would grant him an interview for the documentary. I told him that I had already told Lisa Soloway I would do the background work, but I didn't want to be interviewed on the program. The lawsuit had just ended, and I didn't feel I could face another onslaught. But Alan persisted and said the story wouldn't be as effective without the details an insider like me could provide. "My family's safety is my primary concern," I explained, but Alan assured me that he would do his best to keep us safe. I finally agreed and that fall Tina and I flew back to New York together for interviews with anchor Elizabeth Vargas. I also contacted Rachel Griffiths, another IFB abuse victim, and she bravely agreed to be interviewed for the progras as well.

About six weeks later, Oprah's producer got wind of our efforts and called me to ask if we'd be willing to give her an exclusive. I was within inches of realizing my longtime dream of meeting my TV heroine, but we had already committed to *20/20*. The *20/20* team had put countless hours into researching the IFB with us, we had a great rapport with them, and we respected their work ethic and their high standards tremendously. In the end we had to decline. I was sad, but I knew we were doing the right thing.

As soon as the *20/20* program aired, cult members pounced on us, accusing Tina and me of speaking out "for money." The truth is, neither Tina nor I have ever received a dime for any of our interviews in the national media. We were both loath to step into the spotlight, but someone had to speak out to help the children still trapped in the nightmare we had escaped. We knew that without help from the national media, the IFB's abuses would never be exposed and the laws would never change.

Every day, Tina and I would talk on the phone and encourage each other to ignore the relentlessly vicious accusations against us. "We are doing this for the children," I reminded her—and myself—countless times. We couldn't give up even if the odds seemed insurmountable.

Over the next year Alan, Sean, and I collaborated on the project and they started collecting footage. We worked through reams of documents about the IFB. I spent countless hours compiling pages of research from government organizations, Web sites dedicated to church history, books, academic articles, blogs, Facebook pages, survivor groups, and other sources for *20/20*, doing my part to help them lift the cult's veil of secrecy. I did all I could to help the producers understand the indoctrination, the cover-ups, and the countless links back to Bob Jones University. The producers quickly grasped how dangerous this religious group was for women and children and became emotionally invested in the cause, working tirelessly with us to expose the truth.

Brian Fuller, who had been a student at BJU with Joseph and was now senior pastor of Tina's old IFB church—Trinity Baptist in Concord, New Hampshire—was the only IFB pastor who would agree to grant Alan B. Goldberg and Elizabeth Vargas an interview. When he met with the *20/20* team, one of the first things Fuller said to Alan was, "I always liked Joseph Zichterman, but are you aware that there's a nationwide rumor that his wife, Jocelyn, faked a brain tumor?"

Even after the court had vetted all my medical records, the cult was still on a smear campaign against me. I had already told *20/20* about the allegations and released my medical records to them, but I shouldn't have been surprised. We later heard through friends that board members from BJU had flown to New Hampshire to help Fuller prepare for his interview.

In the months before *20/20*'s investigation aired, the IFB tried repeatedly to sabotage the program. Somehow they persuaded Facebook to shut down our cult-survivor site, which was the key to our networking against the powerful IFB leaders. We got nowhere contacting Facebook, so I called a few of my contacts in the media and before we knew it, the site was back online.

Cult members even harassed Joseph's new employers, making anonymous calls and pressuring them to intervene. One caller threatened that if the university administration wouldn't force me to stop speaking out against the IFB, he would contact its donors and persuade them to stop giving to the school. Fortunately, the university refused to get involved, which flummoxed the IFB. This was a ridiculous request because I wasn't even an employee of the school. The IFB wasn't used to dealing with people who followed the law.

"Shattered Faith" aired on ABC's *20/20* on April 8, 2011, and I consider it a masterpiece. Alan and his producer team (Gayle Deutsch and Sean Dooley) managed to take a mammoth cult, with organizations and churches that spanned the country, and create a documentary that gave the public a concise, yet comprehensive birds'-eye view of its many factions, all in a forty-seven-minute time frame. I was amazed. Our hard work had paid off.

IFB pastor Brian Fuller deftly skirted the issues in his televised interview, though he made a blunder when Elizabeth Vargas asked him whether the "independent" Fundamental Baptist churches were all tightly interconnected.

"You do move from church to church," Elizabeth said in the interview. "To say that you're all islands is a little disingenuous, isn't it?"

"No, I don't think it's disingenuous at all," Fuller replied. "This isn't a network and it just happens you get educated at places that hold many of the same principles that you're going to use in ministry."

This ludicrous statement sent survivors into a frenzy. One of them created a diagram, showing all the connections within IFB churches and all pointing back to Bob Jones University and its "preacher boys." IFB survivors affectionately called it the "notwork" after Brian Fuller's absurd claims.

The genius of the Bob Jones empire was that the system gave the university control without accountability. IFB leaders claimed every church was independent, and technically that was true, so if someone did something wrong, no one could legally connect the university to it. But every insider knew BJU was the linchpin and that its word was law all over the cult, for all intents and purposes.

I realized the only way to illustrate the interconnectivity of IFB churches and, by extension, to expose the cults web of power would be to collect a mountain of evidence. We would need thousands more stories from survivors like Tina and me.

Within twenty-four hours of "Shattered Faith" airing, I received more than twelve thousand e-mails and posts filled with stories of abuse on our IFB Cult Survivors' Facebook group. People came out of the woodwork to talk about abuse they had suffered growing up in the cult. The *20/20* episode included part of my own story and a rumor soon reached me that Jason had stood up in church the following Sunday and publicly admitted molesting me. He never contacted me about it, though, so the story might be apocryphal.

Not everyone was as pleased with ABC as I was. "Shattered Faith" so infuriated Indiana megachurch pastor "Dr." Jack Schaap that he delivered a public rant against *20/20* after the program aired, using it as an excuse to condemn womankind:

> "ABC News called me this week and said, we heard that you believe that men should be in charge of their wives. I says [sic], no sir, no sir, I didn't say that. I said God said that. He said, husbands are the head of the wife. . . . Don't you ever worry about your pastor being rattled, or worried or unsettled or unnerved. I sleep fine. . . . Somebody asked me the other day, this reporter said, I heard you said it would be a cold day in Hell before you get your theology from a woman. He said, don't you kinda think that's demeaning to the genders [sic]. I said, ask Adam what he thought about getting his theology from a woman. I said it damned the whole world. I said the reason your sorry soul is going to Hell is because a woman told Adam what God thinks about things."

At the end of May 2011, Tina headed bravely into her trial against the man who had raped her. Prosecutor Wayne Coull led the jury through the cult network brilliantly and illustrated the incredible abuse Tina had suffered at the hands of the IFB. As expected, Chuck Phelps, former pastor of Trinity Baptist church and BJU graduate, countered as a witness, trying to paint Tina as a liar whose credibility could not be trusted. Numerous cult members showed up in their suits and ties and Sunday dresses, just like always, to back Phelps.

Expecting no less, I had implored our Facebook group members to attend the trial too—to support Tina. Almost thirty of them came in from all over the country, to lend her moral support for the week, which buoyed her spirits enormously. Emotions ran high in the courtroom and several of Tina's supporters left to weep in private when the case triggered flashbacks of their own abuse—along with painful reminders that their own abusers had never been brought to justice.

Tina soldiered through and fielded every question the defense team hurled at her. Their goal was to get Willis off on the forcible rape part of the charges, suggesting that a fifteen-year-old virgin was capable of seducing a thirty-eight-year-old married man. It was appalling, but it was typical IFB Eve-the-temptress thinking, even though Tina had never even been allowed to hold a boy's hand at the time of her rape. She had been much like I was at fifteen, in her ankle-length floral dresses, bobby socks, and tennis shoes, completely naive about sexual relationships. Now she was fighting back on behalf of all the survivors who had ever been blamed for participating in their own abuse. We desperately needed a victory to give countless other victims courage.

The jury came back on May 27, 2011, with a guilty verdict on every count against Ernie Willis. We were exhausted but elated. At long last, a group of IFB survivors had banded together and proved to the cult leaders that they did not have absolute power. The truth could come out no matter how hard they tried to suppress it.

Shortly after the trial, the news spread about Tina's successful prosecution of her abuser and another round of vicious attacks hit the Internet. Tina had won her case, so they left her alone. This time, Melissa and I were in the crosshairs. Our enemies knew we were the ringleaders, the driving force behind survivors' newfound resolve to fight back, and they redoubled their efforts to destroy our credibility. IFB insiders created bogus profiles and sent out messages saying I was "mentally ill" and "unstable."

Three dear friends, Laurie Moody, Hannah Matteson, and Vyckie Garrison stepped up to defend me, but that just brought the cult's wrath down on them. The attacks were relentless, cruel, and exhausting for all of us. Laurie has a held a position in politics for over a decade, and she said it was worse than any attack she had seen on her GOP boss in all the years she's worked on his campaign. I finally took a six-week break and went back to therapy.

It took some intense soul searching, but ultimately I decided other people's opinions of me no longer mattered. I was proud of the work I had done, proud that I had taken a stand. I was going to *own* my role in the exposure the cult was getting, regardless of how many ugly slurs and threats came my way. For a people pleaser like me, who had spent a lifetime trying to be liked, it was a major turning point.

CNN's Ungodly Discipline

By August 2011, Gary Tuchman was ready to start working on a series for CNN's *Anderson Cooper 360* titled "Ungodly Discipline." Gary did a phenomenal job exposing physical abuse in the IFB, combining his own exhaustive research with insights he had gained from our conversations over the past four years. He put Michael Pearl's spare-not-the-rod childrearing philosophy on display and highlighted the beating deaths of Lydia Schatz and Hana Grace-Rose Williams. Survivors of the brutal approach to discipline that killed Lydia and Hana stepped forward to talk about their abuse in IFB Christian schools, colleges, churches, group homes, and in homeschooling families. Two brothers, Doug and Scott Bicknell, bravely described the abuse they endured. I flew to Wisconsin to meet them and felt the same close rapport I had shared with Tina; I now refer to them as my "brothers."

Doug Bicknell reported being beaten so severely at Calvary Baptist School in Wisconsin that he has suffered lasting physical and emotional problems. In one spanking session, during which school principal Marvin Munyon, now a political lobbyist for private schools with an office in the capitol building in Madison, hit Doug fifty-three times using a wooden paddle with holes drilled in it. Munyon has made it his mission to keep spanking legal in private schools in Wisconsin. He's one of many IFB men to insinuate himself into a government position in order to preserve laws that protect child abusers from accountability. Doug's mother, Nancy Bicknell, by contrast, has become an advocate for survivors and has done a remarkable job exposing abuse in the IFB.

Gary and I finally met in person in Seattle and went to dinner, along with his producers, at the Seattle Space Needle. It felt like I was meeting an old friend. There are no words to express how grateful I have been for his efforts in getting the IFB exposed. Without his encouragement and support from the beginning, we would have never seen thousands of survivors speaking out on the Internet, finding freedom from decades of abuse.

Moving Forward

On April 8 2011, *20/20* highlighted the arrest of pastor Phil Caminiti and twelve other church members in Wisconsin featured in the documentary "Shattered Faith." I had flown out to Wisconsin that summer and given law enforcement all the information I could on IFB ideology. They were stunned by the prolific abuse within the group. The professionals working with the families in this case did a tremendous job documenting every detail of the systematic brainwashing—in an attempt to help future cases. Then finally, in the summer of 2012 another significant milestone when Pastor Caminiti was found guilty on eight counts of conspiracy to commit child abuse and sentenced to two years in prison for encouraging his congregation members to use the rod on children as young as infants in his sermons. It was a precedent-setting case—the first time a pastor had been convicted for simply telling church members to abuse their kids rather than committing the act himself. The judge said she was using him as an example to send a message to other pastors that the U.S. legal system would not tolerate advocating child abuse. According to the criminal complaint filed against him and the prosecutor's evidence in the trial, Caminiti encouraged his flock to spank two-month-old children for crying. This strikes me as particularly tragic, given the fact that crying is an infant's primary means of communicating. Babies cry when they're hungry, hot, cold, wet, frightened, or have some other urgent need—not because they're selfish or spoiled.

Full Circle

Another big assault to the IFB structure came when two survivors contacted me to tell me that megachurch pastor "Dr." Jack Schaap of First Baptist Church in Hammond, Indiana, was being accused of having a physical relationship with an underage girl. He had been exposed for misogyny on *20/20* and his tirade after the program convinced many survivors that something was seriously wrong with the man. The survivors who contacted me said the rumor was circulating among church members that he was on "sick leave," but was really in hiding. Upon hearing that, I was sure the church had contacted the police about the incident, since the IFB exposure was so widespread now. But just to be sure, on July 30, 2012, I called the police department and the FBI and spoke to Agent Matthew Chicantek. I was shocked to find out that neither had a report on file about Schaap. Once again, we were facing a scandal on the scale of Tina's. The next morning the police and FBI launched an investigation at the church. To my surprise, men on the church staff told the media that they had known about the relationship for a week, even holding picture evidence against Schaap. Based on all I knew about the IFB's protocol for protecting abusers, I wondered if the girl had been harassed during that long delay. Had Jack told her to keep quiet, having already been confronted by the church? Had church members been told by Jack to keep mum too? Had they been told that their jobs would be in jeopardy if they spoke up about what they knew? Had any evidence been destroyed? If not, why hadn't anybody called the police to report the crime? "Dr." Jack Schaap has now plead guilty to having a sexual relationship with a minor, as well as crossing state lines for the intent of sexual conduct with a minor. As of the time of this writing, he is awaiting sentencing.

What pushed me over the edge emotionally was hearing that David Gibbs from the Christian Law Association had flown to the church and announced that he was doing an "internal investigation." IFB leaders are notorious for claiming they will do their own internal investigations, even though they have no law-enforcement training. He encouraged all the cult members to go to him if they had any information about abuse in the church. I was appalled. David Gibbs has frequently defended IFB churches accused of cover-ups, and he is a master of PR spin. But this was a bold move even for him. Insiders reacted with the same outrage and started sending tips my way, including one about four men in law enforcement who were allegedly either members of Schaap's church or had direct connections to him, information that I quickly passed on to the FBI. Just about every IFB college has been known to have graduates in their local police departments, so they have someone to call when they need a favor.

Social media and law enforcement working together is a relatively new experience for both and it brings its own positives and negatives. On one hand, civilians who understand the cult culture can rally more people to speak out than what would happen normally—as we put their fears about the "evil" law enforcement to rest. On the other hand, using social media enables anyone (even from within the cult) to step up and claim those who are trying to help law enforcement are lying or doing something "wrong" or "unethical." We had our fair share of controversy as we worked to get victims to come forward, but we pressed on and made significant headway in the two weeks following the start of the investigation and, as I write this book, the case is well under way.

Life as a Whistleblower

The IFB never stops its campaign to silence me. In recent months, BJU graduate Jon Ensminger, one of my husband's former deans at Northland, wrote to Joseph's boss at the university, using the old familiar cult lingo that still sends chills down my spine:

> This has become an extremely ugly and public conflagration. . . . All I want to see is a God-honoring resolution to this conflict, and obviously a public Facebook page is not the place to do it. All I ask is that someone from [your university], or someone in the Zichtermans' circle whom they would respect and trust, step in and try to mediate this thing.

We knew from painful experience that the IFB's private mediations were little more than strong-arming sessions meant to force troublesome people like me to knuckle under. It seemed strange to all of us who read the e-mail that Jon hadn't written to Matt Olson, insisting that he contact us to pursue a "God-honoring resolution to this conflict." But neither Matt nor any of the other Northland administrators involved in any of the atrocious attacks on our family has tried to contact us in more than six years. Needless to say, Jon received no reply from Joseph's employers.

On several occasions, IFB members have come to Joseph's workplace to track him down and he has had to put university officials and campus security on alert. Though Northland has stayed conspicuously silent, even after all these years, someone from the cult still contacts Joseph almost every week with either a "hug" or a "slug." We've seen them use every angle imaginable to attempt to insert themselves back into our lives.

Lou Martuneac, who hosts a prominent IFB blog entitled "In Defense of the Gospel," posted the following about the Christian university where my husband teaches on the theology faculty: "[This university] is a sad and tragic example of an allegedly Christian-based school having gone over to the world. I'd suggest they drop any reference to '*Christian*' or '*Bible*' in its literature. . . . [Their] testimony . . . is a blight and open sore on the name of Christ and His church."

Needless to say, Joseph never responds to any of the IFB's attempts to contact him. And with their covert maneuvers and power plays exposed by the social media spotlight, many of the old tactics are much less effective in the lives of countless other survivors too.

After six years, we have still been unable to sell our home back in that tiny, tight-knit IFB community in Wisconsin. We have lowered the price over and over, to the bare minimum of what we need to pay off our debt, but it remains unsold. So though we've been able to extract ourselves from the clutches of the IFB leaders in every other way, they have still managed to create a seemingly unbreakable financial tie with us.

Joseph and I have consistently worked extra jobs since moving to Portland just to cover payments on the long empty house, losing countless hours we could have spent with our children. After this very long journey, we have concluded that there is simply no easy or amicable way to leave a cult. We've been attacked emotionally, financially, relationally, and spiritually—and the attacks show no signs of abating. Carolyn Jessop was right. They try to take everything from you—and they stop at nothing.

That's why I'm telling my story in this book. Our family's heart-wrenching journey out of the IFB is an object lesson for just about everything that's wrong with their ideology. My goal is to shine the light as brightly as possible on all the manipulative tactics of the leaders so they can no longer use them to control others. And until everyone in the IFB is forced to fully and publicly own what they have become, just as we have had to do over the past six years, they will all still have too much to lose to stop hurting people.

17

TRACS* AND ACADEMIC FRAUD

Accrediting associations will not approve our educational process if it does not include the worship of their gods. All education is brainwashing. We wash with the pure water of God's Word, and they wash with the polluted waters of the New Age.

—*Bob Jones III*

We've made great strides in bringing the clandestine subculture of the IFB out of the shadows and into the public eye through survivor forums, legal action, and national media attention. But we've still got a long, long way to go. The cult is working hard to keep the skeletons in the closet and to present the distorted "pure and Christlike" image it always strove to show the outside world. IFB organizations have spent the last four years wiping the Internet clean of sermons, audio files, and other information that could incriminate its members. Many churches have scrubbed their Web sites to hide any ties to the IFB, in an attempt to conceal who and what they really are. All this makes it harder to expose the cult.

At the Heart of IFB Abuse and Indoctrination: Bob Jones University

Even after all the breaking news stories involving inappropriate and illegal acts by Bob Jones University graduates, the school has managed

*Transnational Association of Christian Colleges and Schools.

to avoid the spotlight. Fortunately, numerous BJU graduates see through the spin doctors' attempts to manipulate the facts and refuse to let the school off the hook.

When the university allowed Chuck Phelps—the man who played such an instrumental role in humiliating Tina Anderson and in effect covering up her rape—to remain on its board even after his lies on the witness stand during Tina's case came out, cult survivors were livid. The prosecution team in New Hampshire told me that they wanted to press charges against Phelps, but the seven-year statute of limitations for obstruction of justice had elapsed. Once again, the university was backing an abuser and throwing a victim to the wolves. Finally, after months of protest by BJU graduates, Phelps was pressured into resigning.

As another slap in the face to victims, BJU continued to invite Matt Olson, a graduate of BJU, to speak at the university despite his role in taking Tina into his Colorado IFB church, which kept her from the police.

My brother Jason has been an adjunct professor at BJU, teaching students preparing for youth ministry. He holds nothing more than an unaccredited undergraduate degree from Northland International University. And even after Jason plead the fifth to abusing me, BJU has still endorsed his ministry by publishing his book, *Alone with God,* and they continue to sell his book in the Bob Jones University bookstore.

Now with the IFB controversy garnering national media exposure, BJU added a new rule to its 2012–2013 handbook: "Students should keep in mind that it is not acceptable to disparage BJU through media. Any attempt to do so will not be tolerated and is grounds for dismissal as a student." BJU is sending a clear message: "Speak against us, and we'll find a way to punish you."

Promoting Discrimination

Bob Jones University has subtly continued its racist positions. Most recently, survivors protested one of their dorms' names that was a dedication to the exalted Cyclops chapter president (KKK), Bibb Graves. After two years of raising awareness on the Internet, the school finally removed his name in 2011.

Its homophobic ideology is a constant assault on students. BJU has even gone so far as to tell LGBT alumni they can no longer come on the campus of their alma mater. The only place they are allowed to visit is their art gallery—that is nonprofit and available to the public.

As well, BJU continues their oppression of women, by maintaining women must be in subjugation to men. The female employees must adhere to exceptionally strict regulations on clothing, hairstyles, where they work, and where they attend church—keeping them bound to IFB patriarchal ideology—along with a myriad of other oppressive requirements. A woman's social structure in the IFB is predetermined and decided by the university.

Curriculum Problems

Matt Olson not only believes he did right by Tina, he also continues using his influence as a university president to promote radical positions. In 2006, in a Doctor of Sacred Ministry class at Northland International University, Olson said, "I found this with all three of my kids—this may not be the way it is with yours, but if I get in their face—like this. And I've had to do that. I'm not saying that's always wrong to do. Um, I spanked my daughter when she was seventeen [laugh] . . . and she'll tell you, she needed it [laugh]."

As of fall 2012, BJU's online bookstore still advertised and promoted books by spanking gurus including Richard Fugate, the man who tells parents not to be concerned if their children end up with welts and bruises after a beating because "it is perfectly normal."

In most IFB families, attendance at BJU or another IFB college is the only option for graduating seniors. But even students whose parents are broadminded enough to let them consider other schools can be in for a rude awakening. Some IFB high school students have discovered that their credits don't transfer to non-IFB colleges and have been forced to go back to the drawing board to earn a GED (general equivalency diploma).

In 2008, the Association of Christian Schools International; the Calvary Chapel Christian School in Murrieta, California; and six students sued the University of California system for violating their constitutional rights because UC deemed their high school biology coursework based on BJU and A Beka textbooks inadequate preparation for its college courses. The plaintiffs alleged that the policy set Christian school grads up for discrimination when they applied to UC. A district court in Los Angeles granted the defendants' motion for summary judgment. A court of appeals upheld it, and the Supreme Court refused to review the case. In other words, the courts agreed that textbooks telling you no more than "God created many different and beautiful ferns" probably don't prepare you for college-level botany courses at a non-IFB university.

Lacking Proper Academic Credentials and Misrepresenting Their Accreditation

Endorsing physical abuse while repressing free speech is bad enough, but BJU's greatest Achilles' heel is its lack of regional accreditation, the academic world's gold standard for higher education. In the past BJU had never explained the difference between national and regional accreditation to its students. In our country, national accreditation was designed to evaluate specific types of schools and colleges. Schools apply for national accreditation when their course work is different from traditional degree programs. BJU is promoting itself to its students as a liberal arts school—offering legitimate degrees in every field of study—even though it holds *only* national accreditation through a Christian agency.

I called all fifty departments of education in each state in 2009 and learned that approximately thirty-five states deny BJU teaching degrees because the school is not regionally accredited. Nor does any U.S. state acknowledge the school's counseling degrees. Since teaching and counseling are two of the largest majors at BJU, this sets countless graduates up for failure.

One of the saddest and most disturbing developments in IFB miseducation is that the cult's colleges are now aggressively targeting foreign students. This was the primary impetus for Northland Baptist Bible College's recent name change to Northland International University. Students born abroad have no idea what detriments to their future employability a nonregionally accredited degree will have.

To add insult to injury, the manual of the Transnational Association of Christian Colleges and Schools (TRACS) states that all professors at schools it accredits must have a master's degree to teach at the university/ college level. Yet professors with no more than unaccredited undergraduate degrees teach numerous core classes at both BJU and Northland, often out of their fields of study.

As of fall 2010 (when our public exposure of BJU began), and after receiving their TRACS accreditation, there were 294 faculty members listed on Bob Jones University's Web site. Only 149 had a regionally accredited master's or doctoral degree. The remaining 145 had questionable credentials. The department heads for religion, nursing, and psychology—three of the most popular course areas offered at BJU—lack regionally accredited doctorates. The head of the psychology faculty, Greg Mazak, has the highest credential in his department—a regionally accredited master's degree in counseling and guidance; all other faculty members have unaccredited bachelor's, master's, and doctorates. The school of business has a graduate program, but two of the three faculty members hold unaccredited master's degrees.

Using Honorary Doctorates as Academic Credentials

Not only do the teachers lack credentialing, both BJU and Northland (both TRACS-accredited) have men on faculty who have nothing more than unaccredited undergraduate degrees—who use their honorary doctorates as their academic credentialing. Even as late as 2006, while TRACS-accredited, Les Ollila and Marty Von were teaching core classes at the Northland International University and insisting students call them "Dr." in the classroom. Bob Jones University has done the same with their faculty although in traditional academic settings, to call yourself a "Doctor" with no real doctorate would be considered highly unethical, if not worse. Astounding to us, Jim Berg, now the head of the counseling department of BJU's seminary (as of 2012), has taught undergraduate and master's psychology courses for over a decade. He has been using his honorary doctorate as an academic credential and is referred in the classroom as "Dr." He is currently teaching a master's-level psychology course, Crisis Counseling.

TRACS Investigated

TRACS has been the subject of several investigations by the U.S. Department of Education for its questionable practices, but to date nothing has convinced the group to improve its regulatory methods.

Perhaps this has something to do with its close ties to IFB colleges that would suffer if TRACS got more stringent. Would people like BJU executive vice president for academic affairs Gary Weier—who doubles as commission treasurer and executive board member of TRACS—want to see the rules about master's degrees enforced?

Your Tax Dollars at Work

If you're not a member of the IFB and you have no plans to send your own children to one of the cult's schools or to attend one yourself, why should you care? These schools receive hundreds of thousands of dollars of your tax money in federal grants every year, just as the voucher system diverts your tax dollars for private religious schools. According to 2010–2011 data from the U.S. Department of Education's National Center for Education Statistics (NCES), the Office of Postsecondary Education (OPE), and the Federal Student Aid office (FSA), 66 percent of the full-time students beginning at Bob Jones University get federal student aid. What's more, 49 percent of BJU's incoming freshmen get federal student loans; 49 percent get U.S. Department of Education–sponsored Pell grants, 43 percent get other federal grants, and 18 percent get state or local government grants and scholarships. That adds up to more than $7.5 million of public funds given to college students attending BJU. And that's just for incoming students—those newbies walking around with their "First BJ" buttons while the upperclassmen snicker. Undergrads at Northland International University get almost $2.5 million annually in federal student loans and Pell grants.

Your tax dollars are at work supporting an education in which psychology professors lecture to nursing students that mental illness is a "sin problem," science professors tell students that humans and dinosaurs co-existed, and education professors advocate beating children with a rod. You're also helping to underwrite an education where chapel services are mandatory and commonly include racist, homophobic, misogynist, isolationist, antigovernment rhetoric. These last two are particularly ironic because the government being condemned is underwriting the education many of the students are getting.

18

WHAT NEEDS TO CHANGE?

They are taking faith and crushing it. Why? When
you marginalize faith in America, when you remove
the pillar of God-given rights then what's left is the
French Revolution. What's left is the government that
gives you rights. What's left are no unalienable rights.
What's left is a government that will tell you who you
are, what you'll do and when you'll do it. What's left in
France became the guillotine.

—*Rick Santorum, February 9, 2012*

The Religious Loophole: Understanding Separation of Church and State

After decades of toxic rhetoric, the extremists have a skewed
perspective on what separation of church and state really means. IFB proponents tirelessly trot out the religious persecution argument to defend
the cult, but schools are not churches. I'm all for religious freedom when
it comes to church. If you want to worship trees, worship trees. If you want
to worship the Smurfs and paint yourself blue, go ahead.

But our country needs to distinguish between churches and businesses
operating under a religious banner. Right now isolationist sects run scores
of moneymaking operations and mislabel them "churches." If anyone objects, the religious right claims its freedoms are being eroded. But in its
zeal to uphold "Christian privilege," America has lost its sense of equilib-
rium. Current U.S. laws are so broad that any extremist, even a Charles

Manson–style fanatic, can slap a religious label on his organization and enjoy free rein to abuse children and defraud followers. Corrupt and abusive leaders have exploited the gaping "religious loophole" as an excuse to operate for-profit enterprises cloaked as schools, hospitals, group homes, colleges, and universities—all while demanding the government keep its hands off.

An abuser's most effective strategy is to isolate his victim—and as long as the government enables isolation of children through religious extremism, they will be beaten, brain damaged, and even murdered as a result.

Walking Away from a Cult: A Child's Basic Rights

The religious loophole affects millions of kids in our country, and not just those in the IFB: the Hutterites, Amish, Gypsies, FLDS (polygamous Mormons), Scientologists, or ultra-Orthodox Jewish, among many others. News has come to light in recent years about hidden crimes in many of these communities that rival IFB abuses.

FLDS: It is not right that an FLDS boy can be kicked off the compound at the age of seventeen and leave with nothing more than a fourth-grade education. It is not right that a young girl can be isolated to such a degree that she is convinced she must become the fifth wife of a sixty-five-year-old man when she turns eighteen.

The Amish: It is not right that an Amish child can decide to leave his religious roots, losing all his family and friendships, and walk away with an eighth-grade education. I consider it disgraceful that the Supreme Court ruled in 2011 in favor of Amish leaders who want the "freedom" not to educate their children past the eighth grade.

The IFB: It is not fair that kids from IFB high schools are being denied entrance to college because their IFB curricula lack the quality to pass state scrutiny. It is not fair that IFB students had to go back to college to get new degrees. It is not fair that homeschooled Lydia Schatz was so isolated she ended up murdered at the hands of her own parents. And it is not fair that the IFB Westboro Baptist Church can haul their kids from protest to protest, all while claiming they are "schooling" them. It is not fair to international students, who get sucked into fraud, unaware of job requirements in each state.

In Virginia: It is not fair that seven thousand school-aged children will not receive an education due to a new "religious exemption," in which their religious parents are allowed to opt out of putting their kids in school.

What kind of freedom do any of these children have if they want to leave their communities for a new life?

Children who make a different religious choice than their parents should be able to walk away from their faith traditions with minimal consequences. It's hard enough for people to leave a cult—the financial, emotional, relational, and spiritual damage is dramatic. The least the government can do is protect their basic human rights.

Freedom of Religion for *Some*? Or for *All*?

At the core of our Constitution is the right to worship as we choose and we should never lose that right. Children born into extremist homes have that same right. We will never maintain religious freedom in our country until we determine that the Baptist and the atheist should have equal say and sway. To ensure everyone maintains their personal rights, religion must stay out of the public square. Jesus did not mandate people follow him. He wooed them. The church has lost its mission and it needs to get back to wooing—not mandating.

Christian Dominionists are demanding the Ten Commandments remain in the capitol buildings, but what would they say if Warren Jeffs demanded a portion of the Pearl of Great Price (Mormon book of ethics/values) be hung in each building? They want prayer and the Bible put back in public schools, but what if it was prayer to Allah? Bottom line: Christian Dominionists want freedom for *themselves*, not *all*.

Time for the Laws to Change!

Every child in the United States has a right to a decent education and to live in a safe and healthy environment. That said, it's time to set a *legal* precedent that says *every* child in America should maintain those rights.

Increased government accountability in the school system is a way to ensure that this happens. We need oversight in private religious schools as well as homeschooling environments. Professionals have asked for decades how they could "break down the walls" of these isolated groups—and there's a solution: Regulate all the schools.

How do we make this happen? By requiring that every private religious school have social workers and school counselors on staff and qualified and objective educators to regulate the curriculum being taught. Homeschoolers should be required to take standardized testing every year—at the very least—to ensure the children are really being educated. Group homes (i.e., reform schools) should be licensed in every state. If an organization wants to start a college or university and claim they are giving out academic bachelor's degrees, the government needs to ensure that every credit has marketable value, and in order for that to happen they need to set one standard across the board in our country—regional accreditation.

I believe people should have the right to homeschool. However, I've talked to many homeschooling families who share my concerns. Like me, they argue that if you're doing right by your children, you should have no fear of oversight. The only people with reason to fear regulation are the ones who want to get away with wrongdoing. Responsible homeschoolers realize how easily abusers can sneak into the system and they would like to see laws passed to ensure that all kids are protected.

Extremists are not going to govern themselves. We need federal laws to require it of them.

Unfortunately, when the government lets religious lobbyists and ultraconservative politicians intimidate them like schoolyard bullies, extremists victimize children with total impunity.

It's time now for the government to stand up and say, "No! You can't do that anymore!" and take the religious bullies off the playground.

Toxic Rhetoric and a Christian Militia

If that's not cause enough for concern, the IFB's antigovernment isolationist sermonizing is triggering a significant rise in the militia movement across the U.S. Could all that rhetoric about joining God's army and fighting the evil secular humanists set the stage for a homegrown terrorist attack? It did in Norway. In 2011, a right-wing extremist named Anders Behring Breivik attacked a summer camp and murdered seventy-seven people. Before the massacre he wrote a long manifesto filled with Christian Dominionist rhetoric. He went to the Internet to find much of his well-crafted message about his "personal duty." Certain concepts within his manifesto could have been taken right out of an IFB sermon. He outlines action steps for Christian Dominionists, saying, "They [families] must refuse to turn their children over to public schools. Above all, those who would defy Political Correctness must behave according to the old rules of our culture, not the new rules the cultural Marxists lay down. Ladies should be wives and homemakers, not cops or soldiers, and men should still hold doors open for ladies. Children should not be born out of wedlock. Glorification of homosexuality should be shunned."

It's no exaggeration to envision brainwashed IFB youths taking up arms against the government or average citizens led by one charismatic leader, believing their religious freedoms are at stake. Tens of thousands of Americans share the same extremism. An Internet search for Alex Jones, the Constitutionalists, the Patriot Party, the Christian Militia, or Christian Dominionists, all of whom appeal to members who buy into the conspiracy theories of the IFB, will lead you to a trove of information on dangerous ideologies many Americans would never dream existed within our borders.

Even the government recognizes the dangers lurking in the shadows. The Department of Homeland Security now deems extremist Christian fundamentalists a legitimate terror threat to our country.

The IFB ideology has become commonplace in the political arena as well. As a result, the Republican Party has been hijacked by revolutionary rhetoric. The IFB is being revved up on a steady diet of extremism by men and women like Rush Limbaugh, Glenn Beck, Mike Huckabee, Michele Bachmann, and Rick Santorum.

With systematic brainwashing that "all others are evil" and the continual message thrust upon children that they may need to "take up arms" and "get America back"—Dominionism is rising to the surface. Decades have passed in which abusers have had free rein to damage many young minds—corrupting them. It appears the stage has been set. What type of rhetoric will it take to incite violence?

In the summer of 2012, County Judge Tom Head of Lubbock, Texas, made an appearance on a local television station to generate support for a tax increase and told the public he was expecting civil unrest if President

Obama was reelected. Head, the county's highest-ranking elected official, seemed close to advocating a rebellion when he warned that the president would send United Nations forces into the extremely conservative city of Lubbock to stop any uprising.

> "He's going to try to hand over the sovereignty of the United States to the UN, and what is going to happen when that happens?" Head asked. "I'm thinking the worst. Civil unrest, civil disobedience, civil war maybe. And we're not just talking a few riots here and demonstrations, we're talking Lexington, Concord, take up arms and get rid of the guy. Now what's going to happen if we do that, if the public decides to do that? He's going to send in U.N. troops. I don't want 'em in Lubbock County. Okay. So I'm going to stand in front of their armored personnel carrier and say 'you're not coming in here.' And the sheriff, I've already asked him, I said 'you gonna back me' he said, 'yeah, I'll back you.' Well, I don't want a bunch of rookies back there. I want trained, equipped, seasoned veteran officers to back me."

I don't know what church Judge Head belongs to, but this radical rhetoric is right out of the IFB playbook.

Time for a Healthy Fear

For the last few years I have been calling the IFB the "Christian Mafia" in an attempt to raise awareness of the cult's interconnectedness and menacing message. For real change on a grand scale, citizens of the U.S. need to recognize the sect for what it is: a dangerous mind-control cult. In his book *Thought Reform and the Psychology of Totalism*, psychiatrist Robert Jay Lifton identifies eight factors that define a destructive cult. The IFB meets them all, from Milieu Control (members are isolated and prevented from receiving outside sources of information) to Mystical Manipulation (members are told that God will punish them if they leave the group).

Journalists have been sounding the alarm for a very long time. How long will it take before we pay attention?

As Jeff Sharlet put it in his bestselling book *The Family: The Secret Fundamentalism at the Heart of American Power*: "American fundamentalism's original sentiments were as radically democratic in theory as they have become repressive in practice, its dream not that of Christian theocracy but of a return to the first century of Christ worship, before there was a thing called Christianity."

Sharlet joined "the Family" to gain access to information about Christian Dominionism; I grew up in the middle of it. I was the brainwashed mind ready for my "call to arms"—a "militant fundamentalist"—eager to do what God wanted me to do. I know from firsthand experience what he writes so magnificently about: Christian Dominionism puts *children* in danger, w*omen* in danger, and *you* in danger.

No doubt, because of the IFB's sheer size and influence this group is: The Most Dangerous Mind-Control Cult in America.

Conclusion

Joseph and I are still picking up the shattered fragments of our lives and finding ways to mend them. There have been many times along this twisting and arduous path when I've wondered why all this happened. Why this? Why me? There have been days when the stress, fear, and hurt from the IFB's endless campaign to silence me have overwhelmed me.

Why not just let it go? Why not move on and spare my children, my husband, and myself more grief? Because I've concluded this is a cause worth fighting for, a battle worth winning. This *is* the good fight.

If my story can bring lasting change to the laws in our country and improve fellow victims' lives, then sharing it will have been worth all the anguish, all the tears. To that end, I've made myself an open book until the age of thirty-five, sharing the most intimate and sometimes humiliating details of my past.

As a result, my life has been picked apart, ridiculed, disparaged, and even threatened. That's okay. I have done what I know I needed to do to shed light on this abusive culture—all for the children's sake.

Along this journey, friends have asked about my progression out of this extremism and what I now know for sure.

I know *for sure* that God is *not* a fat, white, angry, Republican, Baptist, male pastor in the sky—with a wooden dowel in one hand and a Bible in the other. I know *for sure* that She/He/Energy/Source/The Divine is good, loving, kind, and compassionate and there is order and purpose in everything.

Bibliography

"1.5 Million Homeschooled Students in the United States in 2007." Issue Brief, U.S. Department of Education, National Center for Education Statistics, Institute of Education Sciences, December 2008, <nces.ed.gov/pubs2009/2009030.pdf>.

"*ACSI et al. v. Stearns et al.*" National Center for Science Education Web site, April 25, 2009; <http://ncse.com/creationism/legal/acsi-v-stearns>.

"*ACSI v. Stearns*—Coursework Subject Matter and Textbooks." University of California Web site, <http://www.universityofcalifornia.edu/news/acsi-stearns/>.

American College Review online. Bob Jones University data. <http://www.americancollegereview.com/getdetails.php?unitid=217749#finaid>.

Amira, Dan. "God Caught Backing Multiple GOP." *New York* magazine, online edition, June 9, 2011, <http://nymag.com/daily/intel/2011/06/god_caught_backing_multiple_go.html>.

Ashbrook, William E. *Evangelicalism: The New Neutralism.* Columbus, OH: Ashbrook, 1966.

Badash, David. "Anti-Gay Pastor: Parents Must 'Squash Like a Cockroach' the Gay Out of Kids." The New Civil Rights Movement Web site, May 1, 2012, <http://thenewcivilrightsmovement.com/anti-gay-pastor-parents-must-squash-like-a-cockroach-the-gay-out-of-kids/politics/2012/05/01/38837>.

Banerjee, Neela. "Dancing the Night Away, with a Higher Purpose." *The New York Times*, online edition, May 19, 2008, <http://www.nytimes .com/2008/05/19/us/19purity.html?_r=1&pagewanted=all>.

Bayliss, Edward E. *The Gypsy Smith Missions in America*. Boston: International Publishing Co., 1907.

Beale, David. *In Pursuit of Purity*. Greenville, SC: Unusual Publications, 1986.

Beardsley, Frank G. *History of American Revivals*. New York: American Tract Society, 1912.

————. *A Mighty Winner of Souls, Charles G. Finney*. New York: American Tract Society, 1937.

Beaven, Jerry. Letter from Jerry Beaven to Robert T. Ketcham, April 20, 1951, "Graham-Ketcham Correspondence." Distributed by R. T. Ketcham, 31 S. Dearborn, Suite 1205, Chicago, IL.

Bennet, James E. "The Billy Graham New York Crusade: Why I Cannot Support It," in *A Ministry of Disobedience: Christian Leaders Analyze the Billy Graham New York Crusade*, ed. Carl McIntire. Collingswood, NJ: Christian Beacon Press, n.d.

Betts, Frederick W. *Billy Sunday, the Man and Method*. Boston: Murray Press, 1916.

Bob Jones University Web site. List of majors. <http://www.bju.edu /academics/majors/biochemistry-and-molecular-biology/> Bob Jones University Press Web site. <http://www.bjupress.com>.

Bonner, Jessie L. "North Valley Academy, Public Charter School in Rural Idaho, Touts Patriotic Focus." Associated Press report on *The Huffington Post*, June 1, 2012, <http://www.huffingtonpost.com/2012/06 /01/public-school-in-rural-id_0_n_1563549.html>.

Branch, Taylor. *Parting the Waters: America in the King Years, 1954–1963*. New York: Simon & Schuster, 1988.

Brown, Elijah P. *The Real Billy Sunday*. New York: Revell, 1914.

Bruns, Roger. *Billy Graham: A Biography*. Westport, CT: Greenwood Press, 2004.

Burnham, George, and Lee Fisher. *Billy Graham: Man of God*. Westchester, IL: Good News Publishing, 1957.

Butler, Farley. "Billy Graham and the End of Evangelical Unity" (dissertation). Gainesville: University of Florida, 1976.

Campbell, Nancy. *Be Fruitful and Multiply*. San Antonio: Vision Forum Ministries, 2003.

Carroll, B. H. *Evangelistic Sermons*. New York: Revell, 1913.

"Chancellor, Bob Jones University: Apologize for Stating That Homosexuals Should Be Stoned to Death." Change.org, <http://www.change.org/petitions/chancellor-bob-jones-university-apologize-for-stating-that-homosexuals-should-be-stoned-to-death>.

Chapman, J. Wilbur. *The Life and Work of Moody*. Chicago: W. E. Scull, 1900.

Chase, Sylvia. "PrimeTime: A Tragic Case of Abuse." Commentary, ABC News online, Jan. 6, 2006, <http://abcnews.go.com/Primetime/story?id=132186&page=1#.UFPv3WglaFI>.

The Church League of America. *Billy Graham: Performer?, Politician?, Preacher?, Prophet?: A Chronological Record Compiled from Public Sources by the Church League of America (1951–1978)*. Wheaton, IL: The Church League of America, 1979.

Clark, Rufus W. *The Work of God in Great Britain: Moody and Sankey*. New York: Harper & Brothers, 1975.

Cohen, Gary G. *Biblical Separation Defended: A Biblical Critique of Ten New Evangelical Arguments*. Philadelphia: Presbyterian and Reformed Publishing Co., 1966.

Colquhoun, Frank. *The Fellowship of the Gospel*. Grand Rapids: Zondervan, 1957.

Conant, William C. *Narratives of Remarkable Conversions and Revival Incidents*. New York: American Tract Society, 1958.

Conger, Krista. "Severe Stress Hurts Children's Brains, Changes Hippocampus, Study Shows." Stanford University Web site, March 7, 2007, <http://news.stanford.edu/news/2007/march7/med-carrion-030707 .html>.

Cook, Charles. *The Billy Graham Story: "One Thing I Do."* Wheaton, IL: Van Kampen Press, 1954.

Daniels, Glenn. *The Inspiring Life and Thoughts of Billy Graham: The Man Who Walks with God.* New York: Paperback Library, 1961.

Daniels, W. H. *Moody: His Words, Works, and Workers.* New York: Nelson & Phillips, 1878.

Dobson, Edward. *In Search of Unity: An Appeal to Fundamentalists and Evangelicals.* Nashville: Thomas Nelson Publishers, 1985.

Dobson, Ed, and Ed Hindson and Jerry Falwell. *The Fundamentalist Phenomenon.* Grand Rapids, MI: Baker Book House, 1986.

Dodd, C. H. *Apostolic Preaching and Its Developments.* Cambridge: Cambridge University Press, 1935.

Dooley, Sean, and Alice Gomstyn. "New Hampshire Man Found Guilty of Rape of Tina Anderson." ABC News online, May 27, 2011, <http://abcnews.go.com/2020/new-hampshire-man-ernest-willis-found-guilty-rape-tina-anderson/story?id=13702833#.UB82tGglZSU>.

Drucker, Dawn, M.S., L.M.F.T., L.C.D.C. "Only Sociopaths Intentionally Hurt Animals: A Professional View." People for the Ethical Treatment of Animals (PETA) Web site, <http://prime.peta.org/2010/04/only-sociopaths-intentionally-hurt-animals-a-professional-view>.

Drummond, Henry. *D. L. Moody, Impressions and Facts.* New York: McClure, Phillips & Co, 1900.

Eckholm, Erik. "Preaching Virtue of Spanking, Even as Deaths Fuel Debate." *The New York Times*, online edition, Nov. 6, 2011, <http://www.nytimes.com/2011/11/07/us/deaths-put-focus-on-pastors-advocacy-of-spanking.html?_r=1>.

Edersheim, Alfred. *Life and Times of Jesus the Messiah.* New York: Longmans, Green and Co., 1900.

Edman, V. Raymond. *Finney Lives On.* New York: Revell, 1950.

Ellis, Wm. T. *Billy Sunday: The Man and His Message.* Philadelphia: Winston, 1914. "The End of *ACSI v. Stearns.*" National Center for Science Education Web site, Oct. 19, 2010, http://ncse.com/news/2010 /10/end-acsi-v-stearns-006258.

Falwell, Jerry. *The Fundamentalist Phenomenon.* Garden City, NY: Doubleday, 1981.

Farwell, John V. *Early Recollections of D. L. Moody.* Chicago: Bible Institute Colportage Association, 1890.

Ferm, Robert. *Cooperative Evangelism.* Grand Rapids: Zondervan, 1958.

Fernandez, Manny. "Official Stirs Texas City with Talk of Rebellion." *The New York Times*, online edition, Aug. 27, 2012, http://www .nytimes.com/2012/08/28/us/lubbock-official-tom-head-stirs-city -with-remark.html?_r=2.

Finney, Charles G. *Memoirs.* New York: A. S. Barnes & Co., 1876.

———. *Revivals of Religion.* Dayton, OH: United Brethren Publishing House, 1910.

Firestone, David. "The 2000 Campaign: The Reform Party; Buchanan Forcefully Strikes Familiar Notes in Speech at Bob Jones University." *The New York Times*, online edition, Sept. 19, 2000, <http://www.ny times.com/2000/09/19/us/2000-campaign-reform-party-buchanan -forcefully-strikes-familiar-notes-speech-bob.html?ref=bobjonesuni versity>.

Fitzwater, P. B. *Preaching and Teaching in the New Testament.* Chicago: Moody Press, 1957.

Foster, Stephen D. "31 Rick Santorum Quotes That Prove He Would Be a Destructive President." Addicting Info Web site, Jan. 5, 2012, <http: //www.addictinginfo.org/2012/01/05/31-rick-santorum-quotes-that -prove-he-would-be-a-destructive-president/>.

Frady, Marshall. *Billy Graham: A Parable of American Righteousness.* Boston: Little, Brown and Company, 1979.

Frankenberg, T. *Billy Sunday: His Tabernacles and Sawdust Trails*. Columbus, OH: F. J. Heer, 1917.

———. *The Spectacular Career*. Columbus, OH: McClelland & Co., 1913.

Fugate, Richard J. *What the Bible Says About Child Training*. Apache Function, Arizona: Foundation for Biblical Research, 1996.

Fund Education Now Web site. Resource Room: School Voucher Programs, <http://www.fundeducationnow.org/resource-room/voucher-school -programs/>.

"Ga. Parents Locked Teen Daughter Inside Chicken Coop as Punishment, Investigators Say." Crimesider staff report, *CBS News Crimesider*, July 13, 2012, <http://www.cbsnews.com/8301-504083_162 -57471913-504083/ga-parents-locked-teen-daughter-inside-chicken -coop-as-punishment-investigators-say/>.

Gillies, John. *Memoirs of George Whitefield*. Hartford: Edwin Hunt & Son, 1853.

Graham, Billy. *Calling Youth to Christ*. Grand Rapids: Zondervan, 1947.

———. "Hate vs. Love." Hour of Decision Sermons, No. 1. Minneapolis: Billy Graham Evangelistic Association, 1951, 1955.

———. *Just as I Am: The Autobiography of Billy Graham*. Grand Rapids: Zondervan, 1997.

———. "Peace vs. Chaos." Hour of Decision Sermons, No. 3. Minneapolis: Billy Graham Evangelistic Association, 1951.

———. "The Pilgrim Pope: A Builder of Bridges." *Saturday Evening Post*, Jan./Feb. 1980, p. 72.

———. *Revival in Our Time*. Wheaton, IL: Van Kampen, 1950.

Greene, Robert. *The 48 Laws of Power*. New York: Penguin, 1998.

Gsell, Brad K. *The Legacy of Billy Graham: The Accommodation of Truth to Error in the Evangelical Church*, revised and expanded edition. Charlotte, NC: Fundamental Presbyterian Publications, 1996.

Halperin, Alex. "Quote of the Day: A Judge in Texas Really Doesn't Want to See Obama Reelected—and He's Ready to Raise Taxes and Take Up Arms." Salon.com, Aug. 22, 2012, <http://www.salon.com/2012/08/22/quote_of_the_day_22/>.

Hamilton, Ron. "Listen to Patch's Story." Patch the Pirate's official Web site, <www.patchthepirate.org/tale>.

Harris, Lynn. "Godly Discipline Turned Deadly." Salon.com, Feb. 22, 2010, <http://www.salon.com/2010/02/23/no_greater_joy/>.

Harrison, Archibald W. *The Evangelical Revival and Christian Reunion.* London: Epworth Press, 1942.

Hennagin, Nate. "47 Organizations Sign National Coalition for Public Education Letter Urging Congress to Oppose DC Vouchers." Americans United Web site, Feb. 11, 2011, <http://www.au.org/blogs/legislative/47-organizations-sign-national-coalition-for-public-education-letter-urging>.

Henneberger, Melinda. "Shoots Bear, Submits to Husband: The Fascinating Marriage of Mike and Janet Huckabee." Slate.com, Jan. 29, 2008, <www.slate.com/articles/news_and_politics/first_mates/2008/01/shoots_bear_submits_to_husband.3.html>.

Henry, Carl F. H. *Confessions of a Theologian: An Autobiography.* Waco, TX: Word Books, 1986

———. "Theology, Evangelism, Ecumenicism," *Christianity Today,* 2:8 (Jan. 20, 1958), pp. 20–23.

High, Stanley. *Billy Graham: The Personal Story of the Man, His Message, and His Mission.* New York: McGraw-Hill, 1956.

Hirschfield, Brad. "Beating Children in the Name of God." *The Washington Post,* online edition. Aug. 18, 2011, <http://www.washingtonpost.com/blogs/for-gods-sake/post/beating-children-in-the-name-of-god/2011/08/18/gIQAqDFGOJ_blog.html>.

Hodson, Jeff. "Did Hana's Parents 'Train' Her to Death?" *The Seattle Times,* Nov. 27, 2011, <http://seattletimes.nwsource.com/html/localnews/2016875109_hana28m.html>.

"Homeschooling Goes Boom in America." *Worldnet Daily*, Jan. 5, 2009, <http://www.wnd.com/2009/01/85408/>.

Home School Legal Defense Association (HSLDA) Web site E-lert Service. Subject: California: SB 1551 Defeated! A Great Victory for all Parents! July 30, 2012, <http://www.hslda.org/elert/archive/2012/07/20120703145541.asp>.

Hood, Edwin Paxton. *The Great Revival of the Eighteenth Century.* Philadelphia: American Sunday School Union, 1882.

Huckabee, Mike. *Character Makes a Difference*. Nashville: B&H Publishing Group, 2007.

Hulse, Erroll. *Billy Graham: The Pastor's Dilemma*. Hounslow, Middlesex: Maurice Allan Publishers, 1966.

The Jack Hyles homepage. <http://www.jackhyles.com/>.

"Jack Schaap Confesses to Sexual Relationship with Teen After Firing from Megachurch." *The Huffington Post*, Aug. 2, 2012, <http://www.huffingtonpost.com/2012/08/02/jack-schaap-confesses-to-_n_1732732.html?utm_hp_ref=chicago>.

James, Susan Donaldson. "Child's Death Sheds Light on Biblical Disciplinary Teachings." *ABC News 20/20*, Nov. 8, 2011, <http://abcnews.go.com/US/childs-death-sheds-light-biblical-disciplinary-teachings/story?id=14897901#.UE9hJWglZFI>.

Janz, Jason. "Fourteen Reasons for Fourteen Years." Fourth Baptist Sojourners ABF Class blog, Aug. 19, 2008, <http://4bya.wordpress.com/2008/08/19/jeremy_janz/>.

Jessop, Carolyn, with Laura Palmer. *Escape*. New York: Broadway Books, 2007.

Klicka, Christopher J., Esq. "The Social Worker at Your Door 10 Helpful Hints." National Center for Home Education, *Issue Analysis*. Home School Legal Defense Association (HSLDA) Web site, Apr. 4, 1999, <http://www.hslda.org/docs/GetDoc.asp?DocID=70& FormatTypeID=PDF>.

Krakauer, Jonathan. *Under the Banner of Heaven*. New York: Doubleday, 2003.

Johnson, Torrey, and Robert Cook. *Reaching Youth for Christ*. Chicago: Moody Press, 1944.

Johnston, Thomas Paul. *Examining Billy Graham's Theology of Evangelism*. Eugene, OR: Wipf & Stock Publishers, 2003.

Kostlin, Julius. *Luther*. New York: Scribner's, 1903.

———. *Theology of Luther*. New York: Scribner's, 1910.

Latourette, Kenneth Scott. *The Expansion of Christianity*. New York: Harper, 1945.

Lizza, Ryan. "The Political Scene: Leap of Faith: The Making of a Republican Front Runner." *The New Yorker*, online edition, Aug. 15, 2011, <http://www.newyorker.com/reporting/2011/08/15/110815fa _fact_lizza?mbid=gnep>.

Loftus, Elizabeth F. "The Reality of Repressed Memories." Abstract. University of Washington Web site. Copyright ©1993 American Psychological Association. http://faculty.washington.edu/eloftus/Articles /lof93.htm.

Ludditeandroid blog at Word Press. "More Quotes from the BJU Textbook." Aug. 31, 2005, <http://ludditeandroid.wordpress.com/2005/08 /31/more-quotes-from-the-bju-textbook/>.

Mainstream Baptist, the blog of Dr. Bruce Prescott. "Huckabee, Gothard and the SBC." Dec. 27, 2007, <http://mainstreambaptist.blogspot .com/2007/12/gothard-huckabee-and-sbc.html>.

Marsden, George. *Fundamentalism and American Culture*. New York: Oxford University Press, 2006.

———. *Reforming Fundamentalism*. Grand Rapids: Wm. B. Eerdmans, 1987.

———. *Understanding Fundamentalism and Evangelicalism*. Grand Rapids: Wm. B. Eerdmans, 1991.

Martin, William. *A Prophet with Honor: The Billy Graham Story.* New York: William Morrow, 1991.

McBeth, H. Leon. *The Baptist Heritage.* Nashville: Broadman, 1987.

McCune, Roland. *Promise Unfulfilled: The Failed Strategy of Modern Evangelicalism.* Greenville, SC: Ambassador Emerald, 2004.

McLachlan, Doug. *Reclaiming Authentic Fundamentalism.* Independence: American Association of Christian Schools, 1993.

McLoughlin, William G. *Billy Graham: Revivalist in a Secular Age.* New York: The Ronald Press Company, 1960.

Mihalcik, Carrie. "Have Mercy: 7 of the Worst Homophobic Pastor Rants." Current Web site, May 23, 2012, <http://current.com/groups/news-blog/93783278_have-mercy-7-of-the-worst-homophobic-pastor-rants.htm>.

"Mike Huckabee Member of Bill Gothard Cult." Daily Kos Web site, Jan. 19, 2008, <http://www.dailykos.com/story/2008/01/19/439174/-BREAKING-Mike-Huckabee-member-of-Bill-Gothard-cult>.

Mitchell, Curtis. *Billy Graham: Saint or Sinner.* Old Tappan, NJ: Fleming H. Revell Company, 1979.

———. *Billy Graham: The Making of a Crusader.* Philadelphia: Chilton Books, 1966.

Moody, Pal D. *My Father, Dwight L. Moody.* Boston: Little, Brown, 1938.

Moritz, Fred. *Contending for the Faith.* Greenville, SC: Bob Jones University Press, 2000.

Morrissey, Tracie Egan. "Cult of Progeny: The Duggars Aren't Just a Family, They're a Cult." Jezebel.com, Sept. 4, 2012, <http://jezebel.com/5939635/the-duggars-are-an-evil-cult>.

Muncy, W. L., Jr. *A History of Evangelism in the United States.* Kansas City: Central Seminary Press, 1945.

N.A. "What's the Next Step?" *Christian Life* (June 1956), pp. 20–23.

National Center for Education Statistics Web site. Institute of Education Sciences. College Navigator: Bob Jones University, http://nces.ed.gov /collegenavigator/?q=Bob+Jones+University&s=all&id=217749#fi naid.

———. Institute of Education Sciences. College Navigator: Northland International University, <http://nces.ed.gov/collegenavigator/?q=N orthland+International+University&s=WI&id=239503>.

"National Coalition for Public Education Coalition Letter to the House Urging Opposition to Restarting and Expanding the DC Voucher Program," Feb. 8, 2011. American Civil Liberties (ACLU) Web site. Linked to PDF "Oppose Restarting and Expanding the DC Voucher Program," <http://www.aclu.org/religion-belief/national-coalition -public-education-coalition-letter-house-urging-opposition-restart>.

"National Coalition for Public Education Submitted to the House Committee on Education and the Workforce Subcommittee on Early Childhood, Elementary & Secondary Education for the Hearing on 'Exploring State Success in Expanding Parent and Student Options.'" National School Boards Association (NSBA) Web site, May 16, 2012, http://www.nsba.org/Advocacy/Key-Issues/SchoolVouchers/Writ ten-Testimony-of-the-National-Coalition-for-Public-Education.pdf.

"N.C. Baptist Pastor Charles Worley's Final Solution: Put Gays Behind Electric Fence Until They All Die." Conservative Babylon Web site, <http://home.conservativebabylon.com/2012/05/21/n-c-baptist-pas tor-charles-worleys-final-solution-put-gays-behind-electric-fence-un til-they-all-die/>.

Needham, George C. *Life and Labors of Charles H. Spurgeon*. Boston: D. L. Guernsey, 1883.

Niebuhr, Gustav. "On the Campus in the Center of the Storm, Life Goes On." *The New York Times*, online edition, March 5, 2000, <http:// www.nytimes.com/2000/03/05/us/on-the-campus-in-the-center-of -the-storm-life-goes-on.html?ref=bobjonesuniversity>.

Nygren, Anders. *This Is the Church*. Philadelphia: Muhlenberg Press, 1943.

Ottman, Fred C. J. *Wilbur Chapman, A Biography.* New York: Baker & Taylor, 1887.

Overton, John Henry. *The Evangelical Revival in the Eighteenth Century.* London: Longmans, Green, 1891.

Pan, Deanna. "14 Wacky 'Facts' Kids Will Learn in Louisiana's Voucher Schools." *Mother Jones,* online edition, Aug. 7, 2012, http://www .motherjones.com/blue-marble/2012/07/photos-evangelical-curri cula-louisiana-tax-dollars>.

Pearl, Debi. *Created to Be His Help Meet.* Pleasantville, Tennessee: NGJ (No Greater Joy) Ministries, 2004.

Pearl, Michael, and Debi Pearl. *To Train Up a Child.* Pleasantville, Tennessee: NGJ (No Greater Joy) Ministries, 1994.

The Pew Forum on Religioun & Public Life: U.S. Religious Landscape Survey, 2007. Pew Forum Web site, <http://religions.pewforum.org/ affiliations>.

Phillips, Holly Adams. "To Cover Our Daughters: A Modern Chastity Ritual in Evangelical America." Religious Studies Thesis, Department of Religious Studies, Georgia State University online archives, Jan 1. 2009. <http://digitalarchive.gsu.edu/cgi/viewcontent.cgi?ar ticle=1029&context=rs_theses&sei-redir=1&referer=http%3A%2F %2Fwww.google.com%2Furl%3Fsa%3Dt%26rct%3Dj%26q %3Ddoug%2520and%2520randy%2520wilson%2520brothers %2520vision%2520forum%26source%3Dweb%26cd%3D4%26sqi %3D2%26ved%3D0CFoQFjAD%26url%3Dhttp%253A%252F %252Fdigitalarchive.gsu.edu%252Fcgi%252Fviewcontent.cgi %253Farticle%253D1029%2526context%253Drs_theses%26ei %3DRYsbUNuLOMv0iwKFzoHoDg%26usg%3DAFQjCNFn2SX hytIRYGo_AGztXHjrc0z8Bw%26sig2%3DOHFlpSnRD-ywJn fEMx-7og#search=%22doug%20randy%20wilson%20brothers %20vision%20forum%22>.

Pickering, Ernest. *Biblical Separation: The Struggle for a Pure Church.* Schaumburg, IL: Regular Baptist Press, 1979.

————. *The Tragedy of Compromise.* Greenville, SC: Bob Jones University Press, 1994.

Pierson, A. T. *Evangelistic Work.* New York: Baker & Taylor, 1887.

Poling, David. *Why Billy Graham?* Grand Rapids: Zondervan, 1977.

Pollock, John Charles. *Billy Graham, Evangelist to the World: An Authorized Biography of the Decisive Years.* San Francisco: Harper & Row, 1979.

————. *Crusades: 20 Years with Billy Graham.* Minneapolis: World Wide Publications, 1969.

————. *To All the Nations: The Billy Graham Story.* San Francisco: Harper & Row, 1985.

Pride, Mary. *The Way Home: Beyond Feminism, Back to Reality.* Fenton, MO: Home Life Books, 1985.

"Publicly Funded School Voucher Programs." National Conference of State Legislators Web site, <http://www.ncsl.org/issues-research/educ/school-choice-vouchers.aspx>.

"Religion: Superchurch." *Time* magazine, Online archives, Dec. 1 1975.

Rice, John R. "Billy Graham and Editor Exchange Letters," *The Sword of the Lord* (May 24, 1957), pp. 2, 9.

————. *Come Out—Or Stay In?* Nashville: Thomas Nelson, 1974.

————. "Cooperative Evangelism," *The Sword of the Lord* (June 20, 1958), pp. 1–3, 5–8, 10–12.

————. *I Am a Fundamentalist.* Murfreesboro, TN: *The Sword of the Lord*, 1965.

————. "Questions Answered About Billy Graham," *The Sword of the Lord* (June 17, 1955), pp. 1, 9–11.

Rodeheaver, Homer. *Twenty Years with Billy Sunday.* Nashville: Cokesbury, 1936.

Ryle, F. C. *Christian Leaders of the Last Century.* London: Thomas Nelson and Sons, 1880.

Sangster, W. E. *Let Me Commend.* Nashville: Abingdon-Cokesbury, 1948.

Scott, Glorianne. "Christian School Principal Charged with Sexual Assault on Child." Examiner.com, June 10, 2009, http://www.examiner.com/article/christian-school-principal-charged-with-sexual-assault-on-child.

Sharlet, Jeff. *The Family: The Secret Fundamentalism at the Heart of American Power.* New York: Harper Perennial. 2008.

Simon, John S. *The Revival of Religion in England.* London: Robert Culley, n.d.

Simons, M. Laird. *Holding the Fort.* Chicago: W. G. Holmes, 1887.

Smyth, Charles. *Simeon and Church Order.* Cambridge: University Press, 1940.

Strober, Gerald S. *Billy Graham: His Life and Faith.* Waco, TX: Word Books, 1978.

Tabachnick, Rachel. "Preview of School Choice: Taxpayer-Funded Creationism, Bigotry, and Bias." Talk to Action Web site, June 27, 2011, <http://www.talk2action.org/story/2011/6/27/151131/081>.

Tulga, Chester. *The Doctrine of Separation in These Times.* Chicago: Conservative Baptist Fellowship, 1952.

Turner, Darrell, "Graham Reflects: From the Early Years to the Pressures of Fame." *Christian News*, March 31, 1986, p. 19.

Webber, Robert. *The Younger Evangelicals.* Grand Rapids: Baker, 2002.

Weber, H. C. *Evangelism: A Graphic Survey.* New York: Macmillan, 1929.

Whitehead, John. *The Life of the Rev. John Wesley.* Boston: Hill & Broadhead, 1846.

Whitesell, Faris D. *Basic New Testament Evangelism.* Grand Rapids: Zondervan, 1949.

Whitney, Arthur P. *The Basis of Opposition to Methodism in England in the Eighteenth Century.* New York: New York University Press, 1951.

Wilder, Forrest. "Rick Perry's Army of God." *Texas Observer,* online edition, Aug. 3, 2011, <www.texasobserver.org/cover-story/rick-perrys-army-of-god>.

Williams, Derek. *One in a Million: The Story of Billy Graham's Missions in England During 1984.* Berkhamsted, UK: Word Books, 1984.

Wilson, Bruce. "Humans and Fire Breathing Dinosaurs? Romney Education Plan Would Fund Bizarre K–12 School Curriculum." *The Huffington Post,* June 27, 2012, <http://www.huffingtonpost.com/bruce-wilson/christian-textbooks-funding_b_1629312.html>.

———. "The Loch Ness Monster Is Real; The KKK Is Good: The Shocking Content of Publicly Paid for Christian School Textbooks." Alternet .org. June 18, 2012, http://www.alternet.org/story/155926/the_loch _ness_monster_is_real%3B_the_kkk_is_good%3A_the_shocking _content_of_publicly_paid_for_christian_school_textbooks.

Wirt, Sherwood Eliot. *Crusade at the Golden Gate.* New York: Harper & Brothers, 1959.

Woodbridge, Charles. *The New Evangelicalism.* Greenville, SC: Bob Jones University Press, 1969.

Zwemer, Samuel. *Evangelism Today.* New York: Revell, 1936.